Information Technology for Library Management and Automation

Information Technology for Library Management and Automation

M. Ram

Information Technology for Library Management and Automation

ISBN 978-93-5111-565-6

Published in 2015 in India by

RANDOM PUBLICATIONS

4376-A/4B, Gali Murari Lal, Ansari Road
New Delhi-110 002
Phone : +9111-43580356, 011-23289044, 011-43142548
e-mail: sales@randompublications.com,
info@randompublications.com, randomexports@gmail.com

Reprinted 2026

Type Setting by : Friends Media, Delhi-110089

Preface

Planning for library automation has been defined as planning for 'integrated systems' that computerise an array of traditional library functions using a common database. While this is still generally true, rapid technological change is forcing a re-examination of what it means to 'automate the library.' As physical, spatial and temporal barriers to acquiring information are crumbling, libraries must plan for a broader and more comprehensive approach to providing automated services.

Libraries should adopt the new sophisticated information technology tools to provide accurate and instant information and to cope up with the demands of new knowledge, the enormous increase in the collection of documents, their problems of storage, dissemination and retrieval of information. Today, the term 'Library Automation' is used to refer "the extensive use of mechanical, electronic or microelectronic equipments to perform the functions and activities associated with the libraries, such as acquisition, serial control, cataloguing and circulation and also to library and information services and networking". Computers are used in libraries to assist in a number of library routines necessary for efficient day-to-day functioning what we call 'house keeping activities'. They are also used for formatting and generation of indexes. Library automation may be defined as the application of automatic and semi-automatic data processing machines (computers) to perform traditional library house keeping activities such as acquisition, circulation, cataloguing and reference and serial control. Finally, library automation is the process of performing all information operations/ activities in library with the help of computers and related information technologies.

The present book is designed to equip the academics and library professionals with basic knowledge about library automation.

I would like to thank my team for standing beside me throughout my career and writing this book. My special thanks go to "Random Publications" who have published the book.

– M. Ram

Contents

1

Information Technology in Library Automation

INTRODUCTION

Libraries should adopt the new sophisticated information technology tools to provide accurate and instant information and to cope up with the demands of new knowledge, the enormous increase in the collection of documents, their problems of storage, dissemination and retrieval of information. Today, the term 'Library Automation' is used to refer "the extensive use of mechanical, electronic or microelectronic equipments to perform the functions and activities associated with the libraries, such as acquisition, serial control, cataloguing and circulation and also to library and information services and networking". Computers are used in libraries to assist in a number of library routines necessary for efficient day-to-day functioning what we call 'house keeping activities'. They are also used for formatting and generation of indexes.

The computers are of great significance with the advancement of telecommunication and reprography technologies in the library automation – when computers interconnected by some of the modern communication vehicles, one can have information over vast distances in no time. The computers are being increasingly used in library and information services for information processing and repackaging of information and on improving products and services of library and information centres. They offer a versatile tool for organization and retrieval of information.

HOUSE KEEPING ACTIVITIES

Library took necessary for efficient day-to-day functioning and falling into the area of 'house keeping' consist of procedure for acquisition, cataloguing, circulate and serial control.

Acquisition: Acquisition and ordering systems in libraries cover the selection, ordering and accessioning of items into the library's collection. Computers are used:

- To send order slips and 'chasers' for unacknowledged or overdue orders to the booksellers.
- To produce lists of books on order
- To keep accounts of money spent
- To produce accession lists of recently acquired books.

The detailed input to an acquisition system covers

- New orders
- Amendments to existing orders
- Bookseller's reports
- Acknowledgement of receipt of items in the library

Selection of new books can be done from commercially available services which disseminate information about forthcoming documents, or directly from MARC tapes or any local inputs.

Two files are maintained in a computer-based acquisition system. One is the main file containing records of all current orders. The second is a file with the names and addresses of booksellers used by the library. A code number for each bookseller links the two files, so that booksellers information is not repeated in the order file. The system prints out the orders addressing the appropriate supplier printing of orders can also be done on special pre-printed stationery that can be sent directly to the book-seller.

By checking with the date of entering the order record into the file, 'chasers' can be sent to the booksellers, if no information regarding the order has been received within a predetermined time.

When the item is received in the library, the order record with the bibliographic details becomes the basis of the catalogue record. The edited record is merely added to the catalogue file in an integrated system.

Other processes that can be performed by a computerized acquisition system are:

- Listing items on order, by author, department or subject;
- New accessions listing;
- Notifying individuals who have recommended a particular book, about the receipt of that book;
- Control of accounts;
- Production of relevant statistics to help management decisions.

Circulation Control: This is one library service that is most accessible to computerization. The advantages are especially seen in the amount of time saved in issue and discharge routines, and the avoidance of bottlenecks, which are the basic of any library. Circulation systems using computers have the details of the book issued and the person borrowing it is entered on files. Dates of return are on the basis of the period of loan (one week, a fortnight etc.). Daily check of the files will identify what books are due or overdue and notices can be typed and sent to the users who have borrowed them. Provision for reservation data will make it possible to pick out these books for which there is a request and a user can be asked to return that particular book.The circulation process in a computerized system depends on giving unique identification codes to books and to users. An accession number or a call number can be used as this is a unique identification key for a book. Users can be given individual identity codes.

Cataloguing: Cataloguing includes the job of describing, recording and displaying details of the holdings of the library. Computers are used to aid in the production, maintenance and updating of catalogues. The quality of the catalogue depends ultimately on the cataloguer. In other words, initial input data is still the cataloguer's work. Bibliographic details are gathered from relevant sources or from the acquisitions system. Usually there is one main or master file for the holdings of the library, and a temporary file for cumulating the additional records, because printing the master file is done only once in while.

After initial input of the records, the computer can perform simple tests on the record structure, and errors can be located and checked. Again, if a basic record structure of a package format as that of the CDS/ISIS is used, entry of data becomes a very simple process. The computer can be asked to generate added entries, if required, which can later be sorted into the main file. Separate listings for authors, subject and key points of access can be created. A postings file and an inverted index helps the computer search and display record relevant to a specific query.

Serials Control: Serial control through the use of the computer is perhaps one of the most complicated tasks of housekeeping. This is perhaps because of the literally unpredictable nature of serial publications. Some of the functions of the serials control system that can be handled by the computer are:

(i) Listing of Serials holdings: is basically producing a catalogue of serials. However with serials, there are problems relating to change in title, periodicity etc. A listing system will depend on the bibliographic record for each serial being available in machine readable form. From a master file of such serials records, individual listing can be made based on title, subject, publishers/ suppliers etc. Union lists of serials holdings by librarians within a geographic region can also be produced by computer.

(ii) Accessioning of serials: must take into account receipt of issues, and periodicity of the serial, likely date or receipt in order to be able to send claims notices to suppliers for items not received, and to update the holding file. To predict the arrival of periodical parts. Each record must contain information about the publication pattern of the serial. This relates to the number of volumes per calendar year, number of parts per volume supplements, if any, the pattern of numbering parts, and the frequencies of publication. Algorithms can be written with reference to the real calendar which use information on the details given above, to predict the arrival of each issue. Prediction cards called 'chaser' notices can be sent to the suppliers when an issue is overdue. Details of the suppliers and the price per volume are necessary for the system to handle subscription, renewals and accounting functions.

INFORMATION SEARCH AND RETRIEVAL

Creation of bibliographic databases has become one of the essential and key activities of library automation. The search process on a computerized database has many advantages over search from a catalogue by manual methods in term of speed, and accuracy.

Any library or information can create first a set of machine readable records of its holdings, based on a structured format, or using a database package like the CDS/ISIS.Users can search the database through key terms of author, subject or title, which are formulated into a search expression using Boolean operators (logical connections AND, NOT OR). Computer will display relevant terms/records that match the terms of the user's request. Current Awareness listings, Selective Dissemination of Information (SDI) and retrospective searches are the services where the computer capabilities can be used very effectively.

Index generation is another area where computer are generally of use. Computer can be used to format the entries in a permuted index and also to generate the entries for an index. Keywords can be derived from the bibliographical description, or assigned to describe the document (subject keys) and then put into the required format. KWIC indexes for instance, can be produced from titles of documents, with keywords and content generation performed by the computer. Stop lists of put forward lists prevent words like 'a', 'the', 'of', etc. from being used as the key terms. Fully automatic indexing can also be done through statistical analysis and word frequency counts with weighting, provided the text is machine-readable form.

ADVANTAGES OF LIBRARY AUTOMATION

Library automation or computer applications in library and information functions and services has the following advantages:

(i) *Speed:* Information processing is done much faster which ensures better work flow through the library.

(ii) *Accuracy:* The degree of precision and accuracy in processing information is high. However, it is dependent on the accuracy of information led into the system.

(iii) *Cost Effectiveness:* Operating costs can be reduced if the system is well designed and well managed.

(iv) *Reduction in Library Work Loads:* Library workloads can be reduced as the computer can do vast amount of work and processing.

(v) *Improved Services to Users:* High rate and better quality in performance is possible through the use of computers.

(vi) Avoids/eliminates duplication of work.

(vii)Easier access to external databases

(viii)Providing on-line access and search of information possible.

Looking at the advantages of Library automation in library functions and services, it is highly recommended that libraries/information centres should follow the same in India, as here more than 97per cent libraries are still using the traditional and orthodox systems in their library services. India should keep pace with the changing scenario and acknowledge and utilize the computers as an internal part of library house keeping and services as libraries in the USA, UK, Japan and other countries are making their full use.

PLANNING FOR LIBRARY AUTOMATION

Library Automation refers to the use of computers to serve the needs of library users. The operations of a library get a quantum jump with the introductions of computers. The computers help to provide fast and reliable access to the resources available in the library as well as elsewhere. The application of computers in the library operations avoids repetitive jobs and saves lot of labour, time, speeds up operations, increases use of library resources. Computers are not only used as a tool for processing the data, but also for data storage and accessing. Planning for an automated system, no matter how big or small, should be part of an overall long-range plan for the library. Automation should always be used as a means to achieve overall better patron service. Careful planning for technology will assure that your automation project is 'sustainable', *i.e.*, enhances the organisation's ability to meet its service mission without disrupting the organisational stability of the institution.

The present scenario of library worldwide is:

- Vastly expanded storage of indexes, statistical data bases, and document databases within the library.
- Full-text storage of documents, complete with full-text keyword searching and on-demand printing.
- Access by users to library databases from home or office, with direct downloading of information and text on demand.
- The ability to access remote databases across the country and the world, and to download information and text on demand.
- Storage of pictorial and graphic material.
- Availability of 'intelligent systems' providing transparent, one-step searching and access to various library in-house and remote databases.

These capabilities and far more have become reality. Accordingly, today's integrated system must not only provide access to the traditional cataloguing, circulation, public catalogue (OPAC) and acquisitions modules, but must be capable of connecting through the local system into the systems of other vendors, remote bibliographic databases, CD-ROM drives on a local area network (LAN), and the Internet.

Users are expecting that their library systems be capable of, among other things:

- Providing seamless integration between system gateway and OPAC modules.
- Providing access for external users on the Internet to the library's OPAC.
- Monitoring the usage of remote databases that have been accessed through the gateway.
- Accessing the Internet using a variety of graphical interfaces.

Essentially, what this means is that libraries must plan to use a local library system as a vehicle for achieving access to resources outside that system. Stimulated by the Internet, which has created universal connectivity to information resources heretofore unknown and/or inaccessible, and by Z39.50 interoperability standards and 'gateways,' users of individual local systems are expecting to access the resources of other systems—anywhere and anytime. Moreover, the traditional definition of 'publishing' has been stretched by the creation and instant availability of informational home pages and Web sites worldwide.

Given such increased complexities and heightened levels of expectation, libraries must learn all the more how to plan for the introduction of automation in an organised and systematic fashion. There is little mystery involved here: It is entirely a matter of building upon what you already know about your library, using tools that are readily at hand and, most importantly of all, involving the people—staff and users—who must live with the consequences of any automation decisions.

WHAT IS LIBRARY AUTOMATION

Traditional library work consisting of acquisitions, technical processing, serials control, circulation and reference services all entail time consuming manual work. Though these activities are essential to proper functioning of a library, they consume professional staff time that might otherwise go towards user services and library development. Library computerisation is now gaining importance necessitating the establishment of profession-wide standards. Comprehensive studies of library computer systems world over include discussions of machine-managed acquisitions, cataloguing, serials control, circulation and bibliographic service modules. The litreature in this area highlights major aspects of computer's role in the library environment. Similar to several aspects of library management, the demand for more and faster information services and the decline in library resources are compelling librarians to appreciate the role of computers within their operations.

In general, librarians are looking to maximize the benefits of automation by spreading computer use to as many aspects of library activities as possible by taking advantage of developments in computer hardware and software and telecommunications.

NEED FOR LIBRARY AUTOMATION

Even though this question seems to be very fundamental it is essential to emphasise this aspect, as the library automation is yet to take off in majority of the Indian libraries. Secondly, while justifying need for library automation more than cost-effectiveness the benefits derived by the library users become the major consideration. To appreciate the advantages it becomes necessary to highlight the different levels of library automation.

Following are considered as important factors for Library Automation:

- Information explosion.
- Increase in the collection of libraries.
- Inability of users to explore the unlimited litreature and information of their interest.
- Advances in the computer and communication technology.
- Wastage of user/ staff time in locating the information.
- Provide wide access to resources within the libraries and elsewhere.
- Better access.
- Quality in service.
- Cooperative efforts (Resource Sharing).

Out of all libraries an academic library has a difficult task of defining its mission and operating objectives. The automation programme will have to mange a wide range of litreature associated with numerous departments and educational programmes of the academic institution. Furthermore, in an academic library the collections will be diverse unlike a special research library where the collection is relatively homogeneous.

The user group will also range widely, including faculty, staff, students, scholars, administrators and the general public. The position of an academic library funded largely by the government further complicates the process of identifying and prioritising objectives. As difficult as the task might at first appear, it is nevertheless essential to the process of establishing automated systems of any type. In addition the overall health of ones library operation will benefit from a modicum of intellectual rigour in this area.

AREAS OF LIBRARY AUTOMATION

As a first step in a planning process, it is desirable to formulate a model for computerisation listing all itemised and prioritised information systems being maintained on a manual basis by the library. For this exercise it is necessary to break down these procedures into their constituent parts. When further subdividing these activities, each item is to be considered of its functional elements. The systems and subsystems listed below are only indicative and may vary with differing library system environments.

These are:

- Acquisitions:
  - — Selection
  - — Ordering
  - — Claiming/cancellation
  - — Receiving/invoice processing
  - — Extended procurements
  - — Gift tracking
  - — Fund Control
  - — Maintains information about all library related funds
  - — Ability to group funds (nesting)
  - — Track fund allocations and adjustments
  - — Fund encumbrance
  - — Fund expenditure
  - — Cash Balance
  - — Free Balance
  - — Automatic updating of fiscal information through recording of specific transactions
  - — Track year-to-date expenditures
  - — Create Purchase Orders
- Technical Services:
  - — Books
  - — Serials
  - — Special Collections
- Cataloguing:
  - — Books
  - — Serials
  - — Special Collections
- Circulation:
  - — Charge/Renewal
  - — Discharge
  - — Loan Periods
  - — Processing schedules
  - — Holds
  - — Messages
  - — Blocks
  - — Notices

  - — Transaction Recording Devices for off-line processing
  - — Member control
  - — Inventory control
- Serials Control:
  - — Receipt (check-in)
  - — Claiming
  - — Bindery control
  - — Replacements
  - — Monographic serials
  - — Invoice processing
- Reference Services:
  - — Desk services
- User tools
- Bibliographic utilisation
- Reprography
- Inter-library communications
- General Administration
- Grants Administratiuon
- Library Publications
- Bindery
- Periodical Citation Searching
- OPAC
- Bibliographic Database

PLANNING OF LIBRARY AUTOMATION

Planning for library automation has been defined as planning for 'integrated systems' that computerise an array of traditional library functions using a common database. While this is still generally true, rapid technological change is forcing a re-examination of what it means to 'automate the library.' As physical, spatial and temporal barriers to acquiring information are crumbling, libraries must plan for a broader and more comprehensive approach to providing automated services.

DEVELOPING A LIBRARY 'PROFILE'

One of the most important planning tools involves collecting basic statistical information on the library and its operations. You will find that the same basic data will be needed again and again—whether for vendors from whom you are requesting cost estimates, or for other libraries with whom you may be seeking to cooperate in implementing automation.

The following are examples of commonly needed data:

- Number of titles and volumes in the collection, current and projected.
- Number of borrowers, current and projected.
- Number of materials circulated, current and projected.
- Number of new materials acquired, current and projected.

- Interlibrary loans, lent to and borrowed from other libraries.
- Description of any cooperative arrangements involving the library.
- Library address and hours of operation.

In addition, it is important to take stock of any existing automation in the library by compiling the following data:

- Percentage of collection that has catalogue records in machine-readable form.
- Description of collection without machine-readable records, by category, (, monographs, audiovisuals).
- Description of currently-automated library functions (if any).
- Estimates of the location and number of workstations (to show where you intend to have equipment in any future system).
- Specifications for any existing equipment to be re-used with any future system (if any).

At the same time that this data is being assembled, it is important to assess user needs and set service priorities. This can be accomplished by undertaking a focused, strategic planning process designed to involve the library's 'stakeholders.'

DEVELOPING A STRATEGIC PLAN

A library planning to automate should undertake a process by which representative staff and users can identify service needs and objectives. The purpose of such an effort is to allow participants to articulate their interests and concerns, share perspectives and learn about possibilities in a collaborative setting. Group interaction is an important contributing factor in the success of the goal, which is to develop and sustain library automation in the years ahead.

Here are the basic steps involved in this process:

- Plan on a two-day, intensive planning effort.
- Ask participants to identify strengths, weaknesses, opportunities and threats in the library's environment (known as 'SWOT' factors in strategic planning) that are characteristic of or that confront the library.
- Group these factors into critical issue areas that are likely to have an impact on the libraries' future in developing and sustaining automation.
- *Ask participants to identify ideas and perceptions in relation to the question*: "How do you see the library providing user-friendly, cost-effective automated services in five years?
- Through a method of your own devising, ask participants to prioritise all of the ideas that come out of the above two 'brainstorming' exercises.
- Ask participants to shape these priorities into the draft of a strategic 'vision' for automation development consisting of a statement of purpose, goals and objectives for the library.

SETTING SERVICE PRIORITIES

Your strategic vision must now provide the framework or context for the next step in the automation process, which is to determine which library functions should be automated and in what order of priority. For example, processes that are repetitive, occupy large amounts of staff time, require retrieving information from large, unwieldy files, or are high-profile functions of the library (such as the public catalogue) are prime candidates for automation. Determining the functions that you wish to automate and their priorities relative to each other is important for all sorts of reasons.

If needs and priorities are clear, functions can be automated in phases, allowing for more effective use of frequently scarce funding. Moreover, it is a way to develop credibility with funding agencies and be able to take advantage of 'sudden' funding opportunities. Finally, evaluations of systems and options will be easier and more productive if you are able to match your highest functional priorities against the corresponding modules available in the marketplace.

A WORD ABOUT COSTS

Speaking of funding, planners need to be aware that there are certain cost elements involved in the installation and operation of any automated system.

These may be summarised as follows:

- Planning and consulting costs include direct, out-of-pocket costs, (*e.g.*, hiring a consultant) and indirect costs, (*e.g.*, training staff) associated with getting started.
- Purchase of the system includes the cost of acquiring the initial system hardware and software, as well as the cost of preparing a site for the computer system.
- Telecommunication costs are those fees paid to telephone companies for connecting remote terminals or workstations to a central computer system.
- Conversion costs are those associated with the creation of machine-readable bibliographic and, for circulation systems, patron, records.
- On-Going Operating costs include:
  - — Maintenance fees
  - — Utility costs
  - — Bar code labels
  - — Miscellaneous supply costs
  - — Telecommunications costs
  - — Salaries and benefits (if extra staff are hired).
- Additions to the existing system may be required to maintain performance specifications, to accommodate new users, or to allow for additional automated functions.

SYSTEM SPECIFICATIONS

At some point, you will need to re-formulate your functional priorities into 'functional specifications,' which may be defined as what you want an automated system to do for you, including things that your current manual system cannot do. 'Technical specifications' must also be established. These include standards that must be adhered to, system performance, operation, and maintenance, as well as infrastructure requirements, such as stable sources of electricity and telecommunications, and sufficient bandwidth. Developing clear and accurate functional and technical specifications that are specific to your library is one of the most important, if not THE most important, activity that you will engage in as you plan for your automated system.

These specifications will carry you through the entire procurement process, and will ensure that the system which most closely matches them will be the most useful and the most responsive to your needs.

DEVELOPING A FORMAL SPECIFICATIONS DOCUMENT

It is very difficult to compare systems sensibly and pragmatically solely by randomly looking at systems, talking to sales representatives, reading litreature or comparing broad cost quotations. For this reason, libraries use a formal document—often known as a 'Request for Proposal,' or RFP—that organises and standardises the information provided to and requested from the various system vendors. Utilising an RFP to solicit written responses from vendors makes it possible for you to systematically compare functionality, cost, maintenance, support, and all the other issues that are involved in system procurements. The process can save you money and will result in a wiser decision.

An RFP document should include these essential elements, among others:

- Background information on the library.
- A description of how the proposals should be arranged and submitted.
- Instructions on receiving vendor business and financial information.
- Criteria the library will use to evaluate vendor proposals.
- Questions regarding vendor training and documentation.
- Your functional and technical specifications.

Also, vendors should be asked to describe:

- How they will create bibliographic, item and borrower databases.
- Their system maintenance programmes and services.
- Their site preparation requirements.
- Their delivery and installation methodologies.
- Their system performance guarantees.
- Their pricing and cost strategies, in detail.

EVALUATING VENDOR PROPOSALS

Upon the receipt of vendor proposals, it will be time to begin the process of system evaluation and selection.

This process involves a number of key steps:

- If possible, form a project team of persons to assist with the evaluations and the selection who have some knowledge of automation or who work in the area(s) being automated. People involved in the strategic planning process would be a good choice.
- Try to weed out proposals that are 'fatally flawed,' *e.g.*, where the vendor fails to reply to any of the functional specifications or the system is missing a module for a high-priority function.
- Begin in-depth reading of the 'surviving' proposals, carefully noting both deviations from the requirements as defined by the RFP and any aspect that is handled unusually well. Make a list of any parts of the response that are not clear and require further clarification.
- Schedule system demonstrations. They are an important component of the evaluation process. Allow the vendors to show off the vendor's system in the most attractive light; however, be prepared with a list of what you want to see along with questions you would like answered. Use the same list with each vendor. This permits more effective cross-comparisons.
- Consider using computerised spreadsheet software in order to compare and evaluate vendor cost proposals. Costs may not be what they seem at first glance.
- Contact some of each vendor's current clients—sites of the same library type, and of similar size, where the hardware and software modules that have been proposed to you are currently in use.
- Assign point values to the criteria listed in the RFP and assign scores to the different proposals. The system with the highest score becomes the number one finalist, the system with the second highest score number two and so on. To maintain a negotiating edge, it is better to cut to two vendors rather than one. If that is impossible, maintain the illusion anyway. Remember: The selection process is not over until the contract is signed. Until that point, never let any vendors know that they have been eliminated, including those with fatal flaws.

PUTTING SYSTEMS INTO PLACE

After the system selection process is complete, there are several important steps which must occur. You and your vendor will have to negotiate and sign a contract. You will want to test the system and make sure it suits your needs. You will want to make provisions for system maintenance. Finally, you will want to train both your staff and your users as much as possible to prepare them for when the system is up and running.

With regard to training, the following must be considered: In thinking of automation planning, there is often a tendency to focus on the hardware and software aspects of planning, and to ignore the human aspects of automation—training and public relations. Without these, however, even the most carefully designed system may not be accepted by library staff or library users. To assure the success of your hard planning work, a training and public relations plan should be part of any automation project.

Fortunately, training can begin long before the system is installed. By involving staff at all levels in the analysis of operations, the identification of needs, the setting of priorities, the development of specifications, and the evaluation of systems, staff will gain much of the knowledge they need as the planning progresses. User acceptance and enthusiasm for your new automated system is certainly an important ingredient in a successful planning effort. If you are implementing a public access catalogue, it is probably the most important measure of success.

Public relations can allow you to accomplish three things:

- Make users aware of your new system and services;
- Motivate them to use the system; and
- Train them in using the new system and services effectively.

RETROSPECTIVE CONVERSION

In the rush to acquire hardware and software, librarians often forget that their most valuable product is the library's database. The creation of a high-quality machine-readable database provides the cornerstone upon which all present and future automation efforts rest. Vendors will come and go, hardware will become obsolete, software will be replaced, but a well-constructed, well-maintained database, with its accompanying local holdings, will be the library's transportable and viable link from system to system. Moreover, as library users begin to access not only their local system but systems in other libraries as well, the quality of respective databases will influence both the outcome of search strategies and the availability of materials.

Database readiness has several important facets:

- Catalogue records must be carefully converted from manual to machine-readable formats.
- Collections must be prepared for conversion through effective and ongoing weeding and inventory programmes.
- Once converted, collections must be properly maintained as titles are added, withdrawn, transferred and recataloged.
- Standards—for bibliographic, item and patron records as well—must be adhered to. In particular, adherence to well-established and accepted standards of description for bibliographic information in a machine-readable database is critical because: without standards, files cannot easily be transferred from one automated system to another.

- It is essential for libraries wishing to participate in resource sharing arrangements with other libraries, who will require such adherence as a condition of participation.

LIBRARY AUTOMATION SYSTEM

Early opinions of the potential uses of computers in libraries varied. One university librarian observed that:

- '. . . computers can be used in library operations. It does not prove that they should.'

Despite such ambiguous attitudes, decreasing library budgets have been a significant factor in persuading the management of many academic libraries of the benefits of computerising library activities. Many librarians have found over the last ten years or so that they have been unable to recruit more staff but their work loads have increased, perhaps by an increase in student number in an academic library, or by acquiring more books, or by the library and its services being used more. In order to cope with such situation many librarians have decided to use computer systems.Librarians have been very careful in selecting, acquiring and installing an automated system. Moreover the setting up of library cooperatives, such as BLCMP, SWALCAP and SCOLCAP, contributed greatly to the development of library automation through a sharing of expertise and requirements. The limited abilities of the early automated systems have in many ways been overcome in the integrated, turnkey systems developed by the cooperatives and the commercial system vendors.

The decision to introduce library automation was usually based on a re-appraisal of the objectives of the library, for example:

- To make the most of effective use of existing library manpower and resources for the benefit of library users.
- To allow for integration of all aspects of information management relevant to the library's work now and in the future
- To create a user-friendly environment in which the information handling and information processing needs of both library staff and library users, as an integral part of the learning process, are addressed
- To facilitate vertical integration of the library's current microcomputer-based systems.

In the early phase of automation, it was common that many academic libraries used their parent institution's computer facilities. Few had their own because of the then relatively high cost. Since computer prices have fallen, many academic libraries have acquired their own computers for library operations.

In the university context:

- 'libraries became less dependent upon their parent institutions for central computing facilities, and most now have their own hardware.'

Current technology may integrate the system in the library with that in its parent institutions, or stand alone.

Although IT systems may be stand-alone:

- 'The complex task of senior management in any field is not necessarily best served by the use of individual software packages. The growth of networks, the provision of information by MIS; and the ability of decision support systems to model decisions and analyse possible effects—these are likely in the long term to prove more useful tools for senior managers. The next few years will probably see a gradual increase in utilisation of these integrated management support systems in academic libraries.'

The advantages of integration are, for senior library managers, enhanced by micro-computers and intelligent terminals:

- 'The importance of these devices for the management information systems lies in their ability to acquire data from the organisation's main computer and to process it, using their own software, within the device itself. Not only is there a saving in processing load on the main machine, but the manager can be assured of a very fast response and of confidentiality and can have the software tailored to his own specifications without affecting other users. In addition many intelligent terminals provide flexible control over the information which is displayed, so that not only text but graphics can be produced and manipulated. This can be a major advantage where complex statistical data has to be presented.'

THE STATE OF AUTOMATION

Automated systems were mostly established in the early 1980s. Now, all librarians were concerned with the cost of maintenance, but recognised that it is offset by improved productivity in the libraries' operations.

Microcomputers had been gradually introduced, but two chief librarians did not yet have them in their own offices, allegedly because they were considered too expensive.

Non-etheless, in one Scottish university it was planned to introduce the use of microcomputers and spreadsheets for financial data systems.

This development was being promoted by the chief librarian even though he did not have a microcomputer in his own office to use that spreadsheet.

There were some indications that the librarians were willing to introduce automated management information systems. Progress had been slow, however, and finance was a major barrier.

PARTICIPATION IN COOPERATIVE ACTIVITIES

The libraries were generally members of some cooperative scheme, particularly SCONUL and COPOL, both of which compile and disseminate comparative information on library performance.

Thus, to some extent, these organisations are already contributing to the development of management information systems.

ACQUISITIONS AND COLLECTION MANAGEMENT

All the libraries were suffering from reduced purchasing power. They could acquire fewer books and serials despite increases in their budgets. Overspending on periodical subscriptions was also a problem in some libraries, and had become the main issue, generally, in senior staff meetings. Most libraries had information on numbers of books borrowed, but similar data on the use of periodicals is not commonly collected, so although the librarians are aware of the reduced power of periodicals budgets, decisions on which periodicals subscriptions to retain could not easily be made. It was believed to be a very critical area that needed to be managed more carefully, and it was hoped that automated management information systems could be established to do this.

READER SERVICES

Two points were made which relate to the need for management information about reader services. First, there is a need to monitor utilisation and opening hours. Clear information on the number of users who come to the libraries in the evening, for example, must be compared against the cost of staff. Second, online services had already been introduced in all academic libraries, since they can be expensive services, charges had been introduced in most libraries. CD-ROMs are increasingly widely available free of charge; as a consequence, the number of inter-library loans has increased. Information is needed by library management on all these areas to enable the most cost-efficient and sustainable solution to be implemented.

STAFFING

All but one of the libraries had increased their expenditure on library staff as a proportion of the total budget. They all currently faced the problem of managing a workload arising from increased numbers of students with a reduced staff. There appeared to be a readiness among library staff to establish automated management information systems to monitor the workload and to simplify some reporting tasks.

EVALUATION PROCESSES

Formal and comprehensive evaluation processes might be supposed to be in place in all the libraries since all the librarians were aware of the need for quantitative and qualitative data about their libraries, but there was only one university library which claimed that it had a formal and comprehensive system for library evaluation. Most libraries claimed to have an informal system and to be trying to introduce formal ones. They were aware of the existence of performance measures and performance indicators which would help them to evaluate their libraries, but only two libraries had experimented with performance measurement, and only one had fully implemented a formal system through the development of an experimental decision support system. Two of the eight libraries had no immediate plans to introduce the use of performance indicators. Neither the chief librarians nor senior librarians were promoting their introduction.

The other five libraries were moving to introduce the use of performance indicators. This was being promoted by chief librarians because of a perceived need for quantitative and qualitative data. There appeared to be little suggestion that it was being done simply because it was fashionable. Three of the five libraries are using mostly paper-based management information systems.

Two others are using microcomputer networks. Of the rest, two libraries had discontinued collecting internal information, and one has never collected information for use as performance indicators. In terms of the use of performance indicators in decision making, the one library which uses performance indicators stated that they had a considerable impact on decision making; most of the others suggested that performance indicators had little impact on decision making. Despite the lack of formal performance measurement in some libraries, all had a financial data system. Current reports from the financial data system are said to be adequate for decision making, and for the libraries' annual, reports, as well as meeting the needs of the institutions' own finance departments.

USE OF EXTERNAL INFORMATION FOR LIBRARY PLANNING

The library plans and objectives in the libraries visited showed that they were aware of current external trends. Their parent institutions' plans were the principal source of information about future developments. In addition, they took account of information from outside institutions such as government departments and, in particular, the higher education funding councils. Other information sources which were mentioned consisted of other libraries' annual reports. *Information UK 2000,* users' comments on the library services, publishing trends, etc.

To obtain comparative data about their libraries' performance, they made heavy use of SCONUL and COPOL data. Most external information is acquired in printed form. Some information sources are kept in the chief librarians' offices, others in the senior librarians': no one had a comprehensive collection of the external information in their own offices.

Two libraries had recorded some external information, *e.g.*, information on price inflation, in their microcomputers. Although there are serious problems in data processing, the range of external information held shows that there was the potential to establish a comprehensive management information system. The external information would, however, have to be tailored with other information in order to be used in decision making.

LIBRARY PLANNING AND OBJECTIVES

All the libraries had produced a statement of their mission, medium-term plans, and specific objectives or targets. One library operated on a planning cycle of three years, and the others on five years. Thus, this was a common management activity, with the potential for providing guidelines for resources allocation, and a basis for management information systems.

FINANCE

As the result of financial pressures, the libraries visited had mostly changed their approach to financial management. Cost centres and budget centres are more commonly used than in earlier years since they provide a means of allocating finance in a way more relevant to the evaluation of the library plans. The libraries which are using budget centres or cost centres have been employing a scientific/quantitative approach to resource allocation. Only three libraries still use their traditional budgetary structures and allocate resources on a historical basis. Despite differences in the schemes used for resources allocation, all the libraries had produced and continue to produce some kind of statistical data. The reasons for producing statistical data vary: in general, the data is intended to contribute information to the institution's finance system, and annual reports, or to meet requests from SCONUL or, formerly, COPOL. A requirement to produce general statistical data about the library for managerial use by its parent institution is not common; it was found in only one library.

BUILDINGS UTILISATION

The librarians were, of course, aware of the self renewing concept promoted in the Atkinson report in an attempt by government to restrict the demand for new university library buildings to accommodate ceaselessly growing collections. Attempts to apply the concept had been tried but then put aside. The reasons were clear. There have been important changes in the institutions, as the government has permitted and encouraged growth in student numbers. The introduction of new courses and an increased number of students represent different and urgent problems for academic library services, and have rendered the self renewing concept redundant—at least for the moment. Consequently, libraries had less need of information to assist decision making on what to do with their collection in order to save space. They have more need of information to assess the adequacy of their collections, study places, and usable space to meet the growing demands on them. Non-etheless, in only one polytechnic and one university did the librarians have information on shelf space available for new materials.

2

Select Library Automation Software

INTRODUCTION

To evaluate a particular software package, a simple procedure is to read the literature supplied by the manufacturer, look at the reviews and advertisements published in various computer magazines and to ask the salesperson for a demonstration of the programme. What is often found to be missing in this procedure is the basic conceptual understanding of what a computer does on a physical level and how the software works. It is not necessary to know the details of computer components, such as accumulators, registers, clock signals, instruction set of 380 microprocessors or computer programming, etc. But, when deciding on the best suitable software, more computer knowledge is required than just how to insert a disc into the slot and press a key.

However, the following general guidelines may be useful in selecting a programme.

- Locate and evaluate a knowledgeable dealer or sales person
- Thoroughly examine the documentation for the software you are considering
- Arrange for a demonstration of the software
- Prepare yourself before the demonstration
- Put the programme through its paces
- Evaluate the quality of support you can expect from the dealer or vendor.

CRITERIA FOR SELECTION: STUDY NO. 1

Glossbrener has given the following twelve sure-fire rules for selecting software.

- *Rule* 1: Do not take anything for granted: There is more hidden in the advertisements than it is revealed.
- *Rule 2:* You are not the stupid one: Don't ever let yourself feel foolish when looking at, reading about, using, or otherwise dealing with a

computer programme. If its creators haven't lived up to their responsibility, it is their fault, not yours.

- *Rule* 3: How many and how long?: How many author names can you put in that file? How long can each name be? Nothing brings a program's limitations to the surface faster than these questions.
- *Rule* 4: Forget about the sizzle and focus on the steak: Ask, what the programme can to do and how well it can do it? The advertisement may say, "This programme contains all the standard word processing features". Note, there are no widely agreed 'standard' features of any programme. In short, concentrate on performance and forget the decoration
- *Rule 5:* Whenever possible, make an effort to visualise yourself using the programme: Visualise, how much work will be involved putting all of your books, records, or magazines into database management files? Will you be able to enter each new book record? The more accurately you visualise the steps involved in accomplishing a task.the more you know about how a given programme will deal with those steps.
- *Rule* 6: Read at least two reviews of any programme before you buy.
- *Rule* 7: Get a demonstration on the identical computer, configured exactly as the one you will be using.
- *Rule* 8: Life will be easier if you stick with proven products offered by major hardware and software firms.
- *Rule* 9: Buy only the four 'building block': programmes to start with. It is easy to master a programme faster and comprehensively, if you concentrate on just one at a time. The four building block programmes are communications, word processing, electronic spreadsheet and personal filing or database management.
- *Rule 10:* Don't drive yourself crazy trying to get something to work. Ask.
- *Rule 11*: Nothing is impossible. But the game may not be worth the candle. Computers and software are so versatile that you can accomplish just about anything you want. But these will not save the time, effort and money.
- *Rule 12:* Whenever you can-WAIT! Make sure the rapidly changing software market place works for you.

CRITERIA FOR SELECTION: STUDY NP.2

There is another monumental work discussing various criteria to evaluate and select library automation software, particularly for the housekeeping operations. The eight volume series publication entitled Library Systems Evaluation Guide, is brought out by Jera. Since, it was published in 1983, the Guide may be a little outdated. However, the principle evaluation criteria discussed are still valid. The coverage in eight volumes of the Guide is indicated in the table.

Table. Indication of Coverage in Library Systems Evaluation Guide.

Vol. No.	Title	No. of Pages	No. of Reference
1.	Serial Control	194	60
2.	Circulation Control	261	97
3.	Public Service	267	117
4.	Acquisitions	252	96
5.	Management Services	234	88
6.	Interlibrary loan	248	98
7.	Cataloguing	261	168
8.	System integration	278	198
	Total	**1995**	**922***

Note: * No effort is made to identify the unique references. The total number of references includes a number of multiple citations.

The Guide presents basic information on the requirements and techniques of evaluation of automated library applications in a concise and easily usable format. The Guide considers 'evaluation' as 'relative in nature'. Therefore, to determine the ability of various systems to meet a library's requirements, the systems must be compared with each other or to some reference model. The latter approach to evaluation is both easier and more objective, provided a reference model is available. The Guide provides such a reference model, which could suitably be adjusted to represent the requirements of a given library and then this model may be used to evaluate one or more number of library automation software packages.

The Guide suggests an eight-phase evaluation methodology.

- *Phase 1:* Setting objectives.
- *Phase 2:* Fine tuning of components of the methodology to agree with objectives.
- *Phase* 3: Selection of candidate systems for evaluation.
- *Phase* 4: Examination of accompanying system literature and documentation.
- *Phase* 5: Comparison of candidate systems with the functions and features table, and with the checklist of data elements.
- *Phase* 6: On-site evaluation of candidate systems.
- *Phase* 7: System selection and acquisition.
- *Phase* 8: Post installation evaluation.

CRITERIA FOR SELECTION: STUDY NO.3

Rowley emphasises the need to identify systems requirements before the selection of either software or hardware. The functional requirements are important. Therefore in the evaluation of any package for a given application, priority must be given to establish whether the software is capable of performing the tasks for which it is to be acquired.

General Criteria

- *Other's experiences*: Useful in indicating the potential and problems of a software package; some users may offer help and advice in implementing the package.
- *Cost*: Comparisons of prices of packages be made. What is included in the price of the package and what is excluded should be understood. Cost of hardware and database creation are additional costs.
- *Originator*: The originator's reputation, and experience in developing software is helpful. An established software house is more likely to be able to offer continuing support.
- *Supplier*: Sometimes the supplier is the same as the originator, if the supplier is a separate agency acting as an intermediary between the user and the originator, it may hinder direct communication between the user and the originator.

Technical Criteria

In addition to the general criteria of the selection, the following technical criteria should be considered, both when selecting between packages and also in assessing whether any specific package is suitable for a given purpose.

- *Language*: The programming language in which the software is written. Whether a compiler or interpreter is available on the given system to run it efficiently in terms of machine time and storage requirements.
- *Operating System*: The package must be suitable for running under the operating system on the hardware being used. Whether it is a single user or multi-user operating system that will function on a network.
- *Hardware*: Compatibility with software, its various versions and also ability to run other necessary or useful software on the computer system.
- *Ease-in-use*: The quality of the operator - machine interface, menus, commands, screen displays, documentation, etc. will enhance ease in use of the software.
- *Supplied format*: Software must be supplied on disks, tapes, etc., that can be run on the system and when required transferred to another medium such as hard disk.

Support Criteria

It is an important criteria for using the software and to fully exploit the various features of the software.

- *Documentation*: It includes both printed documentation and online help facility. The documentation should cover introductory exploration of the basic features, a full account of all features, a list of commands, an online help system, additional tutorial support, choice to interface at different levels depending on user's experience, etc.

- *Advice to setting up*: Assistance in installing and implementing the package must be provided. This may cover creation of databases, input formats, report formats, initialisation, etc.
- Training in the use of software package.
- *Maintenance*: This may include removing any bugs or errors that might become evident in the software as it is used for a greater variety of applications and improving the software so that it incorporates new facilities and concepts (*e.g.,* mouse, windows, popup menus).
- *User groups*: Many of the larger and well-established software packages (*e.g.,* CDS/ISIS, LIBSYS) have user groups or user clubs. These groups share expertise and experience in application of the software, discuss problems and limitations in using the software and present a concerted front to the software supplier for solving problems and asking for improvements.

CRITERIA FOR SELECTION: STUDY NO.4

Grosch discusses some procurement and evaluation factors together market trends that may affect the future of library systems. The major system evaluation and selection according to Grosch is the availability of the capabilities and product enhancements of the application software at the time of its installation. The other criteria include examining hardware platform options, operating system requirements, directions of the system developers towards open systems, conversion support, training, ongoing software support, record of old and new versions of the software, ease-of-use, etc. The advice is: 'Setting realistic goals that are attainable in your selection of a system, biting off only what can now afford but providing a goal enhancement base for future years, will result in an easier systems transition'. Electronic spread-sheets crunch numbers. Word processing programmes crunch words. Library automation and information storage and retrieval programmes crunch information. They help to deal effectively with information explosion. The purpose is important. If the selected software cannot retrieve right information at right time in right format for the right user, the sophistication and decor of the package is worthless. The categories of software explained before help in fixing the appropriate category of the software for the purpose of library automation.

Based on what one has in terms of physical environment (computer) and social environment (users, staff) and what one can afford, suitable software has to be selected. There are many options and a large variety of software packages. It is suggested to acquire a commercially available software package. These are developed for use by a variety of customers. A great amount of skill and effort is put in their development. They are expected to be reliable, easy to use, well documented and they are available for a wide range of applications. Even then the selection of suitable software is difficult because of their availability in large number, over choice, tall claims, varied cost, technicalities involved, etc. It is necessary to know the various criteria that could be applied in selecting the suitable software. The four selected studies, by Glossbrenner, Library Systems Evaluation Guide, Rowley and Grosch provide a variety of selection criteria. This wider perspective of such criteria with be helpful and provide better pitch and outfield to play the serious game of selecting the suitable player-that is, the required software package.

LIBRARY AUTOMATION IN ACADEMIC LIBRARIES

The history of library automation is sufficiently old now. It started in early fifties in the Untied States of America. The landmark was the initiation of MARC project by the Library of Congress. During 1960s some experiments were carried out in India in this field but very sparingly. During late seventies there were some achievements like production of National Union Catalogue of Scientific Serials by INSDOC, production of Union Catalogue of DRDO libraries of Western Region by the Institute of Armament Technology at Pune.

Then came eighties and the whole focus of the librarians shifted towards library automation. A number of seminars were organized on the library automation and still being done so. We graduated from simple library operations to specialized functions including networking. Now we talk about digital libraries and e-journals. We have come a long way. But we are a country where bullock cart and cars are seen on the same road so blocking the fast moving traffic and those bullock carts restrict the speed of the cars to its own speed.

To overcome this problem there are only two ways. First, replace the bullock cart with a car, and second, bypass the bullock cart and leave it behind. The state of library automation in our university libraries is more or less the same. We have the libraries like IIT libraries which are highly automated and also totally manual libraries which are really restricting the speed of academic and research in the country.

FACTORS RESPONSIBLE FOR AUTOMATION IN ACADEMIC LIBRARIES

There are several reasons which can be cited for this difference. Some of them are :

- Attitude and awareness of the management.
- Attitude and awareness of the Users specially faculty.
- Resources available
- Non-availability of suitable software:
- Level and skill of staff
- Geographical locations

Attitude and Initiative of the Management:

Attitude and initiative on the part of the management has played major role in library automation in Indian University Libraries. The management here includes both the university management and the librarian as a secretary of the management whose task is to carry out the decisions taken by the executive bodies of the university, such as Syndicate, Executive Council etc. If the Librarian had the initiative then he was able to convince the authorities about this emergent need. In some of the cases, the initiative also came from top and the Librarian was forced (or bypassed) to do it. But the best blend was when the initiative of both the Librarian and University Authorities was synergized. If there was no initiative on both the ends than there was no progress.

Attitude and Initiative of the Uses

A library may be as smart as its readers. If the readers are smart and well aware they may force the authorities to work towards library automation. If the readers are knowledgeable about the development being taking place in the information technology, they have influenced the use of computers in library to a great extent. This is more true about faculty as they are the people who participate in decision making process. The good examples are the libraries of IITs and other higher engineering educational institutions.

Resources available

The third important factor is the resources available with the university libraries. The resources include both financial as well as human resources. In most of the universities, the librarians are given funds only for books and journals. Some libraries do not want to or are not allowed the funds received for books and journals to be used for any other purpose, even though the University Grants Commission (UGC) guidelines permit the use of a certain percentage towards such activities (In VIII Plan it was 15per cent and in IX plan 10per cent). Most of the libraries depend on the funds provided by the UGC under Inflibnet project. The distribution of the money under this project was not done logically. Big and small libraries were equated at par and as a result while some libraries remained fund starved some were not able to use the funds. Before distributing funds to libraries there should have been a survey of the requirement and certain guidelines laid down. Besides this there are no other financial resources available with the university libraries. In order to save the university libraries from going further down UGC must do something in this direction. Another very serious problem, may be more serious than the financial one, is the lack of trained manpower. Many of our library science schools have not based their curricula on the automation requirement of the university libraries. Some of them are even teaching today what was designed thirty or forty years back although that has become totally outdated. Not many library schools produce a candidate who can straight away go the Automation Department of a University Library and can independently work without any further training. The bifurcation of the library science schools from libraries are perhaps the one of the main important reasons for that. As a result our profession became the only profession where practice went far ahead of the teaching.

In the country people are talking about digital libraries and web-OPACs and we are teaching fundamental of computers in our library schools. This is the only profession where getting a professional degree does not require any professional training. Can you imagine a doctor without hospital training or an engineer without a training in Industry.

Non-availability of suitable software

Non-availability of suitable software has also played an important role. Though there are a number of software available for library management but most of them are Non- standard. The main reason behind is that most of the software have been developed without the help of a qualified librarian. As a result there were a stream of Non--standard software. Some of these soft wares have been developed by big corporations like CMC but have not been proved very successful. The software developed by institutions (for example DESIDOC, INSDOC etc.) could not be successful as they were lacking in marketing and after sales service. The librarian is confused as he is not in a position to decide what to select.

Level of skill of library staff

The level of skill of library staff also played a very important role. In our country there are no standard for level of subordinate staff to be recruited in academic libraries. There educational and professional qualification vary from state to state. In some of the cases the library assistants are recruited with 12th pass and a six months certificate in library science while in Central institutions like IITs and Central Universities it is minimum graduation and degree in library science. The institutions having better stuff went far ahead (though there are exceptions to that). The better qualified staff was better oriented towards progressive thinking which could move the things fast. This point emphasizes the requirement of a uniform qualification policy for the recruitment of staff in academic institutions.

Geographical Location

Geographical location of an institution also played a very important role. The institutions near to a metro city were benefited by the availability of the resources. They were having better approach to hardware and software market and also the manpower for data entry. They were having approach to better training facilities. Hyderabad is a good example which can be cited.

PRESENT STATUS OF LIBRARY AUTOMATION IN UNIVERSITY LIBRARIES

The real boost in library automation came from the establishment of the INFLIBNET Centre. Before Inflibnet scattered efforts were being made in academic libraries specially in the institutions of special characters like IITs, IIMs etc. INFLIBNET proved a real catalyst. Inflibnet started with scratch. At that time there were no financial assistance available to the University Libraries for automation.

For the first time it was established that automation was the need of hour. The finances were allocated for the first time. The standards were established about the data capturing. The format was finalized and the Karvan started. As one estimate at present about 120 university libraries have been using computers in their activities. Some of the University libraries are even establishing digital libraries not only of already available digital resources but are digitizing their own literature.

AREAS WHERE COMPUTERS ARE BEING USED

The following are the areas where computer are being used at present.

- Online public access catalogue
- Circulation
- Acquisition
- Serial control
- Intranet
- Internet
- CD-ROM services

Online Public Access Catalogue (OPACs)

The problem being faced by the users in locating the document was the first to be targeted in the library automation. As a result the work first started in this direction.

There was one more reason for this and that was the availability of CDS/ ISIS software which had the facility of catalogue only. It was in contrast of the special libraries where the work first started on providing information services like CD-ROM search.

Even today this area of automation has more activity than any other area. It has now graduated to Web-OPAC (web based online public access catalogues) where university libraries have made their databases available on their Web sites.

This has eliminated the need of installation of search software on the user's terminal. One potential which remains unutilized is the use of search data for research purpose as the search history can provide very useful tools for the librarians to formulate their collection development plans.

Circulation

Circulation is one of the main activities of a university library or any library per say. In university libraries, however, the number of books issued and retuned are more than in special libraries. Therefore, the next area which was taken up was the circulation. In some of the libraries the number of books issued/ returned may be more than one thousand per day. We at IIT Roorkee (formerly University of Roorkee) has experience of issuing 1500 books in six working hours.

Sometimes there used to be a queue of more than 100 students, since the free hours for all students used to be the same, before automated circulation started. Use of barcodes had made the life very simple due to added accuracy and speed. Besides speeding up the issue/return, printing reports, sending reminders also become very easy. Circulation data also provides a very important insight into the book use pattern. Librarians should try to use this data for research and development purpose.

Acquisition

Use of computers in acquisition remains a low priority area. Not many libraries are using computers in acquisition. On reason may be the continuously reducing budget for purchase of books. But this area needs to be strengthened.

Computerization at the stage can help not only in order processing but also can be a very effective tool in budget control. You can allocate funds to different departments based on a set formula, can send department heads about Non- availability of funds, can control over ordering and also utilize the data entered at this stage for technical processing and OPAC.

Serial Control

Idiosyncracies involved in serial control affects the use of computers in serial control and hence the area is not very well represented at automation scenario. One more reason is the unsuitability of serial control modules available in most of the library Management Softwares.

The procedures developed by these softwares are so cumbersome that sometimes it looks easier to use normal method rather than automation. However, this area provides very good stage for use of computers as it can help tracking the missing issues very efficiently and provide the current awareness services and even the SDI services besides budget control.

Intranet

Making the information available on intranet is also growing popularity as it eliminates the need of installing the software on the users' terminals. Users can access the catalogue through intranet or they can find the status of the books issued to them through web access.

CD-ROM resources and other digital resources can be accessed on intranet. Growing installation of campus wide networks is also playing a positive role in this direction.

Internet

Use of Internet for academic purposes is also increasing day by day. More and more libraries are putting their resources on Internet. Internet is the medium both to access and disseminate information. Internet has emerged as a very big virtual library which has information on practically every subject and in every media may it be text, audio or video. Libraries should use this facility to the best of their capability. They should provide links to similar type of libraries through web pages.

One very good use can be designing of e-gates where user can have access to the electronic resources through a common user interface. I would like to mention that a number of free e-journals are available on the Internet. The prominent among library and Information Science are 'D-Lib Magazine', Issues in science and Technology Libraries", "Cybermetrics" etc.

Digital Libraries

Digital library has recently become the buzzword for librarians. In the last year most of the seminars and the conferences had 'digital libraries' as their theme. Digital libraries can be of two types *,i.e.,* digital libraries of the digital text available in the market such as e-journals, CD-ROM databases, e-books, software etc. or it can be developed from the printed text available in the library.

If a library takes a decision to develop a digital library of its collection specially theses, dissertations and old journals, it can solve the problem of space and preservation both. But the decision about creating such decision is taken to be very carefully as it will prove a very costly venture both in terms of money and manpower.

PROSPECTS

Having talked about the problems and areas of applications let us talk about future prospects. I can definitely say that the things are changing for the good. Now University authorities are realizing that there is no way to escape library automation. They are finding various ways to finance their library automation projects. Librarians are also realizing that they can not remain indifferent to the change, otherwise they will be labeled outdated. One area of concern is the library science graduates being produced by our library schools.

It is surprising that UGC is giving responsibility of refresher courses of library science to the library science school and not to the libraries who are established themselves as advanced libraries and uses the technology far ahead than the library science schools. Existing staff is getting rid of the fear of computerization. They are coming forward to learn and make themselves suitable to face the challenges of the new millennium. Standardization is increasing and the better softwares are available.

PLAN AND MANAGEMENT FOR LIBRARY AUTOMATION

Planning for library automation has been defined as planning for "integrated Library management systems" that computerize an array of traditional library functions using a common database. As physical, spatial and temporal barriers to acquiring information continue to crumble, libraries must plan for a broader and more comprehensive approach to providing automated services. Currently, libraries find themselves confronted with a second computerization wave. The first wave took place during the seventies and turned manual back-room activities, such as acquiring, distribution and cataloguing, into computer-controlled activities. Essential in the computerization wave of the 90s is the deployment of computer networks: campus-wide networks at universities as well as national and international networks.

These networks provide access to remote electronic information by means of library information systems. Furthermore, available electronic information is no longer limited to socalled secondary information (catalogues, bibliographic databases). Also primary information has now become electronically available. Presently, we can refer to the electronic full-text versions of scientific journals. Electronic textbooks and readers enable us to consult information outside the library, ,*i.e.*, at the professional and private work site of the library's traditional customer. We must realize that all traditional library activities are being affected by this innovation: the character of all library tasks is about to change as a consequence of technological developments. Within this context, we can observe a number of trends.

One very important trend is the fact that the physical collection is becoming less important. Of course, in the humanities books will keep playing an important role in the next decades, but the number of electronic sources will gradually increase. The library is shifting its focus from concentrating on supply towards centering on what is asked for by its customers.

In correspondence with this trend, information reference is becoming more and more significant. The library acquires a gateway function, referring to information, irrespective of the location where it has been physically stored. Growing emphasis will be put on navigation. By and large, users will prefer to find their own way across the large amount of available information. To an increasing extent, service will be provided from a distance: the users will choose to consult their sources sitting at their own desk, at their own computer.

This, in turn, implies that the library needs to increase the accessible electronic collection, which is accomplished by disclosing sources elsewhere, but also by electronically providing material that has already been available on paper. Of course, this development entails new problems related to the storage of electronic information.

IMPORTANCE OF LIBRARY FOR ORGANIZATION/R AND D CENTERS IN IT ERA

Special library have been in existence from the beginning of this centuries, whereas information centre engaged from the fifties and have now developed into major group of information institutions. Although special libraries and information centers has over lapping functional characteristics. Special libraries disseminate information and matter acquired by them answers, research questions, and direct users needs details on research information to appropriate some and handle Towards periodicals to keep their user informed current development in this field. Parent organization special libraries after serves a widely distributed group of users who only link being the common subject interest. The concepts of special libraries have been change in all aspects and librarians are known as cyberians.

NEED OF LIBRARY AUTOMATION IN SPECIAL LIBRARIES

In the changing scenario of information storage and retrieval, we have no option but to automate our information and library systems due to various reasons. Consequently, there is urgent need to reply following questions before /and after automation planning. Questions you might ask are basic but important :

- What are the information needs of the organization ?
- Who will access the database?
- What will the content be?
- What is our computing environment or can it be changed?
- Who will maintain the data?
- Who will determine the process and procedural controls and standards?

We have to discuss the said questions with library staff, library committee and with users for better planning for library automation and use of new information technology in library.

STEPS FOR PERFECT LIBRARY AUTOMATION

Redefining and Planning for Library Automation

Library automation is a very complete process and needs exhaustive planning looking to the present and future needs of the users. This includes hardware, software, moony manpower, materials and mechanics (4M's), obsoleteness, updating, adoptability and very fast changing IT environment.

Selection of hardware and others required equipment

- System Purchase: Purchase of the System if not available latest configuration of hardware and software, as well as the cost of preparing a site for the computer system. As having following latest configuration as follow :

- *Processor*: Intel Pentium 4 processors up to 530J with Hyper threading (3.0GHz)
- *Operating system*: Windows XP Professional
- *Memory speed*: DDR2 PC2-4200 SDRAM
- *Memory expansion*: Four DIMM slots for expansion to 3GB memory
- *Graphics*: Integrated Intel Graphics Media Accelerator 900
- *Hard Disk Drives*: Up to 200GB 7200rpm Serial ATA]

- Networking of Computers (LAN) in library: Think and complete the library networking if not already available etc. as Telecommunications dedicate at least one standard (analog) phone line that the vendor can use to dial up to your system. Internet accessibility is become more common for vendor troubleshooting, but you may still need that extra phone line.
- Retrospective data conversion costs are those associated with the creation of machine-readable bibliographic and, for circulation systems, patron records.
- Site Preparation—updating power supply, updating electrical wiring, cable for networking, furniture, remodeling that may need to be done, adequate HVAC system
- Conversion Costs—This includes the costs of converting the catalog and patron records. However, also consider the cost of staff time dedicated to the project. Bar-coding costs also fall into this category.

Operating Costs—This category is often forgotten in automating a library. Typical costs in this category include on-going utility and telecommunications costs, software license renewals, software updates, system maintenance fees, and miscellaneous supplies

SELECTION OF LIBRARY SOFTWARE AND OTHERS REQUIRED SOFTWARE

Following criteria might help the librarians to select the right software for other housekeeping operations:

- Who are the developers, whether an institution, or reputed company or few individuals. The preference is for institution and second preference is for the reputed company. One has to be skeptical about the software developed by individuals as there will be no continuity
- How many times the software has been revised since the time of its first launch.
- How many parameters are available for each module? More the parameters better will be the flexibility and needs no or minimum customization.
- Whether the software has facility to import bibliographic data available in MARC 21 format and similarly export of data in this format

- Training and guidance after installation
- Whether available on major operating systems.
- Whether it is web interfaceble
- Whether it can be interfaced with the e-mail system of the campus network.
- How many installations it has got in the country, since when and major clients.
- Whether it can offer OPAC and different rights to different logins
- Database architecture, Database migration, maintenance, database security, etc,

THE FOLLOWING ARE LATEST TRENDS TO BE CONSIDERED LIBRARY AUTOMATION SOFTWARE

- Integrated library Management system : An automation system in which the various applications share one bibliographic database. Each system comes with a set of core modules as well as additional modules, which can be added on, if necessary (or affordable). The system should not only
- Core modules as : Circulation, cataloguing and online public access catalogue are necessary minimums. Additional modules often cost extra and are therefore not always used by as many of the system's clients which can lead to less responsive development. Additional modules include acquisitions, community information, course reserves, imaging, inter-library loan (ILL), materials booking and serials. Acquisitions and serials are sometimes part of the same module and are often part of the core package, content management, e-learning etc.
- Client-server architecture : Turnkey systems are quickly becoming a thing of the past. A client/server system is identified by a more powerful server machine that handles database manipulation and retrieval while leaving the user interface to the desktop client software. This shares the computational load between the client and server machines and gives the user a better experience through a faster interface.
- Z39.50 : This is a protocol for computer-to-computer information retrieval. It allows users to access dissimilar library catalogues from the host institution's catalogue while using a familiar interface. Both a Z39.50 client and server are needed if you want to visit others and have others visit your catalogue. A Z39.50 client allows access to others' catalogues. A Z39.50 server allows others to access your catalogue. Ideally access works both ways.
- GUI interface for all modules : Graphical and menu-driven interfaces have or are replacing commanddriven interfaces in systems.

- MARC 21 and Non--MARC compliance : First, library systems developed to use MARC records. Now systems must allow for cataloguing formats, such as Internet resources, for which no MARC formats yet exist alongside MARC records.
- Web-based patron catalogue : Patron access is greatly increased when catalogues can be accessed remotely via the World Wide Web. Better systems contain password-protection to allow patrons to access portions of their own records remotely.
- UNICODE : This protocol expands the character set allowed and is essential for collections with materials in Non--Roman languages. UNICODE encodes 65,000 different characters compared to the extended ASCII character set of 256 characters. Not all vendors have fully implemented this yet, but most are working on it.
- RFID (Radio Frequency Identification Technology : RFID is the latest technology to be used in library theft detection systems. Unlike EM (Electro-Mechanical) and RF (Radio Frequency) systems, which have been used in libraries for decades, RFID-based systems move beyond security to become tracking systems that combine security with more efficient tracking of materials throughout the library, including easier and faster charge and discharge, inventorying, and materials handling? Following are the advantages of RFID systems ,*i.e.,* Rapid charging/ discharging, Simplified patron self-charging/discharging, high reliability, High-speed inventorying, automated materials handling, long tag life, etc.

Accordingly, today's integrated system must not only provide access to the traditional cataloging, circulation, public catalog (OPAC) and acquisitions modules, but must be capable of connecting through the local system into the systems of other vendors, remote bibliographic databases, CD-ROM drives on a local area network (LAN), and the Internet. Users are expecting that their library systems be capable of, among other things:

- providing seamless integration between online gateway and OPAC modules;
- providing access for external users on the Internet to the library's OPAC;
- Monitoring the usage of remote databases that have been accessed through the gateway; and,
- accessing the Internet using a variety of online database

Essentially, what this means is that libraries must plan to use a library automation management system as a gateway for achieving access to resources outside campus. Stimulated by the Internet, which has created universal connectivity to information resources heretofore public/society/respected community and by Z39.50 interoperability standards and "gateways," users of individual are expecting to access the resources of other systems— anywhere and anytime. Moreover, the traditional definition of "publishing" has been stretched by the creation and CDROMS, E-books, online databases, informational home pages and Web sites worldwide.

FINANCE MATTER

Finance is an important aspect of any planning and automation is no exception to it, these are: Hardware, Software, Training, Staff, Networking (LAN, WAN, MAN and Internet). Speaking of funding, planners need to be aware that there are certain cost elements involved in the installation and operation of any automated system. These may be summarized as follows: Planning and consulting costs include direct, out-ofpocket costs (*e.g.*, hiring a consultant) and indirect costs (*e.g.*, training staff) associated with getting started, etc.

DEVELOPING A LIBRARY "PROFILE"

One of the most important planning tools involves collecting basic statistical information on the library collection, library in-house activities, user services, users' education etc. The following are examples of commonly needed data of:

- Number of titles and volumes in the collection, current and projected;
- Number of borrowers, current and projected;
- Number of materials circulated current and projected;
- Number of new materials acquired current and projected;
- Interlibrary loans lent to and borrowed from other libraries;
- Description of any cooperative arrangements involving the library; and,
- Library in-house activities and hours of operation.

In addition, it is important to take stock of any existing automation in the library by compiling the following data:

- Percentage of collection that has catalog records in machine-readable form;
- Description of collection without machine-readable records, by category (*e.g.* monographs audiovisuals);
- Description of currently-automated library functions (if any);
- Estimates of the location and number of workstations (to show where you intend to have equipment in any future system); and,
- Specifications for any existing equipment to be re-used with any future system (if any).At the same time that this data is being assembled, it is important to assess user needs and set service priorities. This can be accomplished by undertaking a focused, strategic planning process designed to involve the library's "stakeholders."

DEVELOPING A STRATEGIC PLAN

A library planning to automate should undertake a process by which representative staff and users can identify service needs and objectives. The purpose of such an effort is to allow participants to articulate their interests and concerns share perspectives and learn about possibilities in a collaborative setting.

Group interaction is an important contributing factor in the success of the goal, which is to develop and sustain library automation in the years ahead.

Here are the basic steps involved in this process:

- Ask participants to identify strengths, weaknesses, opportunities and threats in the library's environment
- Group these factors into critical issue areas that are likely to have an impact on the libraries' future in developing and sustaining automation.
- Ask participants to explore their ideas and perceptions in relation to the question: "How do you see the library providing user-friendly, cost-effective automated services as Current Awareness Services (CAS), Selective Dissemination of Information (SDI), online database, online journals etc.
- Through a method of your own devising, ask participants to prioritize all of the ideas that come out of the above two "brainstorming" exercises.
- Ask participants to shape these priorities into the draft of a strategic "vision" for automation development consisting of a statement of purpose, goals and objectives for the library.

SETTING SERVICE PRIORITIES

Your strategic vision must now provide the framework or context for the next step in the automation process, which is to determine which library functions should be automated and in what order of priority. For example, processes that are repetitive, occupy large amounts of staff time, require retrieving information from large, unwieldy files, or are high-profile functions of the library (such as the public catalog) are prime candidates for automation.

DEVELOPING A FORMAL SPECIFICATIONS DOCUMENT:

It is very difficult to compare systems sensibly and pragmatically solely by randomly looking at systems, talking to sales representatives, reading literature or comparing broad cost quotations. For this reason, libraries use a formal document — often known as a "Request for Proposal," or RFP — that organizes and standardizes the information provided to and requested from the various system vendors. Utilizing an RFP to solicit written responses from vendors makes it possible for you to systematically compare functionality, cost, maintenance, support, and all the other issues that are involved in system procurements. The process can save you money and will result in a wiser decision.

AN "REQUEST FOR PROPOSAL" DOCUMENT

The following points should include these essential elements, among others:

- Library Background Information
- Libraries Service Plan, Mission Statement, Technology Plan, other supporting information. Technical Inventory-Inventory of your existing hardware/software, and infrastructure:
- Size of your collection
- number of terminals
- number of patrons
- Network operating system
- number of servers
- Type of wiring
- Existing database that may need to be migrated into the new system—People soft, access database, etc.
- Specifications-Detailed listing of requirements the system should provide.
- Module Requirements : Circulation, Bibliographic Maintenance, Acquisitions, Serials, General System, and Report Generator, etc.
- System Technical Requirements
- Network, System Design, Database Management System, Data conversion requirements, Hardware requirements
- System Performance and Testing Requirements

BE READY FOR THE FOLLOWING UPON THE RECEIPT OF VENDER PROPOSALS AGAINST OUR FLOATED RFP.

- A description of how the proposals should be arranged and submitted;
- Instructions on receiving vendor business and financial information;
- Criteria the library will use to evaluate vendor proposals;
- Questions regarding vendor training and documentation;
- Your functional and technical specifications;
- Also, vendors should be asked to describe:
- How they will create bibliographic, item and borrower databases;
- Their system maintenance programs and services;
- Their site preparation requirements;
- Their delivery and installation methodologies;
- Their system performance guarantees; and
- Their pricing and cost strategies.

CRITERIA FOR VENDOR (FOR HARDWARE AND SOFTWARE) SELECTION

Upon the receipt of vendor proposals, it will be time to begin the process of system evaluation and selection. This process involves a number of key steps:

- If possible, form a project team of persons to assist with the evaluations and the selection who have some knowledge of automation or who work in the area(s) being automated. People involved in the strategic planning process would be a good choice.
- Try to weed out proposals that are "fatally flawed," *e.g.*, where the vendor fails to reply to any of the functional specifications or the system is missing a module for a high-priority function.
- Begin in-depth reading of the "surviving" proposals, carefully noting both deviations from the requirements as defined by the RFP and any aspect that is handled unusually well. Make a list of any parts of the response that are not clear and require further clarification.
- Schedule system demonstrations. They are an important component of the evaluation process. Allow the vendors to show off the vendor's system in the most attractive light; however, be prepared with a list of what you want to see along with questions you would like answered. Use the same list with each vendor. This permits more effective cross-comparisons.
- Consider using computerized spreadsheet software in order to compare and evaluate vendor cost proposals. Costs may not be what they seem at first glance.
- Contact some of each vendor's current clients— sites of the same library type, and of similar size, where the hardware and software modules that have been proposed to you are currently in use.
- Assign point values to the criteria listed in the RFP and assign scores to the different proposals. The system with the highest score becomes the number one finalist, the system with the second highest score number two and so on. To maintain a negotiating edge, it is better to cut to two vendors rather than one. If that is impossible, maintain the illusion anyway. Remember: The selection process is not over until the contract is signed. Until that point, never let any vendors know that they have been eliminated, including those with fatal flaws.
- Compare studies: Do compare study of all received proposal from venders with theirs features etc.

PUTTING YOUR SYSTEM INTO PLACE

After the system selection process is complete, there are several important steps which must occur. You and your vendor will have to negotiate and sign a contract. You will want to test the system and make sure it suits your needs. You will want to make provisions for system maintenance. Finally, you will want to train both your staff and your users as much as possible to prepare them for when the system is up and running. With regard to training, the following must be considered: In thinking of automation planning, there is often a tendency to focus on the hardware and software aspects of planning, and to ignore the human aspects of automation— training and public relations. Without these, however, even the most carefully designed system may not be accepted by library staff or library users. To assure the success of your hard planning work, training and public relations plan should be part of any automation project. Fortunately, training can begin long before the system is installed. By involving staff at all levels in the analysis of operations, the identification of needs, the setting of priorities, the development of specifications, and the evaluation of systems, staff will gain much of the knowledge they need as the planning progresses. User acceptance and enthusiasm for your new automated system is certainly an important ingredient in a successful planning effort. If you are implementing a public access catalog, it is probably the most important measure of success. Public relations can allow you to accomplish three things:

- Make users aware of your new system and services;
- Motivate them to use the system; and,
- Train them in using the new system and services effectively.

ABOUT THE DATABASE

In the rush to acquire hardware and software, librarians often forget that their most valuable product is the library's database. The creation of a high-quality machine-readable database provides the cornerstone upon which all present and future automation efforts rest. Vendors will come and go, hardware will become obsolete, software will be replaced, but a well-constructed, well-maintained database, with its accompanying local holdings, will be the library's transportable and viable link from system to system.

Moreover, as library users begin to access not only their local system but systems in other libraries as well, the quality of respective databases will influence both the outcome of search strategies and the availability of materials. Database readiness has several important facets:

- Catalog records must be carefully converted from manual to machine-readable formats;
- Collections must be prepared for conversion through effective and ongoing weeding and inventory programs;
- Once converted, collections must be properly maintained as titles are added, withdrawn, transferred and re cataloged; and,
- Standards — for bibliographic, item and patron records as well — must be adhered to. In particular, adherence to well-established and accepted standards of description for bibliographic information in a machine-readable database is critical because
- Without standards, files cannot easily be transferred from one automated system to another, and,
- It is essential for libraries wishing to participate in resource sharing arrangements with other libraries, which will require such adherence as a condition of participation.

RESULTS OF YOUR GOOD PLANNING

- Confidence that you have selected the best possible system available, give technological and financial constraints;
- Confidence that you have addressed the priority needs of your library;
- Confidence that you have established a firm basis of understanding and a methodology (the planning process) for future planning;
- Confidence that automation activities are being implemented as part of a clearly articulated, overall plan for the development of library services; and,
- Confidence that you have the ability to respond quickly and effectively to unexpected opportunities and challenges, with a clear understanding of how these unexpected developments may be used to support the library's long range goals.

FEASIBILITY STUDY OF YOUR PLAN

Immediately after the analysis and design for the system has been completed, a feasibility study must be conducted. The aim of a feasibility study is to determine if the project is achievable, if the benefits outweigh the disadvantages and to examine alternative solutions. It is designed to answer these questions:

Is the proposed system realistic? Is it necessary? What other options is available? Is it affordable? The final output of a feasibility study is a report to be presented to the management

DEVELOPMENTS IN COMMUNICATION AND NETWORK TECHNOLOGY

Communication technology, with its ability to transmit data and information from one location to another, serve as a tool to exploit potentials and ability of computer to store and process vast amount of information. A computer communica-tion network is an interconnection of a collection of several computers from which the user can select the service required and communicate with any computer as a local user.

A computer communication networks can be viewed as a collection of nodes with computing resources and nodal-switching computers that facilitate communication through a set of transmission links. Developments in communication technology have made it possible to interconnect geographically dispersed computing resources of different kinds and makes.

Users can access the network through PCs and terminals attached to a node and messages traverse these networks through the switching nodes. Since, computer communicates using digitised signals instead of electric signals, it requires different transmission facilities than those used for transmitting analogue electrical signals. It is, however, a common practice to use conventional telecommunication links for data transmission by converting digital signals into analogue signals using a process called 'Modulation' and the device that performs the conversion is called the MODEM (MOdulator - DEModulator).

Currently, terrestrial, satellite-based data networks, Integrated Service Digital Network (ISDN) and wireless networks are available that can handle all kinds of communication requirements (, *i.e.,* voice, data, telemetry, facsimile and video) without discrimination.

The computer networks can be grouped into four categories based on geographical locations of its computer terminals, , *,i.e.,*,

- *Local Area Network (LAN)*: interconnection of many computers within a given local area, more often premises of a single organisation building. A very high speed of data transmission can be attained within a limited geographic area. LANs are typically configured in a star, bus or ring. Low speed LANs use telephone wires or copper cables, optical fibre cables are used to achieve high-speed transmission of data.
- *Wide Area Network (WAN)*: WAN is used to interconnect a number of widely dispersed computers in various cities of a country or different countries. WANs use communication media maintained by telegraph or telephone companies. These networks usually have land telephone lines, underground coaxial cables, microwave communication and satellite communications.
- *Metropolitan Area Network (MAN)*: MAN refers to inter- connection within geographical limits of a city or town.
- *Gateways*: Gateways consist of software and hardware that are required to interconnect networks amongst themselves. Gateways contend with any differences in packet sizes, protocols and addressing methods between the two networks it connect. Gateways are also used to connect LANs to WANs and WANs, in turn, can be linked through gateways to create national and international data communication networks.

The communications networks can be grouped into the following three categories based on the technology and communication media used by them:

- *Public Switched Telephone Network*: PSTN are managed by common carriers usually telephone companies/departments the world over. The PSTN generally provide two basic services, the normal dial-up connections to the subscribers and permanent leased connection between two subscriber's points. The permanent leased connections provide single traceable line between two subscriber points. The leased lines are generally less prone to noise than dial-up lines.
- *Public Data Network*: Analogous to the public telephone network, many domestic common carriers provide data communications services via a specialised network called a Public Data Network

(PDN). Most Internet Service Providers (ISPs) use combination of PDN and PSTN for providing Internet connectivity.

- *Integrated Services Digital Networks* (ISDN): An ISDN is a network that provides end-to-end digital connectivity to support a wide range of services, including voice and Non-voice services.

Computer networks use physical channels through which information is transmitted between computers in a network. Media may be classified as bounded , *i.e.,* wires (twisted pair telephone wires or UTP CAT 5), cables (co-axial) and optical fibres; or unbounded , *i.e.,* radio waves or microwaves. Data communication is an integral part of the modern information storage and retrieval systems in terms of their online access. Today, network technology works on client server architecture with middleware used for connecting software components or applications on clients and servers.

Technique of packet switching, evolved in 1960s, is used for transferring data between computer systems with an objective to facilitate networked computers to communicate seamlessly across multiple, geographically dispersed locations. The Transmission Control Protocol (TCP) and Internet Protocol (IP), called TCP/ IP suite, is the backbone of Internet and other TCP/ IP based networks.

With developments in communication technology, institutions have options to set-up fibre optic-based gigabit LAN or wireless LAN. Depending on the geographical location, institutions have options to buy terrestrial or satellite-based Internet bandwidth its combinations from a number of Internet Service Providers (ISPs).

DISTINGUISH COMPUTER TECHNOLOGY AND COMMUNICATIONS TECHNOLOGY

Computer Technology

You have certainly seen and, we would guess, used a computer. Nevertheless, let's define what it is. A *computer* is a programmable, multiuse machine that accepts data—raw facts and figures—and processes, or manipulates, it into information we can use, such as summaries, totals, or reports. Its purpose is to speed up problem solving and increase productivity.

Communications Technology

Unquestionably you've been using communications technology for years. *Communications technology*, also called *telecommunications technology*, consists of electromagnetic devices and systems for communicating over long distances. The principal examples are telephone, radio, broadcast television, and cable TV.

In more recent times, there has been the addition of communication among computers—which is what happens when people 'go online' on the internet. In this context, *online* means using a computer or some other information device, connected through a network, to access information and services from another computer or information device. A *network* is a communications system connecting two or more computers; the internet is the largest such network. Information technology is already affecting your life in exciting ways and will do so even more in the future. Let's consider how.

Information Technology and its Used in Education

In her sociology classes at Indiana University, professor Melissa Wilde uses a small wireless keypad linked to a computer to enable students to answer questions not by raising their hands but by pressing buttons, with the results appearing on a screen in the front of the room. Wilde has her students answer multiple-choice questions to see whether they understand her lecture points and to make necessary adjustments.

"I can instantly see that three-quarters of the class doesn't get it," she says. She also uses the technology to get students to answer questions about themselves—race, income, political affiliation—skewed, for example, Towards wealthier or poorer students, an event that fired up a half hour of excited class discussion. Maybe the classrooms at your school haven't reached this level of interactivity yet, but there's no question that information technology is universal on college campuses, and at lower levels the internet has penetrated 99 per cent of schools. Most college students have been exposed to computers Since, the lower grades; indeed, one-fifth of college students report they were using computers between ages 5 and 8, and all had begun using computers by the time they were 16–18 years old. At the college level, the great majority (85 per cent) of students have their own computers, and two-thirds use at least two e-mail addresses.

As you no doubt know, *e-mail* is 'electronic mail,' messages transmitted over a computer network, most often the internet. Three-quarters of college students use the internet 4 or more hours a week, and about onefifth use it 12 or more hours a week. About half are required to use e-mail in their classes. For academic purposes, most students use e-mail to set up appointments (62 per cent) with professors, discuss grades (58 per cent), or get clarification of an assignment (75 per cent). Besides using the internet to help in teaching, today's college instructors also use *presentation graphics software* such as PowerPoint to show their lecture outlines and other materials on classroom screens.

In addition, they use Blackboard, WebCT, and other *coursemanagement software* for administering online assignments, schedules, examinations, and grades. One of the most intriguing developments in education at all levels, however, is the rise of *distance learning,* or *e-learning,* the name given to online education Programmes, which has more than 3.2 million online students enrolled nationwide and grows more than 20 per cent a year. E-learning has had some interesting effects: for example, the home-schooling movement, whereby children are taught at home, usually by parents, has come of age thanks to internet resources. e-Learning has also propelled the rise of for-profit institutions, such as Devry and the University of Phoenix, which 8 per cent of full-time college students now attend.

More than a third of institutions of higher education—and 97 per cent of public universities—offer online courses, and many have attracted on-campus students, who say they like the flexibility of not having to attend their classes at a set time. e-learning has been put to such varied uses as bringing career and technical courses to high school students in remote prairie towns, pairing gifted science students with master teachers in other parts of the country, and helping busy professionals obtain further credentials outside business hours. But the reach of information technology into education has only begun.

In the future, as suggested, see software called 'intelligent tutoring systems' that gives students individualised instruction when personal attention is scarce—such as the software Cognitive Tutor, which not only helps high school students to improve their performance in math but also sparks them to enjoy a subject they might have once hated.

In colleges, more students may use interactive simulation games, such as McGraw- Hill's Business Strategy Game, to apply their knowledge to real-world kinds of problems. And employees in company training Programmes may find themselves engaged in mock conversations with *avatars*—computer depictions of humans, as are often found in online videogames—that represent imaginary customers and coworkers, combining the best parts of computer-based learning with face-to-face interaction.

HEALTH: HIGH TECH FOR WELLNESS

Computers Used in Health and Medicine

Viktor Yazykov, competing in the perilous Around Alone solo sailing competition, found himself in the stormy South Atlantic with a seriously infected arm that needed emergency surgery. So, with the help of step-bystep instructions sent by e-mail from Boston-based Dr. Daniel Carlin to his solar-powered laptop computer, Yazykov operated on his own arm. Yazykov's story is a dramatic example of *telemedicine*—medical care delivered via telecommunications. For some time, physicians in rural areas lacking local access to radiologists have used 'teleradiology' to exchange computerised images such as X-rays via telephone-linked networks with expert physicians in metropolitan areas.

Now telemedicine is moving to an exciting new level, as the use of digital cameras and sound, in effect, moves patients to doctors rather than the reverse. Already telemedicine is being embraced by administrators in the American prison system, where by law inmates are guaranteed medical treatment—and where the increase in prisoners every year has led to the need to control health costs. Computer technology is also radically changing the tools of medicine. All medical information, including that generated by X-ray, lab test, and pulse monitor, can now be transmitted to a doctor in digital format. And image transfer technology allows radiologic images such as CT scans and MRIs to be immediately transmitted to electronic charts and physicians' offices. Patients in intensive care, who are usually monitored by nurses during offtimes, can also be watched over by doctors in remote 'control towers' miles away. Electronic medical records and other computerised tools enable heart attack patients to get follow-up drug treatment and diabetics to have their blood sugar measured. Software can compute a woman's breast cancer risk. Patients can use e-mail to query their doctors about their records.

Various *robots*—automatic devices that perform functions ordinarily performed by human beings, with names such as robo doc, RoboCart, TUG, and HelpMate—help free medical workers for more critical tasks; the four-armed da Vinci surgical robot, for instance, can do cuts and stitches deep inside the body, so that surgery is less traumatic and recovery time faster. Hydraulics and computers are being used to help artificial limbs get 'smarter.' And a patient paralysed by a stroke has received an implant that allows communication between his brain and a computer; as a result, he can move a cursor across a screen by brainpower and convey simple messages—as in *Star Trek.*

Want to calculate how long you will live? Want to go about gathering your family health history to see if you're at risk for particular inherited diseases? These are only two examples of health Web sites available to patients and health consumers. Although online health information can be misleading and even dangerous, many people now tap into health care databases, e-mail health professionals, or communicate with people who have similar conditions. For instance, hours after 10-year-old Robert Lord of San Diego fractured his spine in a fall from a tree, his father found an experimental drug on the internet, saving the boy from lifetime paralysis.

Often patients are already steeped in information about their conditions when they arrive in the offices of health care professionals. This represents a fundamental shift of knowledge, and therefore power, from physicians to patients. In addition, health care consumers are able to share experiences and information with one another. Young parents, for example, can find an online gathering spot at pediatrician Alan Greene's Web site.

MONEY: TOWARDS THE CASHLESS SOCIETY

Computers Affect and Financial Matters

"The future of money is increasingly digital, likely virtual, and possibly universal," says one writer. *Virtual* means that something is created, simulated, or carried on by means of a computer or a computer network, and we certainly have come a long way Towards becoming a cashless society. Indeed, the percentage of all financial transactions done electronically, both phone-initiated and computer-initiated, was projected to rise to 18.4 per cent in 2013, up from 0.9 per cent in 1993.

Besides currency, paper checks, and credit and debit cards, the things that serve as 'money' include cashvalue cards, automatic transfers, and digital money. Many readers of this book will probably already have engaged in online buying and selling, purchasing CDs and DVDs, books, airline tickets, or computers.

But what about groceries? After all, you can't exactly squeeze the cantaloupes through your keyboard. Even so, online groceries are expected to reach $7.5 billion in U.S., sales by 2012. To change decades of shopping habits, e-grocers keep their delivery charges low and delivery times convenient, and they take great pains in filling orders, knowing that a single bad piece of fruit will produce a devastating word-of-mouth backlash. Only about 46 per cent of U.S.,

workers have their paychecks electronically deposited into their bank accounts, but this is sure to change as Americans discover that direct deposit is actually safer and faster. Online bill paying is also picking up steam. For more than two decades, it has been possible to pay bills online, such as those from phone and utility companies, with special software and online connections to your bank. About 19 million American households do some bill paying online, and the number was expected to reach 61 million households in 2008.

Some banks and other businesses are backing an electronic-payment system that allows internet users to buy goods and services with *micropayments,* electronic payments of as little as 25 cents in transactions for which it is uneconomical to use a credit card. Micropayment, suggests futurist Paul Saffo, 'allows you to buy things by the sip rather than the gulp.' The success of Apple Computer's iTunes online music service, which sells songs for 99 cents each, suggests that micro sales are now feasible.

All kinds of businesses and organisations, from independent songwriters to comic book writers to the Legal Aid Society of Cleveland, now accept micropayments, using intermediaries such as BitPass and Peppercoin. Thus, you could set up your own small business simply by constructing a Web site and accepting micropay-ments.

LEISURE: INFOTECH IN ENTERTAINMENT AND THE ARTS

Leisure Activities be Affected by Information Technology

Information technology is being used for all kinds of entertainment, ranging from videogames to telegambling. It is also being used in the arts, from painting to photography. Let's consider just two examples, music and film. Computers, the internet, and the World Wide Web are standing the system of music recording and distribution on its head—and in the process are changing the financial underpinnings of the music industry. Because of their high overhead, major record labels typically need a band to sell half a million CDs in order to be profitable, but independent bands, using online marketing, can be reasonably successful selling 20,000 or 30,000 albums. Team Love, a small music label established in 2003, found it could promote its first two bands, Tilly and the Wall and Willy Mason, by offering songs online fRee for *downloading*—transferring data from a remote computer to one's own computer—so that people could listen to them before paying $12 for a CD. It also puts videos online for sharing and uses quirky Web sites to reach fans.

"There's something exponential going on," says one of Team Love's founders. "The more music that's downloaded, the more it sells." Many independent musicians are also using the internet to get their music heard, hoping that giving away songs will help them build audiences. The web also offers sources for instantly downloadable sheet music. One research engineer has devised a computerised scoring system for judging musical competitions that overcomes the traditional human-jury approach, which can be swayed by personalities and politics.

And a Spanish company, PolyphonicHMI, has created Hit Song Science software, which they say can analyse the hit potential of new songs by "reference to a finely parsed universe of attributes derived from millions of past songs." As for movies, now that blockbuster movies routinely meld live action and animation, computer artists are in big demand. The 1999 film *Star Wars: Episode I*, for instance, had fully 1,965 digital shots out of about 2,200 shots.

Even when film was used, it was scanned into computers to be tweaked with animated effects, lighting, and the like. Entire beings were created on computers by artists working on designs developed by producer George Lucas and his chief artist. What is driving the demand for computer artists? One factor is that animation, though not cheap, looks more and more like a bargain, because hiring movie actors costs so much—some make $20 million a film. Moreover, special effects are readily understood by audiences in other countries, and major studios increasingly count on revenues from foreign markets to make a film profitable.

Digital manipulation also allows a crowd of extras to be multiplied into an army of thousands. It can also be used to create settings: in the film *Sky Captain and the World of Tomorrow,* the actors—Gwyneth Paltrow, Angelina Jolie, and Jude Law—shot all their scenes in front of a blue screen, and computer-generated imagery was then used to transport them into an imaginary world of 1939. Computer techniques have even been used to develop digitally created actors—called 'synthespians.' Actors ranging from the late James Dean to the late John Wayne, for instance, have been recruited for television commercials. And computerised animation is now so popular that Hollywood studios and movie directors are finding they can make as much money from creating videogames as from making movies. But animation is not the only area in which computers are revolutionising movies. Digital editing has radically transformed the way films are assembled.

Whereas traditional film editing involved reeling and unreeling spools of film and cutting and gluing pieces of highly scratchable celluloid together, nearly burying the editor in film, today an editor can access 150 miles of film stored on a computer and instantly find any visual or audio moment, allowing hundreds of variations of a scene to be called up for review. Even Non-professionals can get into movie making as new computerrelated products come to market.

Now that digital video capture-and-edit systems are available for under $1,000, amateurs can turn home videos into digital data and edit them. Also, digital camcorders, which offer outstanding picture and sound quality, have steadily dropped in price.

SOURCE SOCIAL SOFTWARE AS DIGITAL LIBRARY INTERFACE

This article investigates the use of social software applications in digital library environments. It examines the use of blogging software as an interface to digital library content stored in a separate repository.

The article begins with a definition of digital library approaches and features, examines ways in which open source and social software applications can serve to fill digital library roles, and presents a case study of the use of blogging software as a public interface to a project called Digital Forsyth, a grant-funded project involving three institutions in Forsyth County, NC. The article concludes with a review of positive and negative outcomes from this approach and makes recommendations for further research.

A significant portion of digital library literature focuses on issues such as document/technology heterogeneity and the relationship of users and communities in digital libraries. While applications such as MediaWiki and WordPress have been built primarily to support specific types of Web-publishing, they also include a number of structures common to the digital library community, including storage, preservation, and access models.

For this reason, MediaWiki and WordPress can be investigated as acceptable platforms for digital library applications. Some library applications have already been developed using these platforms including Scriblio from Plymouth State University, and The Polar Bear Expedition digital collections. Both of these sites demonstrate the benefits of the incorporation of user services into digital library software.

There are a number of possible approaches to using social software in digital library environments.

Downloadable applications such as MediaWiki or WordPress blogging software lend themselves to data and interface customization.

Other sites, such as Flickr, support data storage and application programming interface functions that could be used to create a digital library application. Through working with WordPress in the digital library application presented in this article, a number of challenges to using social software were discovered including:

- The ability/inability to crosswalk data between the social software application and the primary repository
- A lack of emphasis on metadata by default
- A lack of searching algorithms by default

The remainder of this article presents how a specific social software application (WordPress) was used to implement a public interface to a specific digital library. The article looks at the advantages and disadvantages of this approach as well as what its future potential there may be.

CASE STUDY PRESENTATION

Digital Forsyth is a grant-funded digital library project involving the Forsyth County Public Library, Winston Salem State University, and Wake Forest University. The project is supported by grant funds from the Institute of Museum and Library Services under the provisions of the federal Library Services and Technology Act (LSTA), administered as a multi-year grant by the State Library of North Carolina, a division of the Department of Cultural Resources.The purpose of the grant is to create a digital repository for the historic photographs and collections of Forsyth County, NC institutions. In the first two years, a primary focus of this project has been the digitization and collective categorization of photographs from the archives of each of the institutions.

This process has involved the creation of a digital library using Qualified Dublin Core (QDC) as the metadata standard, with extensive description using a faceted categorization system. Each photograph is described with QDC elements and has faceted analysis completed on the elements and context of the photograph.

On average, each photograph has 11 faceted descriptors.The faceted taxonomy is developed from the 'bottom-up' using the photographs and archival information and is managed using Protégé, an open source ontology management system developed by Stanford University. As the Digital Forsyth project evolved, community participation emerged as one of the goals of the digital library.

The resulting definition of the user interface included goals of community participation in the content, description, and organization of this digital library. While the back-end of the digital library employs a commercial digital library system that enforces authority control and manages metadata well, it did not include a public interface that met the community goals of this project. For this reason, we began looking at alternative platforms that would both allow us to present and manage our data easily and provide a robust community experience.

In short, the basic functional requirements of the software were to have the ability to:

- Store and display QDC metadata
- Store and display hierarchical facets
- Allow user-contributed content, including comments, description, and tags
- Permit the import and export of data in bulk
- Be customized easily both for user-interface and data management purposes

The project team considered several social software or Web-publishing applications including MediaWiki, WordPress, Flamenco, and Flickr. We chose blogging software as a platform because it fills many of the needs of the project, including photo representation, metadata support through use of special fields, category support, and embedded social tools.

While the idea of hosted blogging software was discussed, we felt that a local solution was required in order to achieve the level of customization and data access needed. We ultimately chose WordPress due to our prior experience with the software, which is hosted by one of the project partners for its own user community. The next section includes a discussion of some of the issues and solutions that we encountered.

SOLUTIONS

Using WordPress as a digital library application required the Digital Forsyth team to solve a number of problems related to metadata management, data migration, and user interface management.

Modifying WordPress for metadata representation

In order to work as a digital library interface, WordPress needed to support some level of detail for QDC metadata and provide the capacity to use our hierarchical facets as tags. To achieve this, we utilized custom fields in WordPress, post categories, and manipulation of the WordPress searching and browsing functions.

One of the strengths of WordPress is its support for custom fields that can be used to satisfy rudimentary metadata. We were able to configure these fields to match the Qualified Dublin Core metadata standard and move much of the content out of the blog posting text to these custom fields. In addition, we were able to load the Protégé-based taxonomy of the faceted categorization system into WordPress categories. This allowed us to preserve the relationships of the taxonomy while making terms easily usable in the blog interface.

For loading blog posts using both custom fields and categories, we modified the blog loader scripts to accommodate the new fields. We were able to use internal Protégé IDs to match on category assignments in the metadata records themselves, enabling permanent URLs to be created to point to different sections of the taxonomy. While this provides a unique, customizable link, it does not give the interface 'clean' URLs that would be easily remembered by a user. The use of clean URLs is a popular feature in many social software platforms including Flickr, Del.icio.us and MediaWiki, and allows a user to navigate to different parts of the site using common words rather than cryptic strings.

In order to enable more granular searching of these new fields and categories, we used a pre-developed WordPress searching plug-in called AdvancedSearch. This gave us a suite of defined functions that supported category and custom field limits, which allowed the users of the interface to limit their search/browse experience by institution, date, or other metadata fields.

While the plug-in was modified to support local needs, the existence of the library allowed us to quickly develop search and limiting functionality. While in some cases, we altered specific components of the plug-ins, we avoided making modifications to the core WordPress software. This has allowed us to patch the software several times without negatively impacting local customizations. While future upgrades (particularly the implementation of WordPress 2.3) will require an evaluation of local modifications, the use of locally written plug-ins and minor modifications to third party plug-ins is expected to minimize development required for upgrades.

METADATA ISSUES

While initially we had standardized on Qualified Dublin Core, moving forward with WordPress required us to make two substantial modifications, one to the metadata itself and the other to the WordPress functionality. First, although the libraries had followed the recommended QDC date format wherever possible (but had created Non--standard dates when days/months/ years were not known specifically), WordPress required a well-formed date value. Because of this, we had to zero-fill any un-specified values. This allowed WordPress to make decisions and appropriately place Non--specific dated posts.

The second major issue we faced occurred due to the size of some areas of the taxonomy. The standard functionality of WordPress categories includes a retrieval of all the related child categories when a user is interacting with the category browse interface. While this is preferable in some cases, database response times for our project were leading to time-out issues whenever category values exceeded several hundred.

In order to solve this issue, the category retrieval functions had to be re-written to make this process more efficient and to pull child values only when they were needed.

WordPress allows local implementations to make modifications like this using a local functions file that is related to specific interface themes. While this will require us to re-examine these functions with each WordPress upgrade, it also allows us to continue expanding the use of the taxonomy to create new relationships between the images in our collection.

In general, we used the following four approaches to modify WordPress in the Digital Forsyth project:

- First, the implementers downloaded pre-developed plug-ins. These plug-ins allowed us to quickly extend or modify the functionality of WordPress without significant effort.
- Second, we modified existing functions to fit our local needs. While using pre-defined functions makes these modifications much simpler to do, they can also affect the system when upgrades are made to WordPress.
- Third, in some cases we chose to modify the core functionality of WordPress.
- This was required in special cases where the WordPress default behaviour was not in sync with our expectations for Digital Forsyth. A simple example of this is the fact that blogging software by default returns posts in reverse chronological order. However, for our project we wanted posts to be returned in increasing chronological order; therefore, in such cases we modified basic WordPress functions accordingly.
- Fourth, we created new local functions. While this approach was not used extensively, in the case of category retrieval new functions were required to make data retrieval more efficient. This final approach is probably the most susceptible to issues related to system upgrades.

As the Digital Forsyth project moves into its third year, we are looking Towards merging the library cataloger experience with public feedback and tagging experience. This may allow us to stop using a back-end digital library for record creation and simply use it for archiving, which will significantly simplify the processes of data creation, loading, user-tagging, and updating currently in place.

Creating a user Interface using Themes

We were able to use the theme platform in WordPress to easily create a custom look and feel for our digital library. Two of the major modifications required were modifying the theme to display hierarchical tags more prominently and including our custom metadata fields at the correct place in the blog posting. Other modifications included style and layout customization. Some high level uses and benefits of themes are:

- Enabling multiple user/organization centric views of the data
- Enabling rapid prototyping of interfaces during initial development
- Using splash pages to provide deep links to searching and browsing interfaces.

In general, Word Press themes provide a simple platform for creating user interfaces, and involve approximately 8-10 files. Themes can be based on templates and specific pages where required. In some cases, we found ourselves deciding whether to use external plug-ins for themes or to develop them locally. An example of this is the development of 'photoblogging' style functions without using the photoblogging plug-in that comes with Word Press.

While we found the use of local functions was appropriate at the time we made our decision on this matter, being willing to re-investigate/re-develop this area as upgrades occur is an important component of using social software. Because so many possible features exist and are developed in the blogging user community, deciding which features to include and use can be challenging. Here again, the presence of such a large community of developers and users means that we are able to embed and deploy new services quickly, without a large amount of local development.

We found that using the WordPress software allowed development to start at a much deeper level. For example, rather than writing a batch loader or indexer, we were able to make small modifications to the WordPress software using existing modules. A prime example of modification is the revision to the tag-cloud plug-in. While traditional tag-clouds emphasize the most popular terms, with regard to our project we found that emphasizing the un-common facet categories in the tag cloud using a Term Frequency/Inverse Document Frequency (TF/IDF) approach yielded a more relevant and usable interface.

We accomplished this by creating a function that counted the number of times a facet was used in the corpus of blog posts and comparing those counts against the facets in the individual post. Based on the assigned weights using class definitions in the HTML, the interface uses CSS (Cascading Style Sheets) to modify the style of the resulting tags.

Data Migration

In order to load data from the digital library system to WordPress, we modified the existing RSS loader to support Qualified Dublin Core tags. The RSS loader was used because it already had a framework to support XML and employed a generic approach to the import functions. By adding control structures and modifying the mapping approach of data, we were able to map QDC fields to the appropriate custom fields and categories in WordPress. We also modified the loader in a few ways, such as excluding certain records and category matches in order to ensure that existing records are not overwritten and that duplicate categories are not created. In order to handle record updating, a separate update script was written.

As we begin to collect user-contributed data, data export and archiving is becoming a more significant problem. We are looking at different approaches for exporting and preserving this data, including extending the Qualified Dublin Core data in the back-end digital library system to support new blog-centric fields and storing data in archival packages.

Two fundamental questions arose while we worked on data loading and exporting. First, while we were committed to using external standards to represent and store data, it became obvious that it might be just as useful to define a local standard and then rely on mapping applications to make data available to external systems. Using a locally defined standard could have allowed us to approach some fields (such as record state, cataloger) more specifically while preserving the standard descriptive fields.

A related need to add qualifiers to different types of links could have been achieved via either a local standard or simply a different approach. As the project moves into its third year, we are considering different metadata standards or approaches that might allow more specificity at the administrative levels. Second, we found that the blogging software had sufficient functionality to support all of the data creation, management, and social-contribution needs of the project. It became obvious that using a digital library system for archiving rather than data creation might be a more efficient approach.

While we adapted the WordPress import/export functionality to suit the needs of our digital library, the issue of scalability might make it necessary in the future to take different approaches with large metadata batches. While current loading practices for our project are acceptable, loading larger batches through direct database interaction could lead to more flexible system interoperability.

The Content of the Blog Post Record

For our project, we use the blog record to represent an individual photograph. The QDC record title is mapped to the blog posting title. Post content contains the QDC identifier field mapped to the image HTML element, and the QDC description field is mapped to a Paragraph.

The Post excerpt contains an image element referencing a thumbnail representation of the photograph. The rest of the blog posting uses custom fields to store the rest of the QDC elements. By making extensive use of WordPress's custom fields to store QDC metadata, the interface and search functionality is enhanced.

OBSERVATIONS AND DISCUSSION

Many of the main benefits of using WordPress or other social software as a digital library interface have already been mentioned. Using a pre-developed system can enable rapid and flexible system development, enables the project to be more focused on user-driven functions, and benefits from the development focus of a larger community.

ISSUES

Data Management

One of the primary issues with the use of social software applications as a digital library interface is data management. While digital libraries have multiple goals (including creation, management, and preservation of digital objects and their metadata), the goals of social software are often focused on ease of content creation, user-friendly interfaces, and data presentation.

Making sure that digital objects are accurately represented and displayed means: utilizing primary identifiers from the core digital library system; taking steps to ensure that metadata is accurately represented in the social software application to ensure no degradation of accuracy or specificity; and accurately managing metadata and digital object versions to ensure that the most accurate data is preserved.

While WordPress required us to manipulate some functions to ensure that these goals were met in our project, its flexibility as a content creation and display system has resulted in a significant reduction in the amount of work required to create and manage our user interface. Future developments in the use of WordPress as a content creation and management system are expected to save time and allow Digital Forsyth to employ systems that can focus on metadata management and preservation.

Technical Skills

A common criticism of social software is the skill level required to implement and manage these applications. Using social software in a custom environment such as the one described in this article exacerbates this situation, as specific skills are required to make the software work in specific ways. In general, programming skills, XML skills, metadata skills and digital object skills are essential for a project like ours. In addition, some specific skills are required to work with WordPress and common digital library applications, including skills using:

- PHP
- SQL
- CSS/HTML
- Web server software
- JavaScript

Two issues that took time for us to work through were:

- Lack of familiarity with the WordPress programming framework
- Lack of documentation of software

In addition, while theme creation is relatively straightforward, customizing a theme beyond simple colour and layout decisions required more extensive work. WordPress is rather complicated software, so finding the appropriate function can be difficult at times. Working with these functions can get confusing, regardless of the extent of documentation provided.

SUSTAINABILITY

Project sustainability should be a key concern when selecting software for a digital library project. Commercial systems can have a host of sustainability issues, including vendor support, ease of system use and customization, and system flexibility. Social software and open source software applications have other sustainability issues to consider as well.

These include the inability to guarantee service stability and permanence. While commercial systems typically have market permanence or vendor-supplied migration options, open source and social software is often only as permanent as the user community surrounding it. This means that an organization must be willing to find new solutions when required, and it also means that these organizations will have to carry the burden of system migration on their own.

Further, while there are many hosted low cost and free options for digital libraries (including hosted blogs/wikis, hosted image sites such as Flickr), the system being considered should be compared against the needed stability and uptime of the system. In short, it does not make sense to base key parts of a digital library on a free, hosted service if the digital library cannot sustain itself outside of that service.

In choosing the approach we took for Digital Forsyth, we found that the implementation of the user interface was accomplished quickly and with community-centric features that serve as the centerpiece of the project site. Despite the issues that we experienced with metadata management, system assumptions/limitations, and interoperability, overall the use of WordPress lowered our development and maintenance costs.

We are hopeful that the system will benefit from increased sustainability and portability as future releases of WordPress are installed, and as special functions are developed and deployed. In selecting an existing open source application to serve as an interface to your particular digital library, some key questions to ask are:

- Will the system scale to the level that your data requires?
- Are the data models used in the system compliant with your digital library metadata structure?
- Is migrating data between the applications sustainable?
- What needs can be filled with these social software/open source applications? Is the software appropriate just for user interfaces or can it serve other functions of the digital library system?
- How will system sustainability be ensured with the selected options?
- Will developing the customized parts of the software be more manageable than other solutions?
- What core functional requirements exist, and is this application the best approach?

By choosing the solution we did, we hope to be able to incorporate a number of approaches to public interfaces while keeping our digital library applications centralized and focused on key functions of storage and preservation.

3

Information Systems for Library Management

INTRODUCTION

Three libraries claimed that they had management information systems in their institutions and libraries. One library had a partial system in both the institution and the library, and was trying to develop a comprehensive one in library. One had a partial system in the library, and was attempting to have a comprehensive one, even though there was no management information system in its institution. Of those who did not have management information systems in their libraries, three librarians offered the explanation that this was because there was no management information system in the institution. One commented that its attention was concentrated on selecting and introducing a reliable turnkey automated system. All librarians mentioned that user friendliness and inexpensiveness are priorities in establishing their management information systems.

Apart from the library which has decision support systems, current automated library systems are not fully used for formal management information systems, even though these could perhaps provide enhanced information for performance measurement and could contribute to the establishment of a more comprehensive evaluation of the achievement of the libraries' objectives. In terms of the ability of their automated system to support a management information system, all the libraries stated that existing systems were generally helpful in data processing. However, they produced output data which is crude and which has to be further manipulated before it can be interpreted.

Seven of the libraries' computer systems produce quite complete operational data such as statistics of cataloguing, circulation, etc., but no system provides statistical data on reference services. One university library struggled to collect even crude data since its turnkey system has limited capabilities. It produces only data on circulation and stocks, and lacks compatibility with any other automated system in the library or the institution. Therefore, in order to have data in usable form and when needed, all libraries must at present manipulate them.

Two libraries, however, had microcomputers which had no downloading facilities: they first had to print out the data from larger computers and manipulate it manually before inputting it into a microcomputer to be used with other information. Others did have microcomputers with downloading facilities, and could use them to process the crude data into usable outputs. All the libraries thus employ workable methods of producing management information, but they lack immediacy, and are expensive to operate. The forms of output vary. Those libraries which had formal management information systems had facilities to examine them online, but mostly data is presented in hard copy. Libraries which had informal and/or partial management information systems tended to rely on on-demand reporting. Although most libraries stated that the outputs are easily read, analysing the outputs of the system depends mostly on the abilities of the users to interpret them.

Outputs provide information for junior, senior and chief librarians. Graphical presentations were available to make numerical data understandable in a very short time. Apart from the information provided for junior management, the outputs of management information systems are generally discussed in senior staff meetings on a weekly or monthly basis. With regard to decision making in the areas of library planning and evaluation, in particular budgeting and resources allocation, two chief librarians stated that management information systems had made a great impact in the sense that all decisions were made based on the information from their systems. This is due to the comprehensiveness of the information made available. Their systems can provide only crude data, but it can be interpreted easily so that it assists in answering very specific questions.

APPLICATION IN INFORMATION SYSTEM

Internet is a global information system, consisting of billions of web pages from which we can get information. The major activity on the Internet, that is electronic publishing and information uploading, are being done in quiet an unorganized way. The lack of proper organizing huge quantities of information has not retrieve from the Internet. In any information system, we have followed certain tools and techniques to tell us which document contains what information. These tools and techniques can be classification, cataloguing, indexing, etc., in the case of traditional information systems.

As Internet is a distributed information system with disjoint information sources spread across the globe, we cannot bring the related documents together in the retrieval process. Hence the tools and techniques meant for pinpointing information on the Internet need to be more accurate. XML is significant because it makes it much easier to share and search resources that are in different formats. Until fairly recently, this wasn't much of an issue for libraries. Historically, libraries have served as centralized repositories of information. They purchased books, journals, films, and other information resources on physical media, and patrons found what the library owned by consulting a catalogue that listed holdings. Most catalogs are designed with the assumption that once a library records some descriptive information about each resource it has purchased, this information won't have to be radically altered. For physical resources, this works pretty well, since the authors, titles, subjects, and physical characteristics of a book don't change. Once access to the Internet became widespread, it became clear that providing access to remote electronic resources could be very problematic. Catalogs are designed to provide access to physical resources that are under direct control of the library. However, people want to read journal articles, books, and useful Web pages stored in dynamically updated databases that are maintained and owned by other organizations that might be thousands of miles away. Online library catalogs are poorly suited for providing access to these works; so many libraries do not include these types of resources in the catalogue. As a result, it is often very difficult for patrons to know what electronic resources they can get t1hrough their libraries.

This is where XML comes into the picture. It is impossible to search or display information unless it is structured in a meaningful way. In plain English, this means that information providers need to agree on standards for encoding electronic documents so they can be retrieved in a uniform way. Libraries have encoded bibliographic records in MARC for many years, and that has allowed them to easily share catalogue records, which reduces costs while improving services. For a variety of reasons, it is not feasible to encode the new types of resources patrons want access to in MARC. However, when the information is stored in XML, it is possible to share and combine that data in ways that would not otherwise be possible.

INTERNET AND ITS' SEARCH ENGINES, SEARCH DIRECTORY AND META SEARCH ENGINES

There are many 'search engines'; 'meta search engines' and 'search directory' are available in the Internet. This is obvious from the two following important observations:

- The result of aparticular search is so high in recall and low in precision.
- The output of the search result has no standard of 2any kind.

The search tools on the Internet use robots to collect information about the documents to generate keyword indexes. Generally, these tools use different algorithms to assign keywords to the document. Some of the robots collect keywords from the title whereas some collect from the first few lines of the document. But the very pre-assumption of the search robots, that the titles are expressive and the beginning few lines of a document focuses the content, do not hold good for maximum documents. To give an example, if we search the Internet for term 'data', we should be sure to get results at least regarding 'database', 'data center', 'data warehouse', etc. Certainly the recall will be very high.

The retrieval of irrelevant result can be reduced by subject gateway approach, but cannot be eliminated. The main cause of the problem in *Hyper Text Markup Language* (HTML), the standard for web publication is system-defined tag. This *'tag set'* is mainly for display of the content and HTML provides no tag to address the content precisely. *eXtensible Markup Language* (XML) designed by *World Wide Web Consortium* (W3C) promises a possible solution to this problem. The major advantage of XML over HTML is its extensibility, *i.e.*, provision of user defined tags and attributes to identify the structural elements of a document. XML also provides structural complexity to define document structure that can be nested at any level of complexity.

WHAT IS XML?

XML is a extensible markup language for documents containing structured information. Structured information contains both content and some indication of what role that content plays. Almost all documents have some structure. A markup language is a mechanism to identify structures in a document. The XML specification defines a standard way to add markup to documents.

XML IS JUST LIKE HTML

No. In HTML, both the tag semantics and the tag set are fixed. An <h1> is always a first level heading and the tag <ati.product.code> is meaningless. The W3C, in conjunction with browser vendors and the WWW community, is constantly working to extend the definition of HTML to allow new tags to keep pace with changing technology and to bring variations in presentation to the Web. However, these changes are always rigidly confined by what the browser vendors have implemented and by the fact that backward compatibility is paramount. And for people who want to disseminate information widely, features supported by only the latest releases of Netscape and Internet Explorer are not useful.

XML IS JUST LIKE SGML

No. Well, yes, sort of. XML is defined as an application profile of SGML. SGML is the Standard Generalized Markup Language defined by ISO 8879. SGML has been the standard, vendor-independent way to maintain repositories of structured documentation for more than a decade, but it is not well suited to serving documents over the web. Defining XML as an application profile of SGML means that any fully conformant SGML system will be able to read XML documents. However, using and understanding XML documents *does not* require a system that is capable of understanding the full generality of SGML. XML is, roughly speaking, a restricted form of SGML.

WHY XML

It is important to understand why it was created. XML was created so that richly structured documents could be used over the web. The only viable alternatives, HTML and SGML, are not practical for this purpose. HTML comes bound with a set of semantics and does not provide arbitrary structure. SGML provides arbitrary structure, but is too difficult to implement just for a web browser.

Full SGML systems solve large, complex problems that justify their expense. Viewing structured documents sent over the web rarely carries such justification. This is not to say that XML can be expected to completely replace SGML. While XML is being designed to deliver structured content over the web, some of the very features it lacks to make this practical, make SGML a more satisfactory solution for the creation and long-time storage of complex documents. In many organizations, filtering SGML to XML will be the standard procedure for web delivery.

ORIGIN AND GOALS

XML was developed by an XML Working Group formed under the auspices of the *World Wide Web Consortium* (W3C) in 1996. It was chaired by Jon Bosak of Sun Microsystems with the active participation of an XML Special Interest Group also organized by the W3C. Dan Connolly served as the Working Group's contact with the W3C. The design goals for XML are:

- XML shall be straightforwardly usable over the Internet.
- XML shall support a wide variety of applications.
- XML shall be compatible with SGML.
- It shall be easy to write programmes which process XML documents.
- The number of optional features in XML is to be kept to the absolute minimum, ideally zero.
- XML documents should be human-legible and reasonably clear.
- The XML design should be prepared quickly.
- The design of XML shall be formal and concise.
- XML documents shall be easy to create.
- Terseness in XML markup is of minimal importance.

HOW XML WORKS

In XML, *Document Type Definitions* (DTDs) may accompany a document, essentially defining the rules of the document, such as which elements are present and the structural relationship between the elements. DTDs help to validate the data when the receiving application does not have a built-in description of the incoming data. With XML, however, DTDs are optional. Data sent along with a DTD is known as 'valid' XML. In this case, an XML parser could check incoming data against the rules defined in the DTD to make sure data was structured correctly.

Data sent without a DTD is known as 'well-formed ' XML. With both valid and well-formed XML, XML encoded data is self-describing. The open and flexible format used by XML allows it to be employed anywhere a need exists for the exchange and transfer of information. This makes it powerful. For instance, XML can be used to describe information about HTML pages, or it can be used to describe data contained in business rules or objects in an electronic - commerce transaction, such as invoices, purchase orders and order forms.

XML is separate from HTML, but XML could also be added inside HTML documents. By embedding XML data inside an HTML page, multiple views could be generated from the delivered data, using the semantic information contained in the XML. Moreover, XML can be used for such compelling applications as distributed printing, database searches, and others. When most people think of the things that can be done with XML, they are actually thinking about a family of related technologies rather than a single markup language. On a related note, it is better to think of XML as a grammar than as a language. XML establishes rules for defining new formats. In regular markup languages such as the *HyperText Markup Language* (HTML), authors must use certain tags that make the text bold, create clickable links, draw tables, apply style sheets, etc. With XML, authors are free to make up their own tags and attributes if they don't feel that those that have been created by others meet their needs.

XML AND LIBRARIES

For years, libraries have been quietly using XML to perform functions such as improving access to archival materials, simplifying interlibrary loan processing, and enhancing digital collections, but increased reliance on the Internet for delivering information resources has brought XML into the mainstream, where its impact is starting to be felt by libraries of all sizes. As early as 1993, the library at the University of California- Berkeley started developing a method for encoding archival materials in XML. The outcome of this project was the development of the *Encoded Archival Description* (EAD) standard, which is now maintained by the Library of Congress. Use of EAD has been increasing steadily over the years as a growing number of archival finding aids have been moved to the Web. For the past several years, individual libraries have been improving their services and saving money by developing their own XML applications. Since 1998, Oregon State University has been using an application called *InterLibrary Loan Automated Search And Print* (ILL ASAP) to automatically search interlibrary loan requests and print request forms sorted by location and call number, complete with availability information, scannable Ariel addresses, shipping labels and billing data customized to the borrowing library or consortium involved. This free application has been adopted by dozens of libraries around the country. More-ambitious XML projects have also been successfully implemented. The Washington Research Library Consortium uses XML to provide access to subscription databases, digital collections, materials requested via interlibrary loan, and library catalogs that run on a combination of commercial, open source, and locally developed platforms. This system, known as *Access to Library And Database Information Network* (ALADIN) not only delivers content to seven academic research libraries, but also performs critical related tasks such as patron authentication using XML messages transmitted between applications over the Web. In the spring of 2002, the Library of Congress announced an official specification for representing MARC data in an XML environment, MARC XML.

Even though sharing data between catalogs is relatively easy because of widespread support for the MARC format, the ability to express MARC data in XML is useful for any library trying to develop tools or access mechanisms that combine MARC data with non-MARC resources. Now that a standard has emerged for representing MARC, it is reasonable to assume that vendors and others will develop tools that take advantage of the huge amount of data already stored in MARC format.

As a matter of fact, within a few weeks of the announcement of LC's specification, well-known tools used for manipulating MARC records such as *Java MARC Events* (JAMES) and MarcEdit already contained support for the new standard. As more libraries use XML, they are finding more uses for it. The eScholarship initiative at the California Digital Library not only uses XML to store books in a standardized format, but it also uses XML technologies to allow users to define their own displays. The *Open Archives Initiative* (OAI), an effort supported by OCLC, has developed a protocol that makes it easy to send a query to a database over the Web and receive the results in XML. OAI effectively makes it possible to perform searches of multiple databases simultaneously without the need for proprietary hooks into local databases. While this functionality is very similar to what was promised with Z39.50, OAI is much easier to implement, so the hope is that it will be widely used for many kinds of databases.

STRUCTURE OF INFORMATION SCIENCE

Any field is structured along some distinct, larger areas or subdisciplines of enquiry or practice. Think of a number of areas of medicine, computer science, librarianship, and so forth. Information science is not an exception. It has a distinct, two-partite structure. A number of authors observed that the work in information science falls in two large areas or subdisciplines, each, of course, with further subareas or specialties. White and McCain conducted a monumental bibliometric study of the domain of information science by providing extensive analysis of co-citation patterns for 120 authors over a period of 23 years. Borrowing from

White and McCain, visualize a map of information science as an ellipse with authors inside, distributed or clustered according to their connections. There are two large clusters at each end of the ellipse, with only a few authors spanning both. In other words, there are two major areas or subdisciplines.

I liked their metaphor:

As Things Turn Out, Information Science Looks Rather like Australia: Heavily coastal in its development, with a sparsely settled interior.

In one of the coastal sections, fall authors that worked on analytical study of literatures; their structures; studies of texts as content-bearing objects; communication in various populations, particularly scientific communication; social context of information; information uses; information seeking and behaviour; various theories of information and related topics. As yet, there is no good label for that cluster. Some call it "information analysis." For simplicity, lets call this the *domain cluster,* as did White and McCain, although "basic" may be a good label. In the other coastal section are authors who concentrated on IR theory and retrieval algorithms; practical IR processes and systems; human-computer interaction; user studies; library systems; OPACs; and related topics.

Let's call this cluster the *retrieval cluster,* although "applied" may also be a good label. Basically, most of the areas in the domain cluster are about study of fundamental manifes-tations and behaviour of phenomena and objects that information science is all about. They are centered on the phenomenon of information and its manifestations in literature. The retrieval cluster deals, by and large, with a variety of implementations, on both practical and theoretical levels. It is about implementation, behaviour, and effects of the interface between literatures and people, including, of course, all kinds of retrieval aspects. Unfortunately, these two main clusters are largely unconnected.

Only a very small number of authors spanned the two clusters. In other words, there are very few integrating works. The last text that undertook an integrative approach encom-passing both clusters. A rare example of such an effort in research is the last work by Tague-Sutcliffe, where she related the notion of informative-ness with evaluation of IR systems.

Several modern texts are specifically aimed at IR but none on information science as a whole. I dare to venture a prediction: fame awaits the researcher who devise a formal theoretical work, bolstered by experimental evidence, that connects the two largely separated clusters, *i.e.*, connecting basic phenomena with their realization in the retrieval world. And a bestseller is awaiting an author that produces an integrative text in information science. Information science will become a full-fledged discipline when the two ends are connected successfully. The two clusters are not equally popu-lated.

The retrieval cluster has significantly more authors, not to mention total number of works. As in many other fields, more effort is expanded on the applied side than on the basic side.In part, this is due to availability of funds for given topics—not surprisingly, research goes after moneyed topics. By and large, over the last decade or so, major granting agencies funded only applied research in information science. For instance, I have been unable to identify a single grant addressing any of the topics in the domain or basic cluster from NSF Division of Information and Intelligent Systems since its preceding Division of Information Science and Technology was reorganized and included in the Directorate for *Computer and Information Science and Engineering* (CISE) in 1985. In de Solla Price's concepts and words, the domain cluster is "little science", while the retrieval cluster is "big science," and the connection between the two has presently no science.

PROBLEMS ADDRESSED

General

Webster routinely defines information science as "the science dealing with the efficient collection, storage, and retrieval of information." It is a general definition of problems addressed by information science. The definition follows pretty much an early and popular one given by Borko as a part of a wide discussion and controversy about the nature of the field in the 1960s.

More specifically, information science is a field of professional practice and scientific enquiry addressing the problem of effective communication of knowledge records—"literature"—among humans in the context of social, organizational, and individual need for and use of information.

The key orientation here is the problem of need for and use of information, as involving knowledge records.To provide for that need, information science deals with specifically, oriented information techniques, procedures, and systems. To elaborate, the specific concentration of information science is on human knowledge records as *content-bearing objects*, in all forms, shapes, and media.

The primary emphasis is on content of these objects, in terms of their potential for conveying information. "Literature" may be used as a generic term for these knowledge records, but "literature" has many other connotations, thus requiring a careful restriction in its use in information science. Because of these connotations, "literature" will not become popular in information science.

Realizing this, I am using the term here only as a shorthand, as did White and McCain, when they elegantly stated:

> "The proper study of information science is the interface between people and literature . . . modeling the world of publications with a practical goal of being able to deliver their content to enquirers on demand . . . While many scientists seek to understand communication between persons, information scientists seek to understand communication between persons and certain valued surrogates for persons that literature comprises.

In all of this there is a technological imperative, reflected in efforts to take advantage of modern information technology. While information science is not about technology, the problem of providing effective computer applications pervades the field. Following is a word on the extent and borders of infor-mation science. Focusing information science on the content-bearing properties of literature, and on associated techniques and systems dealing with providing effective access to and use of literature, provides a restriction for information science.

Thus, the field does *not* deal with great many other information systems, such as payroll, inventory, decision support systems, data processing, airline schedules, and a zillion others, nor does it deal with direct communication among and between persons. Information science is about a specific manifestation or type of information that defines its scope and its systems. Information science, as many other fields, also involves a professional component. Starting in 1950s, the profession of information science grew from research and applications in IR, to become a powerful component of the field, and in many ways a leading one in respect to innovation.

As in many other fields, there is an uneasy relation between the scientific or research-oriented component and the professi-onal or practice-oriented one. The profession is responding in its own way to needs of its users and organizations, and chartering its own technological applications, many times independently of research advances, and even in different directions. At present, the connection and feedback between profession and research in information science is not as well established as it is in older fields, such as engineering or medicine. This is a serious inhibitor for progress of both.

More Specific

A number of authors suggested a breakdown of specific areas of information science, beyond the structural analysis offered above. The breakdown among different authors is in significant agreement, although the labels differ somewhat. I will take the breakdown and labels provided by White and McCain. They provided a factor analysis of co-cited authors and extracted 12 factors as specialties.

In descending order of how authors loaded, they labelled the specialties as:

- Experimental *information retrieval* (IR);
- Citation analysis;
- Practical retrieval;
- Bibliometrics;
- General library systems theory;
- Science communication;
- User studies and theory;
- OPACs;

- General imported ideas—other disciplines;
- Indexing theory;
- Citation theory; and
- Communication theory.

While one may quibble with some of the classes and labels, these specialties provide a fairly accurate picture of problem areas in which information scientists worked over the past quarter of a century.

Over time, there were shifts in emphasis and there were movements between specialties. Nothing is permanent. But these are the specialties of information science. New areas are clearly on the horizon. For the 1990s, I would suggest that the major new areas include interaction studies; searching of the Internet; multimedia IR; multilanguage IR; and digital libraries.

These are prime examples of the new significant areas of concentration, not yet evident in the historical record. At the same time, the old area of experimental retrieval is blossoming like never before, courtesy of the *Text Retrieval Conference* (TREC), a government-sponsored mechanism for comparative evaluation of a variety of IR techniques and approaches that involves large test beds. IR was, and still is, the major and most populated area of information science. Thus, a separate discussion of IR follows.

INFORMATION RETRIEVAL

In the early and mid-1950s, a critical mass of scientists, engineers, librarians, and entrepreneurs started working enthusiastically on the problem and solution defined by Bush. By 1960s this became a large and relatively well-funded effort and organized activity. Often, there were heated arguments and controversies about the "best" solution, technique, or system.

These arguments brought on the tradition of evaluation, a major staple of IR research and development. What is now TREC started with Cranfield evaluations in the late 1950s and early 1960s. Remarkably, the basic evaluation principles developed then are still the underpinning of TREC today. Calvin Mooers, an active and highly visible pioneer of information science, coined the term *information retrieval* in 1951. The term took hold, and today is a part of the English language.

At that time, Mooers not only coined the term, but also defined the problems to be addressed:

> "Information retrieval embraces the intellectual aspects of the description of information and its specification for search, and also whatever systems, techniques or machines that are employed to carry out the operation.

Today, we would add that IR also and particularly involves interaction in all of these, with all the contextual-cognitive, affective, situational—aspects that interaction embraces. An expanded Mooers' conception is still valid. As it advanced, IR produced a number of theoretical, empirical, and pragmatic concepts and constructs. Numerous IR systems were developed and successfully deployed. A great many historical examples can be given to illustrate the remarkable evolution of IR systems and techniques, adapting the ever-evolving information technology, from punch cards in the midcentury to the Internet at its close.

Based on IR, an online information industry emerged in the 1970s, and grew through its own version of information explosion, as chronicled by Hahn. IR is one of the most widely spread applications of any information system worldwide. It has a proud history. Surely, information science is more than IR, but many of the problems raised by IR or derived from objects and phenomena involved in IR, are at its core.

Approaches and Paradigm Split

The approach taken by Mooers was to concentrate on the building of systems. This systems emphasis which was formulated early in the 1950s, was the sole approach to IR for some decades. It still predominates in a good part of IR research to this day.

Consequently, most of the IR research and practice concentrated on retrieval systems and processes. However, starting in the late 1970s and gaining steam in the 1980s, a different line of reasoning and research evolved-one that concentrates on the cognitive, interactive, and contextual end of the process. It addressed users, use, situations, context, and interaction with systems, rather than IR systems alone as a primary focus.

The retrieval cluster started splitting into subclusters, as noted by White and McCain, and before by others such as Saracevic and Harter. We now have two distinct communities and approaches to research in the retrieval cluster. They became commonly known as *systems-centred* and *user-centred.* Both address retrieval, but from very different ends and perspectives. The split is not only conceptual, looking very differently at the same process, but also organizational. The systemscentered side is now mostly concentrated in the *Special Interest Group on Information Retrieval* (SIGIR) of the *Association for Computing Machinery* (ACM), while the user-centered cluster congregates around the *American Society for Information Science* (ASIS).

Each has its own communication outlets-journals, proceedings, and conferences. There is less and less overlap of authors and works between the two outlets. We have two camps, two islands, with, unfortunately, relatively little traffic in-between. The systems-centered approach is exemplified by work on algorithms and evaluation based on the traditional IR model, a model that does not consider the users or interaction. The massive research that evaluates a variety of IR algorithms and approaches within TREC is a culmination of this approach.

In contrast, cognitive, situational, and interactive studies and models, involving the use of retrieval systems exemplify the human-centered approach.

Following that approach, interactive models, differing significantly from the traditional IR model, started to emerge. Even in TREC, a group of researchers started an interaction track, but so far have a hard time conceptually and methodologically, thus demonstrating the difficulty in merging the traditional and interactive models and approaches. Let me characterize, in a simplified way, the relationship between the two approaches or subclusters addressing different sides of retrieval.

On the one hand, the human-centred side was often highly critical of the systems side for ignoring users and use, and tried valiantly to establish humans as the proper center of IR work. The mantra of human-centred research is that the results have implications for systems design and practice. Unfortunately, in most human-centred research, beyond suggestions, concrete design solutions were not delivered. On the other hand, the systems side, by and large, ignores the human side and user studies, and is even often completely ignorant of them. As to design, the stance is "tell us what to do and as suggested, do it." But nobody is really telling, or if telling, nobody is listening.

As a rule, in systems-oriented projects, people and users are absent. Thus, there are not many interactions between the two camps. Let me provide some examples. A rough analysis of the 1997 SIGIR proceedings found only 3 papers of some 34 that dealt in some way with people and users; in the ACM's Digital Libraries 1997 conference proceedings, of 25 papers only 3 mentioned people and users. If one reads authors such as Dervin and Nilan, and many of their successors, who champion the human centered approach, one gets the impression that there is a real conflict between the two sides and approaches, and that there is an alternative way to the "dreadful" systems approach.

In a way, this stance is a backlash caused by the excesses, failures, and blind spots of systems-centered approaches not only in IR, but also in great many other technological applica-tions. Unfortunately, sometimes the backlash is justified. All of us who work on the humancentered side are not that dismissive of the systems side. But the issue is not whether we should have systems-*or* humancentered approaches. The issue is even less of human*versus* systems-centered. *The issue is how to make human*and *systems-centered approaches work together.* In this sense, a number of works have addressed integrating usercentered and systems-centered approaches in IR, but this has been discussed mostly by researchers from the usercentered side.

Examples are works by:

- Bates,
- Belkin,
- Cool,
- Stein,
- Thiel,
- Fidel
- Efthimidiadis,

- Robertson and
- Beaulieu.

To reiterate, it is not one camp against the other but how can we incorporate the best features of both approaches and make them work jointly. The issue is how to deliver and incorporate the desired design features that will improve systems orientations towards users, integrate them with systems features, and use advantages provided by both, humans and technology. In other words, the issue is *putting the human in the loop* to build better algorithms and to exploit computational advantages. Real progress in information science, and by extension in IR, will come when we achieve this. Lately, the NSF has championed human-centered design involving an interdisciplinary approach to information systems. Hopefully, this will go beyond rhetoric. It is not easy to do. But, that is what research is for—to address difficult, not only easy problems.

Proprietary IR

By the 1980s, the commercial information industry based on IR became successful and profitable. Out of academe, grants, and government, IR became a money-making propo-sition. This, of course, is another and important sign of success. Not surprisingly, a number of former IR researchers, practitioners, and graduates of IR programmes ventured out to become IR entrepreneurs.

Sure enough, throughout information science history there were many entrepreneurs, and they were highly significant in development of the field. But this generation of entrepre-neurs was different. They ventured to develop and market a variety of IR procedures based on algorithms, applicable and scalable to large files, multiple applications, and/or various advanced technologies. It was knowledge industry at its purest. But, as in all commercial knowledge industries, the product was proprietary. While it was not that hard to guess the base of these various proprietary algorithms and how they worked—after all they were derived from publicly available knowledge and experiences, such as those that came from SMART experi-ments—they remain unpublished and "secret."

A new kind of IR evolved, separate from the rest, not communicating as to intellectual advances with the rest. Non-e of these ventures became a high commercial success, as measured by Silicon Valley standards. But the World Wide Web, emerging in the first half of the 1990s, changed all this. The acceleration of the growth of the Web is an information explosion of the like never before seen in history. Not surprisingly then, the Web is a mess. No wonder that everybody is interested in some form of IR as a solution to fix it.

A number of academic-based efforts were initiated to develop mechanisms, search engines, "intelligent" agents, crawlers, and so forth, to help control the Web. Some of these were IR scaled, and adapted to the problem; others were a variety of extensions of IR. Many had few, if any original, developments, besides new packaging or labeling; and a good number were just the usual hype. The wheel was reinvented a number of times. But out of this, and fast, came commercial ventures, such as the pioneering Yahoo!, whose basic objective is to provide search mechanisms for finding something of relevance for users on demand.

And to make a lot of money. These enterprises pride themselves on having proprietary methods by which they are accomplishing the retrieval tasks. The connection to the information science community is tenuous, and almost Non-existent. The flow of knowledge, if any, is onesided, from IR research results into proprietary engines. The reverse contribution to public knowledge is zero. A number of evaluations of these search engines have been undertaken simply by comparing some results between them or comparing of their retrieval against some benchmarks.

Some evaluations were done within, others outside of information science. Results were not complimentary. The Web-based proprietary IR is expanding and flourishing outside of the field. It is addressing a vexing problem, the like we have not seen before. But as yet, the success is elusive and questionable.

RELEVANCE

As information science pioneers developed IR processes and systems in the 1950s, they defined as the main objective retrieval of *relevant* information. Effectiveness was expressed in terms of relevance. From then to now, IR is explicitly geared not towards any old kind of information, but towards *relevant information*. Various IR approaches, algorithms, and practices were, and still are, evaluated in relation to relevance. Thus, relevance became a key notion in information science. It is also a complex phenomenon with a long and turbulent history in information science transcending IR, going back to early 1950s. Of course, there was a choice.

Relevance did not have to emerge as the key notion. Uncertainty was one choice suggested by a number of theorists to be the base of IR, and thus to reflect effectiveness. But it did not take. In contrast, uncertainty is the basic notion underlying expert systems. If the pioneers had not embraced relevance, but instead, let's say, uncertainty, as the base for IR, we would have today a very different IR, and probably not that successful. In general, relevance, according to *Webster*, means having significant bearing on matter at hand. As with many other concepts, relevance assumes related but more specific meaning in more specific contexts and applications.

In the context of information science, relevance is the attribute or criterion reflecting the effectiveness of exchange of information between people and IR systems in communi-cation contacts based on valuation by people. With relevance as the criterion, and human Judgements of relevance of retrieved objects as the measuring instrument, the measures of precision and recall are widely used in evaluation of IR systems. The strength of these measures is that they involve people—users—as judges of effectiveness of performance. The weakness is the same: it involves Judgement by people, with all the perils of subjectivity and variability. Relevance indicates a relation. For relevance, many relations have been investigated.

An consensus has emerged in information science that we can distinguish between several differing relations that account for different manifestations or types of relevance:

- *System or Algorithmic Relevance:* Relation between a query and information objects in the file of a system as retrieved, or as failed to be retrieved, by a given procedure or algorithm. Comparative effectiveness in inferring relevance is the criterion for system relevance.
- *Topical or Subject Relevance:* Relation between the subject or topic expressed in a query and topic or subject covered by retrieved texts, or, more broadly, by texts in the system file, or even in existence. Aboutness is the criterion by which topicality is inferred.
- *Cognitive Relevance or Pertinence:* Relation between the state of knowledge and cognitive information need of a user and texts retrieved, or in the file of a system, or even in existence. Cognitive correspondence, infor-mativeness, novelty, information quality, and the like are criteria by which cognitive relevance is inferred.
- *Situational Relevance or Utility:* Relation between the situation, task or problem at hand and texts retrieved by a system, or in the file of a system, or even in existence. Usefulness in decision making, appropriateness of information in resolution of a problem, reduction of uncertainty, and the like are criteria by which situational relevance is inferred.
- *Motivational or Affective Relevance:* Relation between the intents, goals, and motivations of a user and texts retrieved by a system, or in the file of a system, or even in existence. Satisfaction, success, accomplish-ment, and the like are the criteria for inferring motivational relevance.

Practically, IR systems assess systems relevance only-that is, they respond to queries-hoping that the objects retrieved may also be of cognitive relevance, and even more so of utility. However, a user may judge an object by any or all types of relevance-for a user they may interact dynamically. Difficulties arise when an object is of system relevance but not of cognitive relevance or utility, or conversely.

If items are of cognitive relevance or utility, but were not reflected in the query, they are not and cannot be retrieved. At the bottom of IR research is a quest to align systems with other types of relevance.

People all over have a strong intuitive understanding of relevance, thus, they intuitively understand, without manuals, what IR is all about. This makes IR systems generally understandable and acceptable-a critical attribute in their widespread application.

DISCIPLINARY RELATIONS

Two things introduced interdisciplinarity in information science. First and foremost, the problems addressed cannot be resolved with approaches and constructs from any single discipline-thus, intedisciplinarity is predetermined, as it is in many modern fields. Second, interdisciplinarity in information science was introduced and is being perpetuated to the present by the very differences in backgrounds of people addressing the described problems. Differences in background are many; they make for richness of the field and difficulties in communication and education. Clearly not every discipline in the background of people working on the problem made an equally relevant contri-bution, but the assortment was responsible for sustaining a strong interdisciplinary characteristic of information science. I will concentrate on interdisciplinary relations with two fields: librarianship and computer science. Obviously, other fields, most notably cognitive science and communication, have also interdisciplinary relations, but these are the most significant and developed ones.

Librarianship

Librarianship has a long and proud history devoted to organization, preservation, and use of graphic records and records in other media. This is done through libraries not only as a particular organization or type of information system, but even more so as an indispensable social, cultural, and educational institution whose value has been proven manifold throughout human history, and across all geographic and cultural boundaries.

Researcher defines the library as:

- . . .Contributing to the total communication system in society. . . Though the library is an instrumentality created to maximize the utility of graphic records for the benefits of society, it achieves that goal by working with the individual and through the individual it reaches society.

The common ground between library science and information science, which is a strong one, is in sharing of their social role and in their general concern with effective utilization of graphic and other records, particularly by individuals.

But there are also very significant differences in several critical respects, among them:

- *Selection of Problems Addressed and the Way they were Defined*: A majority of the problems were not and are not addressed in library science;
- *Theoretical Questions Asked and Frameworks Established*: The theories and conceptual frameworks in librarian-ship have no counterpart in information science, and *vice versa*;
- *The Nature and Degree of Experimentation and Empirical Development*

and the Resulting Practical Knowledge and Competencies Dderived: There is very little overlap in experimentation and development between the two, and professional requirements differ as well to a significant degree;

- *Tools and Approaches Used:* A most telling example is the very different approach undertaken in relation to utilization of technology in IR and in library automation; and
- *The Nature and Strength of Interdisciplinary Relations Established and the Dependence of Progress on Inter-disciplinary Approaches*: Librarianship is much more selfcontained.

All of these differences warrant a conclusion that librarian-ship and information science are two different fields in strong interdisciplinary relations, rather than one and the same field, or one being a special case of the other. This is not a matter of turf battles, or of one being better or worse than the other. Such arguments, while common between many fields, matter little to progress of either field. But differences in selection and/or definition of problems addressed, agenda, paradigms, theoretical base, and practical solutions *do* matter. Thus the conclusion that librarianship and information science, while related, are different fields. The differences are most pronounced in the research agenda and directions.

Interestingly, research on OPACs, now that they are incorporating more and more IR features, is bringing the two fields in closer relation. Probably, so will the research in digital libraries, but at this time, it is too early to tell. The conclusion is not without heated controversy.

Among other authors, Vakkari contends on information science and librarianship being one and the same field, with the now commonly used name of "library and information science." Does it matter? Administratively yes, very much so, particularly in universities and professional societies. Otherwise, no. The issue is, and always will be, in the problems addressed and solutions undertaken. I contend that they differ significantly.

Computer Science

The basis of relation between information science and computer science lies in the application of computers and computing in IR, and the associated products, services, and networks. In the last few years, this relation also involves research on the evolving digital libraries, with their strong technological base.

To illustrate the connection, we use a definition by Denning:

> "The discipline of computing is the systematic study of algorithmic processes that describe and transfer information: their theory, analysis, design, efficiency, implementation, and application. The fundamental question underlying all of the computing is: "What can be automated?"

Computer science is about algorithms related to infor-mation interpreted in the first, whereas information science is about the very nature of information and its use by humans, interpreted in the third or broadest sense. Computer science is about symbol manipulation, whereas information science is about content manipulation, where symbol manipulation is the indispensable infrastructure. The two concerns are not in competition, they are complementary—they lead to different basic and applied agendas. Computer science is also many times larger than information science.

A number of computer scientists have been involved in research and development on information and its many spin-offs, to the point of being recognized leaders in information science. Gerard Salton is a prime example. In addition, there are several streams of research and development in computer science that had no connection with the early evolution of information science, but have addressed information problems similar to those in information science. Among others, these include works on expert systems, knowledge bases, hypertext, and human-computer interaction.

More recently, this involves research and development on digital libraries, a "hot", financially heavily supported area by a host of government agencies in the U.S. and many other countries. Bolstered by heavy support, interest in digital library research exploded on the scene in 1990s, attracting the attention of computer scientists from a wide variety of streams, as well as people from many other disciplines. These areas have a significant informational component that is associated with information representation, its intellectual organization, and linkages; meta-information, information seeking, searching, retrieving, and filtering; use, quality, value, and impact of information; evaluation of information systems from user and use perspective; and the like-all traditionally addressed in information science.Conversely, these streams of computer science research and development provide a different outlook, framework, and approach, and even a different paradigm, not only for information science research and development, but also for its academic and continuing education. Again, as with librarianship, the issue is not about turf. It is about paradigms, theoretical foundations, and pragmatic solutions; and ultimately, it is about their appropriateness to human information problems.

EDUCATION

That education is critical for any field is a truism that hardly needs to be stated. In particular, research lives by education, it cannot be better than the education that researchers receive and then extend and plow back into education. Unfortunately, education in information science has not received the attention that it deserves. This may explain the many difficulties in the field that I have discussed. Educational models that evolved differed to a degree or even substantially from country to country. I am concentrating here on the U.S. models only.

In the United States, two educational models evolved over time. I call them the Shera and Salton models, after those that pioneered them. Both have strengths and weaknesses. Jesse H. Shera was a legendary library school dean from the 1950s until the 1970s at Western Reserve University. Among others, he was instrumental in starting the Center for Documentation and Communication Research in 1955. Shortly thereafter, the library school curriculum started to include courses such as "Machine Literature Searching" and several other more advanced courses and laboratories on the topics of research in the Centre.

The basic approach was to append those courses, mostly as electives, to the existing library school curriculum, without modifications of the curriculum as a whole, and particularly not the required core courses. Information science became one of the specialty areas of library science. The base or core courses that students were taking rested in the traditional library curriculum. Information science education was an appendage to library science. A few attempts to spin off information science as an independent degree and curriculum were not followed widely. But Shera's model was. Library schools in the U.S. and in many other countries imitated Shera's model.

They used the same approach and started incorporating information science courses in their existing curriculum as a specialty. Out of this was borne the current designation "library and information science." Shera's model is still the prevalent approach in schools of library and information science. The strength of the Shera model is that it posits education within a service framework, connects the education to professional practice and to a broader and user-oriented frame of a number of other information services, and relates it to a great diversity of information resources.

The weakness is a lack of a broader theoretical frame-work and a total lack of teaching of any formalism related to systems, such as development and understanding of algori-thms. The majority of researchers in the human-centered side, as I described earlier, came from or are associated with this educa-tional environment. Gerard Salton was first and foremost a scientist, a computer scientist, and the father of modern IR.

As such, he pioneered the incorporation into IR research a whole array of formal and experimental methods from science, as modified for algorithmic and other approaches used so successfully in computer science. His primary orientation was research. For education, he took the time-honoured approach of a close involvement with research. Salton's model was a laboratory and research approach to education.

As Shera's model resulted in information science educa-tion being an appendage to library science education, Salton's model of IR education resulted in it being a specialty of and an appendage to computer science education. Computer science students that were already well-grounded in the discipline, got involved in SMART and other projects directed by Salton, worked and did research in the laboratory, completed their theses in areas related to IR, and participated in the legendary IR seminars.

They also published widely with Salton and with each other, and participated with high visibility in national and international conferences. From Harvard and Cornell, his students went to a number of computer science departments where they replicated Salton's model. Many other computer science departments in the U.S. and abroad took the same approach.

The strength of Salton's model is that it:

"Starts from a base of a firm grounding in formal mathematical and other methods, and in algorithms, and

- Relates directly to research.

The weakness is in that it:

- Ignores the broader aspects of information science, as well as any other disciplines and approaches dealing with the human aspects that have great relevance to both the outcomes of IR research and the research itself, and
- Does not incorporate professional practice where these systems are realised and used. It loses users.

Consequently, this is a successful, but narrowly concen-trated education in IR as a specialty of computer science, rather then in information science. Not surprisingly, the researchers in the systems-centred approach came out of this tradition. The two educational approaches are completely independent of each other. Neither is connected to the other. Neither reflects fully what is going on in the field. While in each model there is an increase in cognizance of the other, there is no educational integration of the systems-and usercentered approaches.

INFORMATION SYSTEMS AND EFFECTS ON DECISION-MAKING

All of the libraries visited already employed automated systems. However, formal and relatively fully automated management information systems existed in only two of the eight libraries visited. They had been established because of the existence of management information systems in the institutions as a whole. In the other libraries, the use of cost centres for resources allocation caused the libraries to have some formal management information. Libraries generally are not fully utilising the capability of their automated systems since some external information remains in printed form, and manual data processing is still a significant element in their analysis of the data available. Those librarians who had 'informal' or 'partial' management information systems had concluded that a management information system would be not helpful for decision making in budgeting and resource allocation, but they still faced a requirement to produce reports for their institutions, particularly for their finance departments, which incorporate management data.

They also produce summary information for various purposes, profiling their parent institution, finance, staff, users, facilities and equipment, programmes and functions. Those libraries which had management information systems possessed information which was deeper in substance and more readily available, so it was easier for them to make appropriate decisions.

DEVELOPMENT OF MANAGEMENT INFORMATION SYSTEMS

There were several reasons why many of the libraries visited lacked management information systems.

The criteria of an ideal management information system are that:

- They must be inexpensive to operate.
- They must not interfere with existing services.
- They must provide reproducible results.

The fact that some libraries claimed to have only 'informal' or 'partial' management information systems or to have no management information systems does not mean that they had no collection of external and internal data. They do collect and use information for establishing library objectives and priorities or for resources allocation, but they have not formalised their management information systems, typically because their institutions had not required them to do so. Other factors which had inhibited development are mainly technical and concern the libraries' infrastructures. The limited capabilities of their computers had resulted in misinterpretation of the output data, and faulty analysis by senior library staff.

This was compounded by a lack of staff training in analysing data. The emphasis on purchasing microcomputers for library users was also a drain on scarce resources which might otherwise have been used to set up automated management information systems. Incompatibility of computer systems also caused problems; for example, in the workload involved in inputting common data such as the identity of students as compared with simply capturing it from a central database. Although they had enough potential to support formal management information systems, less use is made of existing automated library systems than might be possible given some development of their software. Even in the two libraries which had management information systems, there is one evident weakness; neither library has identified a comprehensive range of performance measures.

The contemporary approach casts academic librarians as managers within the higher education system. Planning and controlling development is clearly an important aspect of that role. Academic libraries' objectives have become clearer than in the past, but British academic libraries' attempts to achieve those objectives have been threatened by government financial policies which, in effect, require academic libraries to provide more and better services with less money. Consequently, every aspect of academic libraries' operations has to be reviewed so that they can be managed more effectively and efficiently. It is not easy to achieve this because academic libraries are complex organisations. What academic librarians need, now much more than ever before, is the information which will allow them to plan properly, to know whether or not the library service is meeting the needs of the academic community and to be able to demonstrate that to the internal and external authorities responsible for funding.

Performance measures are also necessary in order to reveal libraries' strengths and weaknesses when compared with internal and external targets, norms and averages. From the survey, it is clear that most library managers are very concerned with the need for management information about their libraries. Libraries have generally established objectives and forward plans; there are still differences in how they allocate resources to fulfil those plans, and clear divergences of opinion on what information is required for library planning and resources allocation. Changing circumstances may call for any aspect of libraries' resources and services to be reviewed, or for them to be considered from a different perspective, often pro-actively or at fairly short notice, and the advantages of a comprehensive management information system should be self-evident.

Similarly, although at present there is much data collection, formal evaluation processes are not common. Performance measures which can compare internal and external information have not been widely utilised and have made little impact in decision making, perhaps because there is no agreement on what constitutes appropriate measures of achievement. Structured management information systems could help library managers in collecting and processing data into a useful form to assist in decision making. Most libraries appear to collect the same data, but only two of the eight selected libraries had established comprehensive management information systems for their librarians' purposes, in particular to support the planning process.

Although they had not fully automated data processing and reporting, and the information from their systems needs to be carefully interpreted, these librarians are making decisions based on outputs from their management information systems. The introduction of computers into academic libraries was largely a response to the problem of dealing with increased workloads with fewer staff, and they are now able easily to handle most of the routine and repetitive work of the library staff.

In addition, they have the capability to enhance the provision of management information, since automated data processing is able to present reports more accurately and much faster than manual systems. A limited range of data processing for management information is currently supported by the computer systems, including microcomputers, available in academic libraries, but there are still significant weaknesses in library automation systems in respect of the production of management information. For example, much remains to be done in monitoring high cost areas such as serials management and staff deployment in reader services.

Consequently, apart from the one library visited which has a decision support system, current library automation systems are not fully used for formal management information systems. It has to be said that most librarians still consider the continuous costs of automation as a worrying expense, and that the development of management information systems is not seen as a high priority compared with the introduction or upgrading of new automation systems for handling routine operations. Non-etheless, most librarians claim that they would now like to install decision support systems, even though they see the expense as a problem. The likelihood of increasing requirements for information to be provided at institutional level to meet government demands that institutions should be accountable may change priorities and foster developments.

While waiting for these developments, and for this new technology to be proved, attempts must be made to find out whether there will be support for the establishment of management information systems or decision support systems, and in particular, whether there will be support from the parent institutions and the library staff. The introduction of automated management information systems seems unlikely to pose a threat to staff in academic libraries, as most already have a 'flat' management structure, but a priority must be training programmes on the use of information in management. Support from parent institutions is also essential since the technology required for decision support systems could be expensive, particularly if they are seen as separate from the replacement of the libraries' existing automated systems.

It will, therefore, be important to convince the vendors who produce turnkey library automation systems to develop new systems which provide more of the management information that meets widely recognised needs in terms of both contents and format. There is a bewildering array of information available from a variety of external and internal sources, and, in addition to the costs of collection and collation, it generally needs tailoring to meet libraries' needs for comparable data. Cooperative groups such as SCONUL have a role to play here in developing guidelines on the information needed, and the format(s) in which it should be presented for comparative purposes. Present outputs from library automation systems are crude, but the work currently being undertaken to develop both performance measures which have wide applicability and credibility, and more effective management information modules as part of library automation systems should eventually resolve that problem.

MANAGEMENT FUNCTIONS

The traditional roles of management are planning, organisation, coordination and control. These can be applied to these change strategies.

RATIONAL-EMPIRICAL

The rational-empirical strategy is primarily concerned with dispensing information, presuming that the plans for change have already been made. It involves the organising function of management, in the sense that the managers determine what information needs to be given to which employees in order to implement the changes. It also involves the control function, in that the management is seeking to influence behaviour through the information it dispenses.

NORMATIVE-EDUCATIONAL

The normative-education strategy is concerned with influencing attitudes and behaviour. As such, it involves the control function of management, but in an indirect manner. That is, rather than controlling behaviour directly, the management attempts to instill attitudes which are likely to result in the desired behaviour. Like the rational-empirical strategy, it also involves the coordinating function, as managers decide who should be involved in which programmes.

POWER-COERCIVE

The power-coercive strategy concerns the management role of control in a straight- forward fashion. It is mainly concerned with seeing to it that the change decisions are carried out as directed. To ensure this, it dispenses rewards or penalties to individuals or groups depending or whether they have implemented the changes. In the extreme, employees who fail to change are fired.

PHASED IMPLEMENTATION

Phased implementation involves both the planning and coordinating functions to a large degree. Planning includes determining the order in which to implement the modules and setting timetables for each phase. Coordination includes meshing together the efforts of different groups associated with each phase, and ensuring that each module is integrated with the previous ones when it is brought into production. As more modules are brought into the 'live' mode, coordination becomes essential in order to see that the different areas function smoothly.

PARTICIPANT-ORIENTED CHANGE

Participant oriented change involves the coordinating function of management. Since, much of the planning and decision making is delegated downward to the staff, management must integrate these plans and decisions. This is particularly important when implementing an integrated library system, as the activities of staff in one area will have more impact on other areas than they are accustomed to.

The actual delegation of these responsibilities to employees involves the organising function. Determining how and to whom these responsibilities are delegated is in important part of the change process.This may involve organising employees into self-managed teams, work groups, or interdepartmental task forces. How these groups are organised, the amount of authority they have, and how they will interact with each other are crucial decisions.

CONCLUSION

The participant oriented change strategy provides the best overall approach to managing library automation and migration projects. Of the strategies which have been outlined, it offers the highest degree of employee communication and participation. These are the same areas that caused the most problems if they were inadequate. One of the chief advantages of this strategy is that it involves the users of the system at the earliest possible stage of the project. That is during the teleological process of identifying reasons for the project and setting goals or criteria for a new system. Involving the employees at this stage reduces the need for normative attitude-adjusting sessions latter in the process.This is not to say that managers who adopt this strategy can just ignore employee attitudes later on. Change will still be stressful, and people may still resist it at various points. But, management will not have to invest as much effort in convincing staff that the new system is better if the staff were involved in selecting it. The rational-empirical strategies of employee training programmes will still have a role to play, as the process moves on. As was demonstrated in the failed attempt at implementing the CASE system, this strategy is not sufficient by itself. But users must learn how a new system works if they are to use it at all. Within the overall context of participant oriented strategy, other employees provide much of that training. With their hands-on experience, employee led training can be more effective than vendor supplied 'canned presentations'.

This also promotes an atmosphere in which employees will be comfortable sharing their learning experiences, tricks and shortcuts following implementation. The other two strategies, phased implementation and power-coercive can not be recommended across the board. The power-coercive strategy is divisive, and is likely make the change harder instead of easier. This strategy aggravates fears about job security, which is one of the sources of change anxiety. While a degree of control needs to be maintained, a threatening approach is not desirable as a general strategy.

The strategy of phased implementation will be helpful for some situations, but not for all. For libraries currently using manual systems or automated systems that are not integrated, this method may help to ease the transition. For libraries that already have a well-integrated system, it could create even more chaos. Within the context of participant-oriented change, the choice of whether to include it rests with the employees who actually work with the system.

LIBRARY AND INFORMATION SERVICES MANAGER

Rather than roll over and accept this, the City of Edinburgh has chosen to harness the very technology cited as a threat and engage with new audiences in new ways. The primary aim has always been to attract physical users to their facilities, however if this is not possible then the next best thing is to engage digitally with their audience. If you think about citizens in a new way, as mobile, digitally accessible, yet unique and focused on receiving the service that they want whenever they want it, technology gives them and you the opportunity to build a new relationship. Once in place, it also enables you to market your services free of charge, increasingly important in these austere times. Liz McGettigan, Library and Information Services Manager at the City of Edinburgh Council, realised the requirement to engage with developments in web 2.0 services, or risk being left behind in an increasingly digital world. She saw the opportunities for promotion that social media enabled and created a team of people within the library to pull all electronic resources into one location. Finally, she employed the best technology available to engage with Edinburgh's citizens, in facilities, on the web, socially and on the go.

- *Your Library*: the Web Portal – This unique portal unites all digital resources including catalogues, databases and other web sites.
- *Tales of One City*: This is an integrated approach to social media, engaging citizens and local communities with Edinburgh's blog, Facebook site, Twitter feed, Flickr and YouTube sites. It's push and pull communication that connects with their audience.
- *SOLUS*: This gives Edinburgh the power to schedule content from their web-based Content Management System to digital signage, web and desktop video players, a library app and to social media channels.

SOLUS, a member of the Capita Partner Programme, provides Edinburgh with a unique digital communications capability and helps maximise efficiency in a market where cost saving and best value is critical. Jim Thompson, Edinburgh's Development and Quality Manager, stated, "The premise behind SOLUS is the ability to create once and schedule many. SOLUS allows us to use one system to upload a promotional video file to our digital signage network, make it available to view across our desktops, embed it into our web portal and intranet, schedule it to our mobile app and distribute it automatically to all our social media channels."

SOLUS has also fully integrated with the Capita LMS to provide functionality for "Your Library App" and this has enabled additional benefits. Most recently added and most popular stock can now be automatically promoted across other platforms managed by SOLUS, such as digital signage and social media. Neil Wishart, Director of SOLUS, was recently at Downing Street, discussing the potential of "Your Library App" with Nick Jones, Director of Digital Communications for No. 10 and The Cabinet Office. Following the meeting Neil commented:

> "One of the key requirements for government at all levels is to engage more efficiently and effectively with citizens. The digital citizen is

real and their dependency on technology is increasing. Rather than being a threat, it provides libraries with the biggest opportunity in a generation to engage with new users in increasing numbers. At the same time, it will let them do this more efficiently and effectively. For the citizen, libraries can offer easy and immediate access to services that can save them money. If people are cutting back due to their personal budgets being squeezed, libraries can take advantage."

To take advantage, access must be 24/7, slick and with instant gratification. V2 of Edinburgh's Library App will allow users to scan a barcode in a shop and automatically search the library catalogue. This is already reality - the recently launched Haringey Library App, which is powered by SOLUS, allows users to scan, search and reserve within seconds. If they don't know how to get to the reserved item, the app will take them there and if an Ebook is available, users can get that instant gratification!

Of course, the proof is in the pudding and Liz McGettigan has solid evidence to prove this innovative use of technology is working. In the last year digital visits have increased by 135,000, PC usage is up by 145,000 sessions, attendance at events has increased, up 32 per cent, and significantly, the decline in physical visits has been reversed with an extra 30,000 people attending libraries. Wishart stated, "It's a classic case of inbound marketing, where effective online positioning has a direct impact on offline behaviour. It's fantastic for Liz to be able to report back to her stakeholders that she has improved access to services and achieved a direct return on investment, both in relation to time and money."

What's next? Creating an app, using social media and installing a digital signage network are all great foundations, but maximum uptake can only be ensured through effective ongoing promotion. The next step in the partnership between Edinburgh Libraries and SOLUS is to develop a range of collaterals to shout about libraries. Liz commented, "There is no point in having the world's best kept secret, we want as many physical and digital users as we can possibly attract. We are actively working on materials with SOLUS to promote our App and these will be resources that can be shared with other libraries across the UK. There is no point replicating spend - if we can all make further efficiency savings and at the same time develop really exciting material, it benefits the whole library community."

Libraries now lead the way in Edinburgh, with other departments continually looking to implement their successful strategy.

QUESTION ANSWERING SYSTEMS IN LIBRARY

Marill's Report, 'Libraries and Question Answering Systems,' laid the groundwork for subsequent research on question-answering systems. The report consists of three parts:

- Two Concepts of a Library,
- Question-Answering Systems and
- Semantic Nets: Informal Introduction.

The first of the 'two concepts of a library' is a schematisation of a present-day library. In the schema, the library consists of the collection of documents, the 'tag' system, and the retrieval system that makes use of the tags to retrieve desired documents. The contributions that technology can make within this first concept are acceleration of document handling, automation of the process of 'tagging' and improvement of the retrieval process.

Marill argues that this first concept, instrumented on a modest scale, would yield unsatisfactory results, and that, carried to its logical limit, it would be absurd. The second concept of a library is one in which the primary function is to provide not documents but information. The 'system' of the second concept will be able to 'read' and 'comprehend' the documents themselves and not merely their tags. It will have a high capability for organising the information internally. It will be able to accept questions worded in natural English. If it has the requisite information available, it will answer the questions in natural English. Thus Marill advocates a very sophisticated pro-cognitive system. He is concerned that people may believe the goal unreachable because it will be thought to require that inanimate mechanisms 'think.'

Marill refers to the question-answering system called 'Baseball' to forestall that misconception. In his discussion of question-answering systems, Marill defines the primary concepts: the corpus, the question, and the answer. The corpus consists of a set of quantificational schemata and their attendant predicate definitions, one definition for each predicate in the corpus. Thus Marill immediately seizes upon a predicate calculus as the formalism for representation of the information in the body of knowledge.

There are two kinds of questions: questions satisfied by yes-no answers, and questions that require sentence answers. Answers, therefore, are also of two types: yes-no answers and sentence answers. The answer to a yes-no question is 'yes' if the question can be deduced from the corpus - if there exists a deduction that has the sentences of the corpus as premises and the question as the last line. The answer is 'no' if the negation of the question can be deduced from the corpus. There is no answer if neither the question nor its negation can be deduced from the corpus.

A sentence qualifies as a sentence answer if the sentence can be deduced from the corpus and if the schema of the sentence is the same as the schema of the question when the question is in statement form. There can be only one yes-no answer, but there can be any number of sentence answers. Marill's treatment of semantic nets is an extension and formalisation of the discussion of relational networks given in Part 1. Marill takes the view that the proper structural analysis of a sentence is given by the quantificational schema of that sentence, as understood in symbolic logic. To this, he adds the view that the meaning of a one-place predicate is identified, ultimately, with the set of objects of which the predicate is true, and the meaning of a two-place predicate is identified with the set of all ordered pairs of objects of which the predicate is true, and so forth. Finally, he adds the notion that the meaning of an object is identified with, first, the set of one-place predicates that are true of the object, and, second, the set of two-place predicates that are true of it and something else, and so forth. The sets with which meanings are identified are extremely large. The machine cannot be required to prove its 'understanding' of a meaning by producing all the members of the sets. Marill maintains that it is enough for the machine to produce a convincingly large sample. The usual representation of a quantificational schema has the form of a string of symbols. Marill views the semantic net as an alternative notation, equivalent to the string notation, but more promising for computer exploitation. To demonstrate the relation between semantic nets and string-form schemata, Marill starts with three simple statements in string notation and transmutes them, by degrees, into diagrams in which lines tie together the several instances of a variable. The elements of a semantic net in Marill's exposition are the following:

- *Rectangles*—which represent the truth functions corresponding to logical operators and their arguments. Each rectangle has one terminal for each argument.
- *Diamonds*—which represent quantifiers. There are two types, corresponding to 'some' and 'all.'
- *A triangle with point down*—which represents 'sentence.' This triangle contains an 'S.'
- *A circle*—which represents a predicate. The circle has as many terminals as there are places in the predicate.
- *A triangle with point up*—which represents an individual.

Mariu gives six rules governing the combination of elements and the formation of semantic nets. The rules are:

- Connecting a predicate to a sentence symbol forms a sentence.
- Inserting a negation rectangle between the sentence symbol and the predicate negates the sentence.
- To connect two sentences, divert their predicates to a two-place truth-function rectangle and connect it to a single sentence-symbol triangle.
- To add a quantifier to a sentence, insert it in the line between the sentence symbol and its nearest neighbour.
- To terminate an unterminated predicate, attach an individual object to the unused terminal, or connect that terminal to a quantifier that is already in the diagram of the sentence.
- To merge two or more networks into one: for each individual, overlay all the triangles that represent the individual, retaining all the lines that are attached to any of the triangles; associate all the occurrences of the same predicate by connecting them with 'association lines.'

In 'Semantic Nets: An Informal Introduction,' Marill presents diagrams to illustrate the rules and to demonstrate the interpretation of moderately complex semantic nets. Marill's diagrams and discussion make it clear that the semantic net is formally equivalent to the conventional representation of a system of statements in predicate calculus. Marill believes that semantic nets afford a promising path into computer representation and processing of complex systems of relations.

EFFECTIVENESS OF INFORMATION-RETRIEVAL SYSTEMS

To some information-retrieval systems, a particularly simple schema is appropriate. The system is a 'black box' that contains a collection or set of items and that, from time to time, either spontaneously or in response to a request, offers a subset of its contents to one of its subscribers and withholds the complementary subset. An item may be thought of as a document. A subscriber may be thought of as simply a criterion: to the subscriber, an item is either pertinent or not pertinent. If one considers a single item of the collection and focuses his attention upon a particular occasion—a particular request from a subscriber or a particular spontaneous offering by the system.

Note that only two of the relative frequencies are independent, for the sum over the four categories must be unity, and the fraction of the items that meets the subscriber's criterion of pertinence is assumed to be fixed. Note, also, that there has to be some way to ascertain the pertinence or Non--pertinence of withheld items. Investigating the problem of evaluation of effectiveness, Swets found that eight of the ten studies that met his criterion of pertinence reduced the analysis to two-by-two contingency tables. However, in none of the studies was advantage taken of the fact that evaluative procedures have been developed for, and found useful in, other fields of application in which performance may be summarised in two-by-two contingency tables. Swets therefore adapted some of the apparatus of statistical decision theory to the information-retrieval context and proposed a measure of merit, a measure that quantifies the ability of the system to maximize the expected value of a retrieval trial, *i.e.*, of an offering or withholding of an individual item on a particular occasion. The measure takes into account the relative frequency and the utility of each of the four categories in the two-by-two table. We shall not review here Swets's explanation of its derivation.

Let it suffice to say that an assumption of normality of distribution is involved, that the measure is based on maximum-likelihood statistics, and that, given the relative frequencies of hits and false drops in a particular sample, one can read the value of the measure from an available table or graph. The measure is simple, convenient, and appropriate. It gives definite meaning to the concept, the 'basic discriminating power' of an information-retrieval system. The measure clearly separates discriminating power from mere willingness to yield output, thus avoiding a confusion that has been rife these last several years and that appears to be at the root of many informational difficulties. Moreover, the measure brings with it a well-developed system of procedures that facilitate analysis and interpretation of data. We expect Swets's measure to prove useful in evaluation of information systems. The main obstacle may lie in determination of the pertinence of withheld items. That obstacle is wide. It causes trouble for all the approaches to evaluation of performance in retrieval of information from large collections.

LIBRARY INFORMATION SYSTEM AND INFORMATION TECHNOLOGY

In library information system, information technology has had a clear and persuasive impact in almost every area of the library. The most significant development in information technology over the last few years or so is digital technology. Digital technology is revolutionizing the traditional concepts of preservation and access in library and archive communities. The applications of digital system and computing system in the libraries have been a subject of interest to present day professional librarians.

More recently the libraries have sought to implement increasingly complex solution that involved distributed networking and access to remote information resources. During the eighties, the whole focus of the librarians shifted towards library automation but in the nineties it has shifted towards digitization. The phrase library automation has been generally accepted within the profession to encompass early automation activities, yet it does not do justice to the current state of affaires as libraries have move well beyond the automation of internal procedures. In Manipur, however, applications of technologies in libraries are lagging far behind.

There are two university libraries, 74 affiliated colleges, nine public libraries, one state central library at Imphal and others at different districts of Manipur and many high and higher secondary schools libraries. But most of the libraries function in the traditional way with conventional printed shelf collection except some libraries like Manipur University library, Central Agricultural Library, RIMS Library, DOEACC Library etc. These libraries have initiated automation. Manipur University Library started automation since 1989 in the areas such as cataloguing, serial control, information retrieval and circulation recently.

This library provides internet facility, OPAC and has become one of the important nodes in the academic libraries system. As far as college libraries are concerned collections of information resources which support the faculty and students are not up to the mark because of lack planned systematic approach to the development of resources. Many of college libraries built up their collection of printed materials as activities and services are yet to be automated. Only one college library *i.e.* Modern College library has started Data entry using CDS/ISIS.

Books are still the only important channel for dissemi-nation of information. The librarian and other supporting professional staff are not well qualified and trained with the new modern technology. As far as infrastructures are concern a large majority of libraries have not yet automated their activities as they are handicapped to switch over to computeri-zation and modernization because of lack of infrastructural facilities like computer hardware, software, and human-ware. And most of the libraries are not provided internet facility.Regarding school and higher secondary school libraries, majority of school libraries are not able to provide even the facilities of a traditional library. From the discussion it is evident that the libraries in Manipur, except some, automation of the operations and services progressing very slowly. Automation as well as conversion of digital library will not be possible within five year though plan for automation exist. In Manipur it is not an easy task to develop digital library system as automation in the library is totally absent. Keeping in views of the reasons, authority should take initiative for promoting library automation by implementing new IT in the libraries of Manipur so that users from different communities can get the universe of knowledge available in the digital format.

PROBLEMS OF DIGITAL LIBRARIES SYSTEMS

Problems faced while entering into a digital libraries systems in Manipur can be summarized as:

- Libraries exist only in the traditional form and there is no electronic library/digital resource;
- Most of the libraries function with inadequate number professional staff required for smooth functioning and there is a general unwillingness to develop digital library system;
- Even if the librarian and some professionals are qualified they certainly lag behind because of lack of awareness about value of information, cooperation and coordination in the resource building and sharing of information and poor communication skill;
- Total absence of hardware, software and trained human power is another reason;
- A highly irregular and unpredictable power supply; and
- Libraries lack standardization of methods due to unwillingness to adapt to new requirements;
- Presently large majority of library have no computer and no internet facility and other infrastructural facilities required to exploit the opportunities provided by electronic media. Therefore, the best use of electronic publication on-line and network access are not possible;
- Lack of financial support due to the acute financial problem the state is facing.

In fact, the main problems faced seem to be lack of financial resources and lack of computer education without which automation in the libraries are not possible.

The dawn of information revolution is considered to be one of the marvelous achievements of the 20th century. The rapid growth and development of IT has resulted in the development of digital library, tools and skill relating to encoding information objects in digital format. The application of digital technologies within the library comes along with the development of computer technology. Keeping the points in view it is necessary to consider some perspective of digital library. Digital library not only creates and develops modern libraries but also transforms many existing libraries.

Digital Library introduced the concept of hypertext, facilitates networking in order to communicate and exchange digital information from source location to destination. It also facilitates preservation, storage, and communication of diverse multimedia objects but also provides intensive access from multiple locations and enrich teaching and learning environment which is not possible with the traditional library. Due to information explosion and existence of information society, everybody is aware of the newly developed technologies. This new developments are reflected in LIS education and in those libraries with existing infrastructure, services and network. In fact, there is a complete change in activities, role of library, librarians and other professionals (staff).

Most of the librarians in Manipur have now entered in the technological era of communication dominated by film and electronic media. The libraries are expected to be an automated information system having pervasive impact in almost every areas of library-be it the online catalogue, online database, online searching, document delivery, inter library loan, circulation etc. Clearly, the impact of automated system in libraries has been pervasive and significant.

INFORMATION EXPLOSION AND THE DIRECT RELATION OF INFORMATION TO DEVELOPMENTS

The present information explosion and the direct relation of information to developments in all walks of life emphasizes the need to give greater priority to the planning of systems which give library and information services to the people. Such systems can only be planned at national levels, if the total information resources of the nation is to be pooled together in a federal country like India, and shared between the cons-tituent states to make it available to all the users who require it in an equally and unbiased way at optimal cost.

Such library and information systems are to be founded upon sound legislation, if they are to attain their objectives the Society's information need has become so imperative that, many of the national and international library organizations has started to stress the urgent need for national library systems working together and sharing their services and materials at international level to provide better services to the people. Better can be defined here in quantitative and qualitative terms. Such national level and international level networking and resource sharing between library systems make possible service at lower cost, convenience of access, access to more materials and more rapid availability of materials.

PREAMBLE OF STATE ACTS

The preamble of a Library Act should summarise and state the aims and objectives of that Library Act. Even though the preamble of KPLA went on to explain the existing situations and the intentions with which the Act was initiated in an elaborate and vague form, it has given what is to be in preamble just before the preamble in precise and clear words as a long title ofthe Act. This summary or long title of the Act which we have to consider as preamble contains the basic concept of modern public library service which the actual preamble failed to state and the KPLA in its totality failed to support.

Like the Model Act, this summary provides for the establishment and maintenance of a system of public libraries and for the comprehensive development and organisation of all kinds of library and information services required for the people. The long title that follows the title of the Act in KPLA states, it is: An Act to consolidate and unify the library laws in the State and to provide for the reorganisation of the entire library system in the State of Kerala with a view to the develop-ment and maintenance of a comprehensive rural and urban library service and for matters connected therewith or incidental thereto.

Ranganathan has laid clear emphasis on legislation for public library service and for the organisation of a comprehensive library system. But all other Acts except KPLA provides for establishment and maintenance of public libraries only. They all cling to the obsolete concept of treating public libraries as independent units in their collection and services. So in this statement of the purpose of the Act, KPLA has accepted the most modern concept of Public Library legislation and the statement is a distinct improvement over those in all other existing State Acts.

THE MODEL ACT OF S.R. RANGANATHAN

To attain these objectives Dr. S.R. Ranganathan had framed the first model public libraries Act in 1930 which he placed for discussion at the Educational Conference at Banaras. Before framing the Act, this internationally reputed library scientist had travelled through most countries of the world where library legislation existed and had evaluated them and in many countries his ideas helped them to improve the systems.

In his Library Development Plan which he submitted in 1947 to Government of India he had included a union library bill and a revised state library bill also which envisaged the national public library and information system according to the most modern principles. Another model library Act was drafted in 1963 by a committee under the chairmanship of D.M. Sen on behalf of the Ministry of Education, Government of India. In 1966 the Library Legislation Sub Committee of the Planning Commission also prepared a model bill. The library Acts that came into existence in Madras, Hyderabad, Andhra,

Karnataka and Maharastra totally or partially accept the ideas of Rang ana than as reflected in his Model Acts and bills. These States became the laboratories where the ideas evolved by Ranganathan were experimented and observed.

In the light of these observations and suggestions contained in the other model bills and Acts, Ranganathan has improved his model Act by rectifying the clauses found to be defective in working and by adding new provisions that seemed essential. This model libraries Act was published in 1972. This is the latest and most advanced Model Act. Ten States out of the 25 States and 7 union territories have enacted library legislation. They are Madras 1948, Andhra 1960, Karnataka 1965, Maharastra 1967, West Bengal 1979, Manipur 1985, Kerala 1989 and Haryana 1989.

Others are Goa and Mizoram. But none of them are considered perfect or efficient. So in this comparative analysis of the essential aspects of State Public Library Acts, the Model Public Library Act, 1972 of Dr. S.R. Ranganathan is taken as the measuring rod or ideal situation with which the State Act is compared. Whenever some notable additional provisions or improvements are found in other existing Acts the same is discussed at the concerned contexts. The Kerala Act to which stress is given in this study and Ranganathan's Model Act of 1972 will be referred herein after as KPLA and Model Act respectively.

PURPOSE AND ADVISING OF STATE LIBRARY COMMITTEE

The Model Act provides for a *State Library Committee* (SLC) for the purpose of advising the SLA on all matters arising under the Act. All existing State Acts and Model Bills enacted or drafted in India provide for appointment of such a Committee or Council. KPLA names it as Kerala State Library Council. All Acts of the states except Kerala's have prescribed its membership on somewhat similar lines. All Acts provides that this body will be headed by Minister for Education. Despite differences in nomenclature and composition the function of this committee or council envisaged everywhere is basically the same *i.e.,* to advise the SLA or State Government in all matters arising out of the Act.

Kerala State Library Council (KSLC)

A careful analysis of the Kerala State Library Council (KSLC) in comparison with the SLC as provided in the Model Act or other State Acts will reveal that it is not a councilor committee of advisory nature as SLCs are. KSLC is an SLC and at the same time an SLA by itself. Naming it as a council is a difference in terminology only. Instead of appointing a Minister as SLA as in Mysore it appoints a body as SLA. But the Act fails to name it as SLA. The duties, powers and functions assigned to KSLC is inclusive of all those assigned to SLA and SLC in Model Act.

Sub-section 1 of the Section 3 of KPLA dealing with the constitution and composition of KSLC states9; KSLC shall be a body corporate having perpetual succession and a common seal with power, to acquire hold and dispose of property, both movable and immovable and to enter into contracts and shall by its name sue and be sued. This is an adaptation of the class related to Karnataka State Library Authority of Karnataka Act. No other Act including Model Act has so clearly defined the nature of this body and assigned so much powers as this like the Acts of Kerala and Karnataka. The powers and functions assigned to KSLC includes both the advisory functions of the committees and councils provided by Model Act and other Acts and the duties assigned to SLA by Model Act and Karnataka Act.

Sub-sections of section 8 of KPLA provides that the KSLC may:

- Advise the government of all matters connected with the administration of that Act and . . . the overall library policy of the State.
- Co-ordinate the working of the District Library Councils and Taluk Library Unions and...supervise and direct all matters relating to library service in the state.
- Establish one or more State Libraries . . . at such place or places in the State as may be considered necessary.
- Appoint and control such officers and servants as may be necessary for the efficient performance of its duties and functions under this Act and the rules made there under.
- Give to the District Library Councils and Taluk Library unions directions in the performance of their functions under this Act and . . . they shall not in-the discharge of their functions under this Act depart from directions given by the KSLC.

While we consider these classes and compare them with the parellel sections of the Model Act or other Acts it becomes clear that the classes which assigns the duties, powers and functions of KSLC is a distinct improvement from all others. KPLA has identified most of the functions and duties expected from such a body and very clearly assigned them to it without giving space for doubt and vagueness.

Composition of KSLC

If KSLC is to become able to fulfil such duties and functions expected from it, the composition of the body should be done accordingly. Membership of such a body should include persons who have contributed to the growth of knowledge, who has evolved or developed methods and techniques for collecting, organising and disseminating information and who have wide experience in related fields of activity. It is not the method of representation but the quality of representation that will make possible the efficient functioning of the system.

The sections which prescribe the membership of SLA in Karnataka Act and SLC in Model Act and other State Acts prescribe their membership on somewhat similar lines. Prof. P.B. Mangla in his study of library legislation opines that it should be a body having representatives from various institutions, organisations, government etc. interested in and connected with the growth and development of library and information services in the State.

The Model Act, the opinion of experts and recommen-dations of committees set for studying library legislation agrees that such a body should include among its members; the Minister for Libraries if there is one, otherwise Minister for Education, then Minister in charge of Local-Self-Government, Director of Libraries, State Librarian, sufficient number of representatives from State Legislative Assembly by election from among themselves, Secretary to Government for Education, representatives elected from Local Library Authorities by rotation to limit size of the body, representatives of associations of library profession and experts with specialization in library and information services and represen-tatives of Universities of the State.

It would be essential that the Minister in charge of Libraries should act as *ex-officio* chairman and the Director of Public Libraries or State Librarian should act as ex-officio secretary of the committee.

The rationale behind such a composition of this body is that it is a body which is to advise the government and discuss continuously on a most important responsibility of the government, that is organisation and dissemination of information required by the society. But disregarding all these principles KPLA provides for constituting a body of members who were not suitable to undertake this work.

The section 3 sub-section (2) related to the composition of the KSLC in KPLA provides: The KSLC shall consist of one member each from Taluks, elected by the general body of the District Library councils, and five members of whom one shall be a librarian, another a person belonging to the scheduled caste or scheduled tribe and another a woman nominated by the government. Library and information service is an intellectual service. It goes without saying that this body as provided in KPLA will not be able to fulfil satisfactorily the purpose for which it is intended.

In these days of information explosion and flooding of vast and varied types of books and other printed materials that originates every minute without wide familiarity of all spheres of knowledge and expertise in handling their information in most effective way at minimum cost the body which heads such a system will be having a mere formal and useless existence. As we have seen in section 8 of KPLA the most important function of KSLC is to advise the government on all matters connected with the administration of this Act and overall library policy ofthe State.

It is not clear how this committee will be competent to render such expert technical advise when it has only persons as members, who has come through election without expertise or knowledge about information work and without even any educational qualifications. Library and information service to the peopleif provided efficiently will be the continuously active service of government and will require expert advise everyday on many matters. The KSLC's inability to provide such expert advise will make government's efforts futile and to overcome this, govern-ment will be forced to create a continuous chain of Advisory Committees which is also not very practicable. While no hard and fast rule can be laid down about the size of this body it is generally felt that it should not have more than twenty members. The KSLC may remain a supreme body in name only for real powers of the council have been passed over to a smaller body which is the executive committee. But it also becomes an unwieldy body with membership of 25 persons.

Thus KSLC has acquired all the defects existing in SLAs and SLCs into one body. This Executive Committee is a new addition in our library Acts. But the findings of Ashok Mehta Committee and various committees appointed by many State Governments to study Panchayat Raj Institutions advise us against such an elected body like KSLC for organising important service as library and information service to the people. Instead of adopting the constitution and composition of SLA and SLC provided by the Model Act or followed by the other State Acts KPLA gave legal sanction to the organi-zational set up of an association that was already existing there, that is Kerala Granthasala Sangham.

The constitution and composition of KSLC and its Executive Committee is the same followed by Sangham for its general body and Bharanasamithi. In all other provisions KPLA follows the same pattern of Sangham with some minor alterations. For more than half a century Sangham was pressurizing the Government to give legal sanction to Sangham to be the SLA and to accept its system as it is,as State's Library System.

But experts have continuously pointed out during this period the futility of such a system for library and information service. But Sangham objected government's all other attempts to enact a modern library system legislation and at last come out successful in legalizing its own system. But this in fact totally prevents the State from having an advanced library legislation and developing its library and information services in conformity with the requirements of the time.

CONCEPT OF THE STATE LIBRARY AUTHORITY

The concept of the *State Library Authority* (SLA) underwent an evolution from State Library Committee to Minister of Education or Libraries; everywhere in the world. The Model Act recommends that for the purpose of promoting and organising a library system in the State the Ministry for Education of the State shall be the SLA.

It shall be the duty of the SLA to provide; for an adequate library and information service in the State and, for the progressive development of the institutions devoted to the purpose and to secure the effective execution by *Local Library Authorities* (LLA) of the national policy for providing adequate library service to the people in every locality. In the existing' State Acts only Karnataka Public Library Act, 1965 provides and clearly names SLA.

The Act provides for the constitution and composition of the SLA.6 SLA shall be a body corporate having perpetual succession and a common seal with power, to acquire, hold and dispose of property and to contract and may by the same time sue and be sued. It consists of twenty members from the fields concerned with information creation, organisation and services, with Minister for Education who shall ex officio be the President and State Librarian who shall ex officio be the Secretary of SLA. But it is desirable to make only one person, instead of a corporate body to be the supreme authority for providing this very important service, for that gives a unified command from administrative points of view. And this person should not be any person less than the Minister for Education, because he is directly responsible to the legislature and his term of office being limited to a period of five years he is ultimately responsible to the people. Hewit who made a study of the library legislation in India; it will be observed that two kinds of supreme authority are favoured in existing legislation and in the drafts of the model bills framed in India. One is a body of persons *i.e.,*

State Library Councilor Committee and second is a Minister of State. He suggests the second as the better of the two, mainly because a Minister is responsible to his legislature, and through it, to the electors and many be called to account therein. A body of persons even though a Minister may be President or Chairman thereof is not so easily questioned.

In any case; so important an activity as the provision for public library and information service to the people fully justifies direct representation in State Legislature. So all the studies on library legislations and the evaluation of existing legislations throughout the world and especially in third world counties, like that of Gardners's study comes to the conclusion that providing up of a body or a person as SLA and clearly naming and defining its powers and functions is certainly essential for the successful working of library Acts. But KPLA is very vague in this aspect and it fails to name a person or body as SLA.

DEPARTMENT OF PUBLIC LIBRARIES AND OFFICIALS

It is generally emphasized that in order to develop a system of public libraries in a State or country on proper lines, it is essential that a separate department of public libraries be created at par with the department of education and that the former should not be a part of the later or any other' department. The Acts of Andhra, Maharashtra, West Bengal and Karnataka prescribe for the creation of separate department of Public Libraries.

Director of Public Libraries

Most of the recommendations related to public library system legislation emphasizes that the department of Public Libraries should be headed by a

Director of Public Libraries (DPL), whose rank must be equivalent to that of Director of Education. He must be a person with qualification and experience in Library and Information Science. Emphasis on his being a professional is laid because it is he to whom the whole public library system in the State would look for guidance and inspiration and his professional outlook would normally greatly help the development of the system on desired lines.

The first public library Act in this country; the Madras Public Library Act, 1948 provided for the appointment of DPL. Andhra, Maharastra and West Bengal also prescribes for the creation of DPL. In Madras and Andhra the Director of Public Instruction is made the ex-officio Director of Public Libraries also.

The disadvantages of such an administrative set-up are quite obvious. The Department of Public Libraries becomes an additional burden to the Director of Public Instruction. This new department will be looked upon as an uninvited guest. A. R. Hewit has rightly pointed out that many of the duties of Director of Public Libraries would require technical knowledge and skill in librarianship. So professional experts only can undertake this responsibility efficiently.

State Library

All the Acts except KPLA which is not providing for these offices, combines the responsibilities of developing and managing the State Central Library Superintending and directing all matters related to the State library system in a single person called State Librarian or DPL.

The Model Act also recommends this pattern. But the Sinha Committee report suggested the creation of two separate posts for this purpose when it said "The DPL may have the overall responsibility to organize develop and supervise the public library system as the Head of the Department of Public Libraries.

The State Librarian should have the responsibility to manage supervise and develop State Central Library and should be the Chief Technical Advisor of the DPL, with no responsibility for the administration of the service in the State. This responsibility should be entirely that of DPL. But in KPLA there is no provision for appointing a Director of Libraries or State Librarian. While the class by class discussion of the Bill was going on in Assembly Mr. V.M. Sudheeran; member presented an amendment to add a new clause in the Act providing for appointment of a Director of Libraries. But was not considered.

Administration

For the administration of public libraries all the State Acts have created a department or directorate of public libraries. It is put under the charge of Director of Libraries or State Librarian who is to be the *ex-officio* Secretary of SLA. The functions of these posts as prescribed by all Acts including the Model Act are: to supervise and direct all matters relating to public libraries, to direct and control the working of LLAs, submit reports to Government and deal with schemes and plans relating to libraries. Many of the highly technical and specialized works of State Central Library also is to be supervised by them.

So it is clear that these posts which are carrying heavy responsibility concerning various matters-financial, advisory, administrative, technical, supervisory and so on-under the Act would require technical knowledge and skill in library and information service. So the Secretary or High Officer of this body should be a whole time officer having the prescribed qualifications to practice the library profession. Disregarding all the facts KPLA assigns all these duties and powers to a Secretary elected by members of the Executive Committee ofKSLC.

Section 3 sub-section (5) of KPLA provides that the elected members of the Executive Committee shall elect a President, Vice-President, Secretary and Joint Secretary from among themselves to be the President, Vice-President, Secretary and Joint Secretary respectively of the State Library Council and of the Executive Committee. Their term of office will be for three years.

KPLA assigns to the Secretary of KSLC the duties and powers which other State Acts assign to State Librarian or Director of Libraries. Section 9 Sub-section (1) States: the Secretary of the State Library Council shall be Chief Executive Authority of KSLC.

The nature of the office of Secretary of KSLC requires professional knowledge and experience as well as continuity of office for the successful operation of the Act, so it is inevitable that this provision will prevent KPLA from fulfilling the objectives for which a modern library legislation should exist. This serious defect of the Act has been pointed out by many members during the discussion of the bill.

Dr. M.Kuttappan has brought to the notice of the Assembly that such an important system like that for library and information service requires qualified government officials as their secretaries at State, District and Taluk levels. The period of an elected Non--official member may be over by three years and if he misappropriates government fund allotted for library development it will not be possible for the government to take action on him. Sri Ishac Kurikkal suggested an amend-ment to the Bill to provide that the Secretary of the SLC shall be appointed by the Government on the advice of the Kerala Public Service Commission.

Another member Sri Kodiyeri Balakrishnan opined that the Secretary of KSLC should be appointed by Government and the Act should specify the qualifications and method of appointment for this post. Sri Ramesh Chennitthala presented an amendment to add the following sub-clause in KPLA namely: The Secretary shall be a person not below the rank of a Joint Secretary to Government appointed by Government from among persons qualified and competent to hold such post. But all these suggestions were rejected and principles were disregarded to maintain a democratic system for constituting the SLA.

Library Co-operation

To make the best possible use of the document resources not only in the public library system but also in other types of libraries in the State such as universities, special libraries etc, a system of inter library co-operation needs to be developed in the state as a whole. It would also be useful and economical if centralization of different aspects such as acquisition programme, technical processing etc. of documents should be introduced at State level or at different levels of the system. The KPLA gives no such provision for co-operation or centralized processing and the institution which is to give leadership in such activities that is SCL is absent in KPLA.

State Central Library

The existing State legislations and the Model Act provide for a State Central Library (SCL) as an integral part of the Public Library Service. The SCL is normally the copy right collection. It should collect as far as its resources allow, expensive work and literature published abroad, material for which the local public library would have little need and could not afford. All the countries of the world possessing adequate library systems, have national library systems and all have national central library as distinct from the other libraries in the system, but is accessible to all through any library of the system.

The same role of National Central Library to the National system is done by SCL to the State system. Usually the library legislations designate the biggest collection available in the State as SCL and makes its resources and services available to the system. Even though various Acts and Model Act give different names to SCL like State Service Library, etc. in a public library system only one such library will be maintained and its resources will be shared by all participating units. Maintaining more than one SCL is unnecessary duplication of work and waste of resources.

Most of the State Acts and Model bills drafted, designate the biggest public library existing in the State as SCL and adopts it to the system and shares its resources among participating units. But instead of designating Trivandrum Public Library, the oldest and biggest collection in the State as SCL, the KPLA deems it to be one of the many State libraries it will establish.

The Act provides for no SCL in its system. Instead it provides that KSLC shall establish one or more state libraries at such place or places in the State as may be considered necessary. The relation of State libraries with other state libraries and different level service units and the purpose of more than one such institution is not defined in the Act.

State Library Service

State Library Service brings the manpower of the State in one pool and thus avoids the waste of time and money involved in filling up posts that would otherwise involve, if every Local Library Authority were to appoint the staff independently. A State Library Service further avoids the influence of members of the Local Library Authority in day-to-day management of libraries. Mysore Act has created a special state library service and it ensures proper administration and economy through State Library Service. But KPLA gives to KSLC and Local Library Authorities that is DLC and TLU the powers to appoint and control required officers and servants.

4

Library Automation of Descriptive Cataloguing Addresses

INTRODUCTION

The automation of descriptive cataloguing addresses only one part of the cataloguing activity. In addition to using computers to facilitate access to cataloguing copy, libraries are interested in computer-based solutions to the much discussed problems of card catalogues. The most frequently cited of such problems include substantial space consumption; the purchase of expensive cabinets and supporting furniture; labour-intensive and time-consuming catalogue maintenance routines which are intensified by changes in cataloguing rules affecting the choice and form of entries; and limited convenience and retrieval capabilities.

These problems can be minimized or eliminated by the replacement of card catalogues with computer-based book-form or online catalogues. Broadly defined, a book-form catalogue contains successive bibliographic records listed in a page format on paper or microforms. Among the earliest applications of library automation, computer preparation of book-form catalogues can lower production time and costs while eliminating the labour-intensive file maintenance routines associated with card catalogues.

As an alternative to computer printed or typeset catalogues, computer-output microfilm catalogues have been widely implemented by libraries and library systems since, the early 1970s. A number of service bureaus, book jobbers, bibliographic utilities, and other vendors have developed software to produce COM catalogues from library-supplied data, thereby eliminating the need for in-house COM recorders and customised programming catalogues. Broadly defined, an online catalogue is an organised, machine-readable accumulation of bibliographic records which are maintained on disks or other direct-access computer storage media for retrieval by library users and staff members working at inter- active terminals or appropriately configured microcomputer workstations. In addition to saving space and automating file maintenance, online catalogues permit remote access by authorised persons equipped with compatible terminals, and they can support information retrieval operations—such as keyword searching of titles and series names—which are not conveniently possible with card or book-form catalogues.Online catalogues may be custom-developed for specific library installations or purchased as prewritten software packages or turnkey systems. Examples of custom-developed online catalogues include the Library of Congress Computerised Catalogue, the MELVYL system at the University of California, the LIAS system at Pennsylvania State University, the Library Computer System (LCS) at Ohio State University, and the Dartmouth College Online Catalogue. Prewritten software packages suitable for online catalogue implementations include BRS/SEARCH from BRS Information Technologies, a powerful information retrieval programme that is available in mainframe, minicomputer, and microcomputer versions; INMAGIC, a versatile data management programme for dominated by integrated library systems which combine database management and catalogue access capabilities with circulation control, acquisitions, serials control, and other operations.

Such systems may be implemented as complete turnkey configurations of hardware and software or as prewritten software packages designed to operate on a library owned mainframe, minicomputer, or microcomputer. Vendors include CLSI, Geac, Notis, Dynix, OCLC, Virginia Tech, Data Research Associates, Carlyle, Comstow Information Systems, Universal Library Systems, Sobeco, Sigma Data/Centel, George- town Medical Library, Washington University, IBM, Inlex, Sirsi, Utlas, Innovative Interfaces, Eyring Research Institute, Easy Data, Data Trek, and Unisys. Among the newest and most widely publicised approaches to online catalogue implementation, a growing number of vendors offer public access catalogue systems which employ CD-ROM storage technology. Examples include the IMPACT system from Auto-Graphics, LASERGUIDE from General Research, THE INTELLIGENT CATALOGUE from the Library Corporation, and the LEPAC system from Brodart.

In such implementations, the library provides a machine- readable version of its catalogue, typically consisting of MARC format records on magnetic tapes obtained from bibliographic utilities or other sources, to a CD-ROM system vendor who indexes and otherwise prepares it for conversion to one or more CD-ROM disks. The disks themselves are created by a mastering process in special manufacturing facilities, and the library receives a specified number of disk copies plus menu-driven software designed for public catalogue access at microcomputer-based workstations. Updated by periodic replacement in the manner of book-form catalogues, such CD-ROM catalogues are increasingly mentioned as an alternative to computer output microfilm for union catalogues and similar implementations.

LIBRARY AUTOMATION CATALOGUING

Descriptive cataloguing is an intellectual activity requiring considerable decision-making and one that is time-consuming. As a result, many libraries experience cataloguing backlogs which impede the flow of materials into circulating and reference collections thereby preventing library catalogues from representing those collections fully and accurately. Recognising that the cost of descriptive cataloguing can approach or even exceed the value of certain materials, many libraries do not catalogue paperbound books, low-cost government publications, or other relatively inexpensive items.

In some research libraries, materials of presumably limited interest may be placed in off-site storage facilities with only an abbreviated catalogue record created. In most libraries, conventional descriptive cataloguing is not even considered for individual titles in large microform sets, even though such materials may significantly augment a library's resources in particular subject areas, and the failure to catalogue them impairs their utility. To simplify decision-making, to save time, and to reduce costs associated with descriptive cataloguing, libraries have historically relied on cataloguing copy, *i.e.*, descriptive cataloguing information prepared by other libraries, especially the Library of Congress.

The automation of descriptive cataloguing depends on the availability of such cataloguing copy in computer-processible form. In the late 1960s, the Library of Congress developed the MARC format for the communication of bibliographic data on magnetic tape and began distributing machine- readable cataloguing copy through its MARC Distribution Service. Since, the late 1960s, MARC formats have been developed for various types of library materials, and the scope of the MARC programme-once limited to English-language monographs—has broadened steadily and significantly. The LC MARC database-the accumulation of Library of Congress cataloguing data in machine-readable form-now contains more than 2.5 million records, most of them catalogued since, the inception of the MARC programme.

Although MARC tapes can be purchased from the Library of Congress for input to local computer systems, most libraries obtain access to MARC data through products and services developed by publishers, computer system developers, time-sharing services, and other intermediaries. Among the earliest of these MARC-derivative products were computer-generated micro publications such as MARCFICHE, produced by MARC Applied Research, and Books in English produced by the British Library. Created by Computer-output Microfilm (COM) technology, both products provided more timely and varied access to LC cataloguing data than could be obtained through the conventionally printed National Union Catalogue, which was itself discontinued in favour of a COM implementation in the early 1980s.As an equally timely and flexible alternative, several search services, including DIALOG and WILSONLINE, offer online access to the LCMARC database.

A growing number of vendors supply the MARC database on CD-ROM disks or digital optical videodiscs accompanied by software which supports the retrieval of specific cataloguing records and the printing of card sets. Examples include the BIBLIOFILE system from the Library Corporation in Washington, D.C., the LASERSEARCH system from General Pesearch Corporation, and the MINI MARC II system from Library Systems and Services Incorporated. Although these products and services are important, most libraries obtain access to machine-readable cataloguing records through one of the bibliographic utilities-organisations which maintain large databases of cataloguing records and offer online access and other services to subscribing libraries.

Examples include the Online Union Catalogue implemented by the Online Computer Library Centre (OCLC), the Research Libraries Information Network (RLIN) operated by the Research Libraries Group, the cataloguing support service operated by the Western Library Network (WLN), the Cataloguing Support System (CATSS) offered by Utlas International, the LIONS system operated by the New York Public Library, the AGILE II service offered by Auto- Graphics Incorporated, and Brodart's Interactive Access System (IAS).

While they differ in database size and composition, the number and nature of their subscribers, and the specific capabilities they support, these bibliographic utilities each maintain a database of MARC records obtained from the Library of Congress and other sources, supplemented by original MARC-format cataloguing contributed by subscribing libraries. Working at local terminals, participating libraries can retrieve cataloguing copy, modify it to meet local requirements, and order printed card sets, machine-readable cataloguing records on magnetic tape, and other bibliographic products.

Local workstations are also used to input original cataloguing records for use by other subscribers. Supporting thousands of online terminals accessing millions of machine-readable records, the bibliographic utilities are among the world's largest and most intensively utilised computer-based information services.

NEED FOR LIBRARY AUTOMATION

Even though this question seems to be very fundamental it is essential to emphasise this aspect, as the library automation is yet to take off in majority of the Indian libraries. Secondly, while justifying need for library automation more than cost-effectiveness the benefits derived by the library users become the major consideration. To appreciate the advantages it becomes necessary to highlight the different levels of library automation.

Following are considered as important factors for Library Automation:

- Information explosion.
- Increase in the collection of libraries.
- Inability of users to explore the unlimited litreature and information of their interest.

- Advances in the computer and communication technology.
- Wastage of user/ staff time in locating the information.
- Provide wide access to resources within the libraries and elsewhere.
- Better access.
- Quality in service.
- Cooperative efforts (Resource Sharing).

Out of all libraries an academic library has a difficult task of defining its mission and operating objectives. The automation programme will have to mange a wide range of litreature associated with numerous departments and educational programmes of the academic institution. Furthermore, in an academic library the collections will be diverse unlike a special research library where the collection is relatively homogeneous.

The user group will also range widely, including faculty, staff, students, scholars, administrators and the general public. The position of an academic library funded largely by the government further complicates the process of identifying and prioritising objectives.

As difficult as the task might at first appear, it is nevertheless essential to the process of establishing automated systems of any type. In addition the overall health of ones library operation will benefit from a modicum of intellectual rigour in this area.

PLANNING OF LIBRARY AUTOMATION

Planning for library automation has been defined as planning for 'integrated systems' that computerise an array of traditional library functions using a common database. While this is still generally true, rapid technological change is forcing a re-examination of what it means to 'automate the library.' As physical, spatial and temporal barriers to acquiring information are crumbling, libraries must plan for a broader and more comprehensive approach to providing automated services.

DEVELOPING A LIBRARY 'PROFILE'

One of the most important planning tools involves collecting basic statistical information on the library and its operations. You will find that the same basic data will be needed again and again—whether for vendors from whom you are requesting cost estimates, or for other libraries with whom you may be seeking to cooperate in implementing automation.

The following are examples of commonly needed data:

- Number of titles and volumes in the collection, current and projected.
- Number of borrowers, current and projected.
- Number of materials circulated, current and projected.
- Number of new materials acquired, current and projected.
- Interlibrary loans, lent to and borrowed from other libraries.
- Description of any cooperative arrangements involving the library.
- Library address and hours of operation.

In addition, it is important to take stock of any existing automation in the library by compiling the following data:

- Percentage of collection that has catalogue records in machine-readable form.
- Description of collection without machine-readable records, by category, (, monographs, audiovisuals).
- Description of currently-automated library functions (if any).
- Estimates of the location and number of workstations (to show where you intend to have equipment in any future system).
- Specifications for any existing equipment to be re-used with any future system (if any).

At the same time that this data is being assembled, it is important to assess user needs and set service priorities. This can be accomplished by undertaking a focused, strategic planning process designed to involve the library's 'stakeholders.'

DEVELOPING A STRATEGIC PLAN

A library planning to automate should undertake a process by which representative staff and users can identify service needs and objectives. The purpose of such an effort is to allow participants to articulate their interests and concerns, share perspectives and learn about possibilities in a collaborative setting. Group interaction is an important contributing factor in the success of the goal, which is to develop and sustain library automation in the years ahead.

Here are the basic steps involved in this process:

- Plan on a two-day, intensive planning effort.
- Ask participants to identify strengths, weaknesses, opportunities and threats in the library's environment (known as 'SWOT' factors in strategic planning) that are characteristic of or that confront the library.
- Group these factors into critical issue areas that are likely to have an impact on the libraries' future in developing and sustaining automation.
- *Ask participants to identify ideas and perceptions in relation to the question*: "How do you see the library providing user-friendly, cost-effective automated services in five years?
- Through a method of your own devising, ask participants to prioritise all of the ideas that come out of the above two 'brainstorming' exercises.
- Ask participants to shape these priorities into the draft of a strategic 'vision' for automation development consisting of a statement of purpose, goals and objectives for the library.

SETTING SERVICE PRIORITIES

Your strategic vision must now provide the framework or context for the next step in the automation process, which is to determine which library functions should be automated and in what order of priority. For example, processes that are repetitive, occupy large amounts of staff time, require retrieving information from large, unwieldy files, or are high-profile functions of the library (such as the public catalogue) are prime candidates for automation. Determining the functions that you wish to automate and their priorities relative to each other is important for all sorts of reasons.

If needs and priorities are clear, functions can be automated in phases, allowing for more effective use of frequently scarce funding. Moreover, it is a way to develop credibility with funding agencies and be able to take advantage of 'sudden' funding opportunities. Finally, evaluations of systems and options will be easier and more productive if you are able to match your highest functional priorities against the corresponding modules available in the marketplace.

A WORD ABOUT COSTS

Speaking of funding, planners need to be aware that there are certain cost elements involved in the installation and operation of any automated system.

These may be summarised as follows:

- Planning and consulting costs include direct, out-of-pocket costs, (*e.g.*, hiring a consultant) and indirect costs, (*e.g.*, training staff) associated with getting started.
- Purchase of the system includes the cost of acquiring the initial system hardware and software, as well as the cost of preparing a site for the computer system.
- Telecommunication costs are those fees paid to telephone companies for connecting remote terminals or workstations to a central computer system.
- Conversion costs are those associated with the creation of machine-readable bibliographic and, for circulation systems, patron, records.
- On-Going Operating costs include:
  — Maintenance fees
  — Utility costs
  — Bar code labels
  — Miscellaneous supply costs
  — Telecommunications costs
  — Salaries and benefits (if extra staff are hired).
- Additions to the existing system may be required to maintain performance specifications, to accommodate new users, or to allow for additional automated functions.

SYSTEM SPECIFICATIONS

At some point, you will need to re-formulate your functional priorities into 'functional specifications,' which may be defined as what you want an automated system to do for you, including things that your current manual system cannot do. 'Technical specifications' must also be established. These include standards that must be adhered to, system performance, operation, and maintenance, as well as infrastructure requirements, such as stable sources of electricity and telecommunications, and sufficient bandwidth. Developing clear and accurate functional and technical specifications that are specific to your library is one of the most important, if not THE most important, activity that you will engage in as you plan for your automated system.

These specifications will carry you through the entire procurement process, and will ensure that the system which most closely matches them will be the most useful and the most responsive to your needs.

DEVELOPING A FORMAL SPECIFICATIONS DOCUMENT

It is very difficult to compare systems sensibly and pragmatically solely by randomly looking at systems, talking to sales representatives, reading litreature or comparing broad cost quotations. For this reason, libraries use a formal document—often known as a 'Request for Proposal,' or RFP—that organises and standardises the information provided to and requested from the various system vendors. Utilising an RFP to solicit written responses from vendors makes it possible for you to systematically compare functionality, cost, maintenance, support, and all the other issues that are involved in system procurements. The process can save you money and will result in a wiser decision.

An RFP document should include these essential elements, among others:

- Background information on the library.
- A description of how the proposals should be arranged and submitted.
- Instructions on receiving vendor business and financial information.
- Criteria the library will use to evaluate vendor proposals.
- Questions regarding vendor training and documentation.
- Your functional and technical specifications.

Also, vendors should be asked to describe:

- How they will create bibliographic, item and borrower databases.
- Their system maintenance programmes and services.
- Their site preparation requirements.
- Their delivery and installation methodologies.
- Their system performance guarantees.
- Their pricing and cost strategies, in detail.

EVALUATING VENDOR PROPOSALS

Upon the receipt of vendor proposals, it will be time to begin the process of system evaluation and selection.

This process involves a number of key steps:

- If possible, form a project team of persons to assist with the evaluations and the selection who have some knowledge of automation or who work in the area(s) being automated. People involved in the strategic planning process would be a good choice.
- Try to weed out proposals that are 'fatally flawed,' *e.g.*, where the vendor fails to reply to any of the functional specifications or the system is missing a module for a high-priority function.
- Begin in-depth reading of the 'surviving' proposals, carefully noting both deviations from the requirements as defined by the RFP and any aspect that is handled unusually well. Make a list of any parts of the response that are not clear and require further clarification.
- Schedule system demonstrations. They are an important component of the evaluation process. Allow the vendors to show off the vendor's system in the most attractive light; however, be prepared with a list of what you want to see along with questions you would like answered. Use the same list with each vendor. This permits more effective cross-comparisons.
- Consider using computerised spreadsheet software in order to compare and evaluate vendor cost proposals. Costs may not be what they seem at first glance.
- Contact some of each vendor's current clients—sites of the same library type, and of similar size, where the hardware and software modules that have been proposed to you are currently in use.
- Assign point values to the criteria listed in the RFP and assign scores to the different proposals. The system with the highest score becomes the number one finalist, the system with the second highest score number two and so on. To maintain a negotiating edge, it is better to cut to two vendors rather than one. If that is impossible, maintain the illusion anyway. Remember: The selection process is not over until the contract is signed. Until that point, never let any vendors know that they have been eliminated, including those with fatal flaws.

AREAS OF LIBRARY AUTOMATION

As a first step in a planning process, it is desirable to formulate a model for computerisation listing all itemised and prioritised information systems being maintained on a manual basis by the library. For this exercise it is necessary to break down these procedures into their constituent parts. When further subdividing these activities, each item is to be considered of its functional elements. The systems and subsystems listed below are only indicative and may vary with differing library system environments.

These are:

- Acquisitions:

— Selection
— Ordering
— Claiming/cancellation
— Receiving/invoice processing
— Extended procurements
— Gift tracking
— Fund Control
— Maintains information about all library related funds
— Ability to group funds (nesting)
— Track fund allocations and adjustments
— Fund encumbrance
— Fund expenditure
— Cash Balance
— Free Balance
— Automatic updating of fiscal information through recording of specific transactions
— Track year-to-date expenditures
— Create Purchase Orders

- Technical Services:
  — Books
  — Serials
  — Special Collections
- Cataloguing:
  — Books
  — Serials
  — Special Collections
- Circulation:
  — Charge/Renewal
  — Discharge
  — Loan Periods
  — Processing schedules
  — Holds
  — Messages
  — Blocks
  — Notices
  — Transaction Recording Devices for off-line processing
  — Member control
  — Inventory control
- Serials Control:
  — Receipt (check-in)
  — Claiming
  — Bindery control
  — Replacements

  - Monographic serials
  - Invoice processing
- Reference Services:
  - Desk services
- User tools
- Bibliographic utilisation
- Reprography
- Inter-library communications
- General Administration
- Grants Administratiuon
- Library Publications
- Bindery
- Periodical Citation Searching
- OPAC
- Bibliographic Database

CIRCULATIONCONTROL

Library interest in automated circulation control is, in large part, based on a long-standing awareness of the problems inherent in manual circulation systems. These problems include Labour-intensive and time- consuming recordkeeping work routines, inaccuracy, high personnel turnover, an inability to generate statistics about circulation activity, and the lack of an interface between circulation files and other library files which contain much the same bibliographic data. Circulation control is one of the most widely automated library operations, and it is often the first and simplest activity to be automated in a given library, possibly because circulation control systems bear an obvious resemblance to inventory management, retail charge card operations, and other transaction processing activities which have been successfully automated in general business applications.

While specific circulation policies and procedures may be subject to considerable local variation, the major component of circulation control-the check-out/check-in procedure-is typically performed in a straightforward manner that is easily understood by computer application developers and systems analysts lacking formal library training. As library users, many data processing professionals have experienced the circulation activity firsthand and are at least broadly familiar with its purpose and nature. Because the bibliographic data required for automated circulation control are often less extensive and complex than those required to computerize such activities as cataloging and acquisitions, data conversion costs, software development time, and storage requirements may be substantially reduced. Perhaps more than any other library activity, the historical development of automated circulation control has reflected changes in state- of-the-art data processing technology. Through the mid- 1970s, most automated circulation control systems were custom-developed for a single library or library system. As early as the 1930sandextendinginto the 1960s, a number of libraries used keypunched cards in combination with sorters, collators, and other unit record equipment as an alternative to manual record keeping. Tabulating keypunched cards with information about books, borrowers, and due dates could be sorted to select overdue items or to identify all books on loan to a given person.

Such "precomputer" data processing systems, several of which were developed for academic libraries by methods and procedures analysts and operations research specialists, were typically based on inventory control models used in business. With the introduction of computers for business applications in the mid- 1960s, a number of libraries developed computerized circulation control systems based on batch processing techniques. Such systems were usually implemented on a computer located in a data processing center operated by a university, municipality, corporation, or government agency with which the library was affiliated. In the typical installation, keypunch or key-to-tape devices were used to convert information about individual circulation transactions to computer-processible form. The resulting data were then hatched for processing at predetermined intervals, a computer writing individual borrower numbers into item records contained in a master circulation file maintained on magnetic tape and printing a list of all items in circulation for library reference.

While some of these batch-processing circulation control systems remain in use, they are now mainly of interest for their limitations and impact on the design of subsequent systems. As a particular disadvantage, the printed lists produced by batch-processing systems necessarily reflect the status of a library's circulating collection at the time when the last batch of transaction records was processed. Part of the information contained in such lists is necessarily invalidated by circulation transactions occurring after that time. By the mid-l970s, library automation specialists had begun to concentrate on the development of online, real-time circulation control systems which process circulation transactions as they occur.

Because pertinent data files are updated immediately, such real-time systems accurately reflect the status of a library's circulating collection. Printed lists are replaced by online terminal Enquiries to determine the circulation status of specific items. While real-time circulation control systems have been custom- developed for individual libraries, a number of vendors offer generalized, preformulated approaches to the computerization of circulation control that eliminate the need for customized system development and speed the implementation process. Such preformulated approaches, currently the dominant method of automating circulation control, can be divided into two related groups:

- Prewritten circulation control software intended for execution on a computer system operated by or for a given library; and

- Turnkey systems, consisting of preconfigured combinations of hardware and software marketed as self-contained products.

Introduced in the early 1970s, the earliest prewritten circulation control software packages and turnkey circulation systems were single- purpose products designed specifically and exclusively for library circulation activities. While such single-purpose systems remain available, library administrators, systems analysts, automation planners, and pro- duct developers are increasingly emphasizing integrated, multifunctional turnkey systems and software packages which combine circulation control with other capabilities. In addition to circulation control, the most complete integrated system implementations include interrelated application modules for cataloging, online catalog access by library users and/or staff, acquisitions, and serials control, a community bulletin board sys- tem, and electronic message transmission.

In some cases, circulation is a standard integrated system component which may be implemented alone or in conjunction with other functions; in others, circulation control is an optional application module which must be purchased separately. Whether designed as single-purpose products or as integrated sys- tem components, prewritten circulation software packages and turnkey systems can be implemented far more quickly than customized circulation control systems which may require months or perhaps years to develop. Speed of implementation is an especially important consideration in applications where automation of the circulation activity will result in a cost reduction.

Similarly, prewritten software packages and turnkey systems minimize or eliminate requirements for local software expertise. Libraries acquiring such products usually do not need to hire programmers. In fact, customer programming is specifically prohibited by most vendors. Because the system design is predetermined, user training is limited to operational considerations. As a distinctive advantage of turnkey implementations, procurement-related tasks are greatly simplified by the availability of a preconfigured combination of hard-ware and software components that are specifically designed to work together. With a single source for central processing equipment and peripheral devices, the necessity of dealing with multiple hardware vendors is eliminated, as are potential problems of equipment compatibility.

While prewritten circulation control software packages are avail- able for computers of all types and sizes, medium-sized and larger public and academic libraries have typically relied on mainframe-and minicomputer-based products. Examples for IBM mainframes include the NOTIS software package, originally developed by Northwestern University for its own use; IBM's own DOBIULIBIS Progamme; and the TECHLIB/STATS implementation of the BASIS software package which is marketed by the Information Dimensions subsidiary of Battelle. Originally developed by libraries in the Minnesota State University system, the PALS software package is marketed by Unisys for use with its own mainframe computers, while the LIAS system, developed by Pennsylvania State University, operates on Honeywell computers.

Examples of circulation software packages for popular minicomputer systems include Comstow's Bibliotech system for Digital Equipment's VAX product line; the Georgetown Library Information System (LIS) for Digital's PDP-11 Series models; the Washington University BACS system for Data General and other minicomputers which run under the MIIS operating environment; and the VTLS and Index systems for the Hewlett-Packard HP-3000 product line. Minicomputer- based turnkey circulation control systems are available from CLSI, Geac, Data Research Associates (DRA), Dynix, OCLC, Universal Library Systems, and other vendors. Reasonably priced and designed for readily available hardware configurations, microcomputer- based circulation control programs have proven particularly popular with small public, school, and special libraries. Vendors include Follett, Gaylord, Easy Data, Data Trek, Aball Software, Nichols Advanced Technologies, Scribe Software, Winnebago Software, and Richmond Software. While the earliest circulation control programs and turnkey systems forced libraries to accept predetermined loan periods, borrower categories, and other operating parameters, most newer products flexibly support a varied range of library requirements.

Unlike earlier systems which contained rigidly coded procedures to control charging, discharging, and related activities, all newer products are parameterized, i.e., they allow libraries to specify the conditions under which items will be circulated, file Enquiries made, and printed output produced. Rather than being written into programs, particular operating parameters are selected by libraries from a range of possibilities. The resulting flexibility broadens the range of applications which a given system can address and is particularly important in installations where a single prewritten software package or turnkey system will be shared by many libraries.

AUTOMATED REFERENCE SERVICE

Since, the late 1960s, many publishers of printed bibliographies, indexing and abstracting journals, and other reference works have offered machine-readable versions of their products for use in computer assisted reference applications. Initially intended for government, corporate, and academic libraries supporting research in scientific and technical disciplines, such machine-readable reference sources have become widely available in business, the social sciences, and the humanities. In addition to databases which correspond to printed publications, a growing number of reference sources have been developed specifically for use in computer-based systems and have no printed counterparts.

While the earliest machine-readable databases were bibliographic in character, Non--bibliographic numeric and directory-type databases are increasingly commonplace. During the late 1960s and early 1970s, a number of libraries purchased machine-readable bibliographic and Non--bibliographic databases for processing on in-house computers using custom-developed information retrieval software. Most libraries, however, lacked access to the hardware and software resources required to implement such systems.

Through the early 1970s,the needs of such libraries were addressed by fee-based search services operated by the producers of machine-readable databases or other organisations such as large research libraries. Such services, which operated in the offline, batch processing mode, were replaced in the mid-1970s by services offering online database searching on a time sharing basis to libraries equipped with conventional terminals.

Now widely utilised by libraries of all types and sizes, online search services can be divided into two broad groups:

- Multidisciplinary services—including DIALOG, BRS, ORBIT, WILSONLINE, DATA- STAR, and ESA-IRS-that provide database coverage of a varied range of subjects for a broad clientele; and
- Specialised services-such as the NLM SEARCH SERVICE, STN INTERNATIONAL, LEXIS, and WESTLAW-that provide online access to one or more databases relevant to a single subject discipline, profession, or activity, such as medicine, law, or engineering.

Various types of specialised search services provide online access to databases containing a specific type of information such as news. Examples include the NEXIS, VUITEXT, DATA TIMES, and NEWSNET search services. While they differ in the number and type of databases offered and in the specific retrieval capabilities supported, multidisciplinary and specialised search services share a common operating methodology: they purchase or otherwise obtain bibliographic and Non--bibliographic data-bases in machine-readable form from their producers, convert the dataases to a form required for storage on their computers, and allow libraries or other subscribers to perform various retrieval operations on such data using prewritten data-base management software.

The software features a Non--procedural query language which permits a user at an online terminal to initiate litreature searches or other information retrieval operations by entering specified commands.

While their query languages are relatively easy to learn, online search services are more often providing menu-driven interfaces for novice users. Some services also offer private file capabilities which allow libraries to establish their own databases. As a recently implemented supplement or alternative to online search services, an increasing number of bibliographic and non-bibliographic databases are available on CD-ROM disks.

Accompanied by information retrieval software, such CD-ROM reference products permit database searching at local microcomputer workstations (over 100 titles were available at the time of this writing). Offered on a subscription basis, they can prove less expensive than online searching for databases that are accessed frequently, although infrequent updating, slow response time for complex searches, and other performance limitations may make them unsuitable for some applications. As a hybrid implementation with potentially attractive cost/performance characteristics, several vendors combine CD-ROM searching of back file data with online access to the most current information.

ORIGINAL CATALOGUING AND COPY CATALOGUING

Entering ISBD Punctuation

The General International Standard Bibliographic Description (ISBD) prescribes punctuation between elements or areas of bibliographic description for current cataloguing (i.e., AACR2):

- Supply ISBD punctuation that occurs within variable fields. Enter punctuation and spaces between elements within a field as prescribed by AACR2.
- If punctuation separates data that occur in separate subfields, enter the punctuation at the end of the first subfield.
- Do not supply ISBD punctuation (space-dash-space) that occurs between variable fields, *e.g.*, between the 250 and 260 fields.
- Do not supply parentheses around transcribed series statements.

Space-dash-space

The OCLC catalogue card print programme supplies a space-dash-space (-) before the following fields:

- 250 Edition Statement
- 254 Musical Presentation Statement
- 255 Cartographic Mathematical Data
- 256 Computer File Characteristics
- 260 Publication, Distribution, Etc. (Imprint)
- 362 Dates of Publication and/or Volume Designation (First indicator value *0*)
- 4xx Series Statements (First 4xx field)

If the field that precedes one of the listed fields ends with final punctuation (.? !), the print programme supplies a space-dash-space (-). If the preceding field does not end with final punctuation, the print programme supplies period-space-dash-space (-).

Verifying Headings

You must use AACR2 or AACR2-compatible forms for all headings and uniform titles for current original cataloguing. Search the OCLC Authority File to verify forms of entry.

Use current Library of Congress (LC) AACR2 or AACR2-compatible forms. If those forms are not in the OCLC Authority File, construct the heading or uniform title according to AACR2.

INCLUDING NON-ROMAN SCRIPTS

The OCLC provides the capability to include Arabic, Bengali, Chinese, Devanagari, Cyrillic, Greek, Hebrew, Japanese, Korean, Tamil, and Thai scripts in bibliographic records. Include these scripts in your current original cataloguing if you have the knowledge and expertise to do so.

ROMANIZED DATA

If you provide Romanized (Latin-script-equivalent) data, Romanization should follow guidelines in the ALA-LC Romanization Tables on the Library of Congress Web-site.

GENERAL MATERIAL DESIGNATIONS

Use General Material Designations (GMD) for current original cataloguing. GMDs are generic terms describing the medium of the item. OCLC defines subfield ‡h (Medium) in field 245 (Title Statement) for GMD information. Enter GMDs in lowercase letters enclosed in brackets. Example: ‡h [electronic resource].

GMDs and Library of Congress Rule Interpretations

Library of Congress Rule Interpretations (LCRIs), rule 1.1C, lists GMDs and provides standards for use. The LC applies rule 1.1C for only certain types of materials. LCRI 21.29 limits the use of GMDs to the title area only. Follow LC practice except: If one of the following GMDs is applicable, it is mandatory for I-level, Core-level, and K-level records in field 245 subfield ‡h.

Dublin Core users apply different codes:

- ‡h [art original]
- ‡h [microscope slides]
- ‡h [art reproduction]
- ‡h [model]
- ‡h [chart]
- ‡h [motion picture]
- ‡h [diorama]
- ‡h [picture]
- ‡h [electronic resource]
- ‡h [realia]
- ‡h [filmstrip]
- ‡h [slide]
- ‡h [flash card]
- ‡h [sound recording]
- ‡h [game]
- ‡h [technical drawing]

- ‡h [graphic]
- ‡h [toy]
- ‡h [kit]
- ‡h [transparency]
- ‡h [microform]
- ‡h [videorecording]

Notes:

* Use the "graphic" GMD only when applying the "Graphic Materials" descriptive conventions, indicated by the presence of the value *gihc* in subfield ‡e of field 040.

LIBRARY DESCRIPTIVE CATALOGUING

International Efforts

The major contribution in cataloguing at the international level is that of IFLA. This is in the form of international standard bibliographic descriptions (ISBDs) which have influenced almost all existing cataloguing rules.

IFLA has so far issued the following ISBDs and is continuously subjecting them to revision:

- ISBD (G)-General
- ISBD (M)-Monographs
- ISBD (NBM)-Non-book Materials
- ISBD (CM)-Cartographic Materials
- ISBD (A)-Antiquarian Books
- ISBD (PM)-Printed Music
- ISBD (S)-Serials
- ISBD (CF)-Computer file, Machine-Readable files (MRF)
- ISBD (CP)-Component parts
- ISBD (ER)-Electronic Resources (replaced ISBD (CF)

Other international efforts include those of Unesco particularly the creation of the International Serials Data System (ISDS). ISDS seeks to develop a registry of world serials publications. containing sufficient bibliographic information for their identification and bibliographic control.

The cornerstones of ISDS are the ISSN and a corresponding "key title", to which geographic qualifiers may be included in parentheses at the end of the title when necessary to make the key title unique.

Another international organization is the International Standardization Organization (ISO) which is responsible for many relevant international standards, in addition to those previously cited on filing rules:

- ISO 690, Bibliographic references: contents, form and structure.
- ISO 9115, Bibliographic identification (biblid) of contributions in serials and books.

- ISO 2108, International standard book numbering (ISBN).
- ISO 3297, International standard serial numbering (ISSN).
- ISO 3901, International standard recording code (ISRC).
- ISO 2709, Format for bibliographic information interchange on magnetic tape.
- ISO 10444, International standard technical report number (ISRN).

AACR2

AACR2 incorporates the ISBD system aiming at eliminating inconsistency in the descriptive treatment of various types of materials. It allows local cataloguers to choose among three levels or degrees of detail in constructing descriptive cataloguing data and also includes some optional rules. This flexibility improves the utility of the rules by a wide range of sizes and types of libraries.

Levels of Description

Rule 1.OD of AACR2 specifies these levels as follows:

- *First level:* Title proper/first statement of responsibility if different from main entry in form or number or if there is no main heading.—Edition statement.—Material (or type of publication) specific details.—First publisher, etc., date of publication, etc.—Extent of item.—Note(s).—Standard number.
- *Second Level:* Title proper [general material designation] = Parallel title: other title information/first statement of responsibility.—Edition statement/first statement of re-sponsibility relating to the edition.—Material (or type of publication) specific details.—First place of publication, etc: first publisher, etc, date of publication, etc.—Extent of item: other physical details. dimensions.—(Title pro-per of series/statement of responsibility relating to series, ISSN of series. numbering within the series. Title of subseries. ISSN of subseries. numbering within subseries).—Note(s).—Standard number.
- *Third Level*: All the elements set out in the rules that are applicable to the item being described.

The information stated here is considered the minimum to be given by the cataloguer, as he may add additional elements in the first two levels. Moreover, the cataloguer may use different levels for different materials. if he does he must be consistent. It is noted that a punctuation pattern is used, which is very important element in bibliographic standardization. This pattern is defined for every element of description.

Areas of Description

The description is divided in both AACR2 and ISBDs into eight areas or fields. *They are as follows:*

- *Area 1:* Title and Statement of Responsibility Area
  - 1.1 Title proper
  - 1.2 General material designation
  - 1.3 Parallel title(s)
  - 1.4 Other title information
  - 1.5 Statement(s) of responsibility
- *Area 2:* Edition Area
  - 2.1 Edition statement
  - 2.2 Parallel edition statement(s)
  - 2.3 Statement(s) of responsibility relating to the edition
  - 2.4 Statement relating to a named revision of an edition
  - 2.5 Statement(s) of responsibility relating to a named revision of an edition
- *Area 3:* Material (or Type of publication) Specific Details area (Used only for cartographic materials, printed music, computer files, and serials).
- *Area 4:* Publication, production, Distribution, etc, Area.
  - 4.1 Place(s) of publication, distribution, etc.
  - 4.2 Name(s) of publisher, distributor, etc.
  - 4.3 Date of publication, distribution, etc.
  - 4.4 Place of manufacture
  - 4.5 Name of manufacturer
  - 4.6 Date of manufacture
- *Area 5:* Physical Description Area
  - 5.1 Specific material designation and extent of item
  - 5.2 Other physical details
  - 5.3 Dimensions
  - 5.4 Identification of accompanying material
- *Area 6:* Series Area
  - 6.1 Title proper of the series
  - 6.2 Parallel title(s) of the series
  - 6.3 Other title information of the series
  - 6.4 Statement(s) of responsibility relating to the series
  - 6.5 International Standard Serial Number (ISSN) of the series
  - 6.6 Numbering within the series
  - 6.7 Enumeration and/or title of subseries
  - 6.8-The same as for 6.2 through 6.6 for subseries
  - 6.12
- *Area 7:* Note(s) Area (repeatable, each note being a separate area)
- *Area 8:* Standard Number, etc Area (a repeatable area)
  - 8.1 Standard number: ISBN, ISSN, ISRC etc.
  - 8.2 Key-title (associated only with an ISSN)

- 8.3 Terms of availability and/or price
- 8.4 Qualification(s) following 8.1 and/or 8.3

Access Points (Headings) and References

AACR2 is of two parts: The first covers descriptions as stated before and consists of (13) chapters where the first covers all types of materials, and chapters 2-12 cover a certain type each, while chapter 13 concerns analytical cataloguing. The second part starts with chapter 20 which is an explanation of the rules of this part, while no chapters 14-19 exist.

Chapter 21 covers the choice of access points, chapter 22 deals with headings for persons, chapter 23 deals with headings for geographic names, chapter 24 deals with headings for corporate bodies, chapter 25 deals with uniform titles, while chapter 26 collects together the various rules for references.

The rules are completed by four appendices:

1. *A:* Capitalization
2. *B:* Abbreviations
3. *C:* Numerals
4. *D:* Glossary

Numerous handbooks and illustrations have been published in different languages, as well as in the local formats adopted such as CEHANET procedures manual.

ROLE OF TECHNOLOGICAL INNOVATIONS IN IMPROVING LIBRARY SERVICES

Once librarians were considered only the custodians of the library collection, but the change in information media from print to electronic has shown the new sunrise in the life of librarians. The basic aim of a library is to meet the teaching, learning, scholarly-research and other information needs of its faculty, students and research scholars and that too effectively and with efficiency. Medical library and information professionals ensures that health care providers have access to reliable, relevant, accurate, up to date and timely information that enhances the quality of health care.

The migration of information from paper to electronic media has changed the whole nature of research. With the easy availability of office computers and the transformation of media, the popularity and usage of digital and virtual libraries has been increased. World Wide Web has totally changed the meaning of a library. Physical presence has been decreased rapidly with the invention of virtual library. There is a universal assumption that man was born innocent or ignorant and should actively seek knowledge. "Information seeking is thus a natural and necessary mechanism of human existence". Information seeking behaviour is the purposive seeking for information as a consequence of a need to satisfy some goal. In the course of seeking, the individual may interact with manual information systems or with computer-based systems. Information seeking behaviour involves personal reasons for seeking information, the kinds of information which are being sought and the ways and sources with which needed information is being sought.

Information seeking behaviour is expressed in various forms, from reading printed material to research and experimentation. Scholars, students and faculties actively seek current information from the various media available in libraries, *e.g.* encyclopedias, journals and more currently, electronic media. In this era of 'E', a sea change can be seen in the information-seeking behaviour of the users of library. In the phase of print media, users had no choice except going to the library and search for the material in books, journals and archives for hours. Search was very time consuming in print phase. Changing needs of users have changed the role of a librarian, which has transformed a librarian into information professional. Librarians have always acted as a link between knowledge source and its users.

In this era of 'E', librarians are playing the role of an electronic middleman. They are now helping the readers in the best possible way by using the latest technology and searching techniques. Users are being connected to the information resources via Internet for hyper-links and for many more options and choices for advance search. The change in the information-seeking behaviour is the result of the invention of E-resources. Readers felt relaxed with this invention and inclination towards these resources was natural.

There are many types of E-resources like Ebooks, E-journals, various open sources, gateways and databases. Chronologically we can divide these resources specifically journals as, in-print journals, on-line journals free with print, only on-line journals, on-line databases. In the era of 'E', readers demand has become significant as they ask for an article or topic in place of a book or journal and at the same time they prefer to search online databases to fulfill their needs. With the invention E-resources quantity and quality of research both have been affected. Different search techniques are undertaken by library users to search and locate relevant information. To understand how users of libraries search and locate relevant documents, we librarians, need to understand the search techniques and what resources and sources of information they generally use and require. Information professionals and users both suffer from the problem of exhaustive information, from a wide range of sources and shortage of time to find, manage and evaluate.

Sometimes users search internet indiscriminately without knowing the facts. Here librarian plays an important role by making the users aware of the importance of the evaluation of the retrieved information by guiding them, how to retrieve, what to retrieve and how to further use that retrieved information, which is called evaluation of information. The challenge posed by the information explosion is being successfully met by electronic information sources. Further this information explosion, diversity of user need, financial crunch and impossibility of self-sufficiency has led to the formation of consortia at local, regional, national and international level.

OBJECTIVE

The main objective of this study is to know the changing needs and information-seeking behaviour of the users and further various methods and resources being adopted by the librarians to fulfil these needs, which is the result of various technological innovations. Information seeking is a fluid and situation dependent activity where a seeker's actions are influenced by access to information, perceived quality and trust in the information source. This reminds the necessity of regular study and development of information system and management information services in North Indian Medical Institutes.

This work intends to study followings in libraries as a prototype of North Indian Medical Institutes:

- To examine information seeking behaviour of library users of North Indian Medical Institutes.
- To study the problems faced by the library users of North Indian Medical Institutes while seeking and using information.
- To explore the role of the library consortia's for providing service to the library users.
- To review the use of E-databases in this era of information explosion.

HYPOTHESIS

In this study it is hypothesized that:

- Physical visit to the libraries has been declined.
- Preference of users has been shifted to online documents from print one.
- Lack of knowledge about IT is the main problem the user face in the information searching process.

METHODOLOGY AND SCOPE

There are many ways to get information. The most common research methods are: literature searches, talking with people, focus groups, personal interviews, telephone surveys, mail surveys, e-mail surveys and internet surveys. A survey has been conducted on North Indian Medical Libraries through a questionnaire to know the changes in the information-seeking behaviour and needs of the users in this era of 'E'. So the medical professionals who were enrolled as member in the various medical libraries of Chandigarh and adjoining areas were considered for the study in hand. Further it can be stated that there were about 720 active library users of these libraries, so these users were taken as the subject for the study.

Through the stratified random sampling technique 72. Questionnaire method was used as it can be completed in one of the two basic ways. Firstly, respondents were asked to complete the questionnaire with the researcher not present and thus data was collected from 72 medical professionals, out of which 33 were students and 39 were senior residents, Assistant professor and professors. Secondly, respondents were asked to complete the questionnaire by verbally responding to questions in the presence of the researcher. This variation is called a structured interview and this method was applied on 28 librarians to know their observations.

FINDINGS (USERS)

Visits to the Library

Twenty-nine respondents (40per cent) reported frequently visiting a medical library, 18 (25per cent) rarely visited and 24 (33per cent) never visited; one respondent did not answer this question. Respondents in their first year reported frequent visits to the library more often than those did in their second year. In the overall group, those who never or rarely visited a library indicated that E-resources are not sufficient; documents that they needed were not available or libraries were not needed because of the Internet.

So the main observation regarding visit to the library is that students visit library more frequently in their initial years of college/ institute. Overall group of users prefer to search Internet as they are not satisfied with the available E-resources in their library. They only visit the library after making sure that this required information is available in the library. This service is being provided through WEB OPAC in most of the libraries today. So hypothesis 1 stands proved.

Preference of Information Sources

Most respondents reported performing database searches independently. Among those who did their own searches, MEDLINE and PUBMED was the bestknown and most frequently used database: only 1 of 72 respondents did not know of MEDLINE. HINARI is being used by some users but the main problem with this database is that site is very slow. When asked about criteria for selecting references, the most important feature was free full-text availability with the demand of online database and formation of consortia. Regarding access to the full text, few respondents said they visited a library to check document availability and ordered articles through a library. More than half of respondents preferred electronic tools for literature searching. Yet most indicated they preferred to print documents rather than read them online. Respondents were further asked about their preferences about the form of the document. An online database is the most preferred format (39per cent) in contrast to the print only format that is the least preferred one (10per cent). This observation directly shows the shift of the preferences of the users from print to the online formats. It is strongly supported by the findings in which online journals and databases have become the most preferred form of document as 75per cent users need only online resources in form or the other. Further users prefer taking print of the required information as they feel discomfort in reading directly from the screen. So hypothesis 2 stands proved.

Problems in Information Seeking

Several problems were identified in the information searching process. Many respondents found difficulties in choosing among the large number of documents retrieved in searches and lack of time was also noted as a problem. Common obstacles in the information-seeking process identified by respondents include lack of time, doubt about the existence of relevant information, retrieval of too much information and difficulties with navigation and searching. Since latest innovations have made the search easier with the latest options like E-mail alerts, send articles etc., but problem in information searching still persists due to the lack of knowledge of I.T. So the hypothesis no. 3 also stands proved.

OBSERVATIONS (LIBRARIANS)

According to the librarians, Internet search engines, E-print services, author Web sites, full-text databases, electronic journals and print resources are all used to some extent by most of the users. Convenience remains the single most important factor for information retrieval. Speed of access, ability to download, print and send articles are top advantages of electronic journals for all groups. All these services and facilities are possible with the application of IT.

These observations reaffirm that important opportunities remain for librarians and libraries in providing both access to information resources and educating clinicians in how to effectively utilize such tools. Determining the relevance of a document or source is solely an individual's perspective, so the library or librarian is not a determining factor in differentiating sources. It would, however, be advantageous for a library to know and have the relevant material available for use. Library users expect their libraries to obtain new electronic resources while simultaneously maintaining or growing traditional print collections until the electronic resources are fully stable. Libraries are expecting to do this with no additional funding. Research has also concluded that information sources like electronic databases are of fundamental importance in a clinical environment giving their direct contribution to decision making in health issues, often making the difference in patient survival. Increasing demand of E-databases can be met with the formation of consortia only, as E-databases are the main feature of consortia these days. Important observation is that these databases have become addiction for the users.

Library Consortia

Information explosion, diversity of user need, financial crunch and impossibility of self-sufficiency has led to the formation of consortia at local, regional, national and international level. A library consortium is an association of a group of libraries to achieve mutually the common objective. Working in an atmosphere, which is fully affected by *Information Communication Technology* (ICT), librarians are mastering the use of electronic resources to better understand and meet the information needs of the users and further train them in using new searching tools for better search.

Consortia provide the following common benefits to the libraries involved:

- Access to otherwise un-subscribed reading materials.
- Scope for electronic archives.
- Getting deep discounts through joint pricing negotiations.
- Developing common resources databases.
- Effective document delivery system.
- Enhanced search facilities
- Better scope for developing a union catalogue among participating libraries.
- By forming consortia, librarians are contributing to the economy of their country by saving Government revenue to a great extent. Following are some of the big and successful consortia's of India.

E-DATABASE

Understanding the user needs play an important role in growing the libraries and librarians; otherwise the library profession may grey in future. To meet the increasing and advanced demands of the user, consortia are playing an important role. Secondly to avail full fruit of consortia a very sincere suggestion to library professionals is to be in touch with whole of the new technology, bridging the libraries through I.T and ICT. One should know the inside out of all the E-databases and involved I.T application.

An E-database is an organized collection of information, of a particular subject or multidisciplinary subject areas; Information within an Edatabase can be searched and retrieved electronically. Edatabase can be full-text or bibliographic. Full-text databases contain the whole content of an article such as citation information, text, illustrations, diagrams and tables. Bibliographic databases contain only citation information of an article, such as author name, journal title and publication date and page numbers. There are many Edatabases and all these databases have various features of searching techniques and tools, which are being used by the librarians to help the users in finding best information in less time.

Some of the popular medical E-databases are mentioned below:

- Academic Search Premier:
  - BMJ
  - MEDLINE
  - OVID

- PROQUEST
- PUBMED
- SCOPUS
- WEB OF SCIENCE
- HINARI

Almost all the reputed publishers have come up with the Edatabases like Oxford University Press, American academy of Pediatrics, Cambridge University press and many more. All these e-databases can be considered as the latest technological innovation in the field of information.

5

Automated Reference Service in Library Technology

Since the late 1960s, many publishers of printed bibliographies, indexing and abstracting journals, and other reference works have offered machine-readable versions of their products for use in computer assisted reference applications. Initially intended for government, corporate, and academic libraries supporting research in scientific and technical disciplines, such machine-readable reference sources have become widely available in business, the social sciences, and the humanities. In addition to databases which correspond to printed publications, a growing number of reference sources have been developed specifically for use in computer-based systems and have no printed counterparts. While the earliest machine-readable databases were bibliographic in character, non-bibliographic numeric and directory-type databases are increasingly commonplace.

During the late 1960s and early 1970s, a number of libraries purchased machine-readable bibliographic and non-bibliographic data- bases for processing on in-house computers using custom-developed information retrieval software. Most libraries, however, lacked access to the hardware and software resources required to implement such systems. Through the early 1970s,the needs of such libraries were addressed by fee-based search services operated by the producers of machine-readable databases or other organizations such as large research libraries. Such services, which operated in the offline, batch processing mode, were replaced in the mid- 1970s by services offering online database searching on a time sharing basis to libraries equipped with conventional terminals. Now widely utilized by libraries of all types and sizes, online search services can be divided into two broad groups:

- Multidisciplinary services-including DIALOG, BRS, ORBIT, WILSONLINE, DATA- STAR, and ESA-IRS-that provide database coverage of a varied range of subjects for a broad clientele; and
- Specialized services-such as the NLM SEARCH SERVICE, STN INTERNATIONAL, LEXIS, and WESTLAW-that provide online

access to one or more databases relevant to a single subject discipline, profession, or activity, such as medicine, law, or engineering.

Various types of specialized search services provide online access to databases containing a specific type of information such as news. Examples include the NEXIS, VUITEXT, DATA TIMES, and NEWSNET search services. While they differ in the number and type of databases offered and in the specific retrieval capabilities supported, multidisciplinary and specialized search services share a common operating methodology: they purchase or otherwise obtain bibliographic and non-bibliographic data- bases in machine-readable form from their producers, convert the data- bases to a form required for storage on their computers, and allow libraries or other subscribers to perform various retrieval operations on such data using prewritten database management software.

The software features a non-procedural query language which permits a user at an online terminal to initiate literature searches or other information retrieval operations by entering specified commands. While their query languages are relatively easy to learn, online search services are more often providing menu-driven interfaces for novice users. Some services also offer private file capabilities which allow libraries to establish their own databases. As a recently implemented supplement or alternative to online search services, an increasing number of bibliographic and non-bibliographic databases are available on CD-ROM disks. Accompanied by information retrieval software, such CD-ROM reference products permit database searching at local microcomputer workstations (over 100 titles were available at the time of this writing).

Offered on a subscription basis, they can prove less expensive than online searching for databases that are accessed frequently, although infrequent updating, slow response time for complex searches, and other performance limitations may make them unsuitable for some applications. As a hybrid implementation with potentially attractive cost/performance characteristics, several vendors combine CD-ROM searching of back file data with online access to the most current information.

TECHNOLOGICAL PROBLEMS IN LIBRARY AUTOMATION

Technological problems include both the hardware, *i.e.*, the computer as an instrument for information processing, and the software, *i.e.*, the methodology which is applied. The major problems faced today in terms of the hardware are due to the variety of computers being used in different types of research and business institutions. The computers, manufactured by various firms are not compatible. Developing countries sometimes receive sophisticated technology like computers as gifts from more developed countries; these often become obsolete from the manufacturer's point of view.

Such machines are not only unsuitable for most complex work but any technical problems which come up cannot be repaired. Information retrieval work requires machines more sophisticated than those manufactured indigenously, and few imported machines are capable of handling information retrieval applications. The random access facility and disks large enough for storage of bibliographic information are not readily available.

In most institutions, organisational goals receive priority over the library's requirements, meaning that the librarian must use the computer available rather than what is actually required according to specifications. Library activities in all institutions are done through sharing disk space as well as computer time. Therefore, when the storage capacity is not large enough to accommodate various types of data, bibliographic data are given the lowest priority. On-line facilities are rare in India. In fact, only TIFR's library has access to an on-line terminal for bibliographic data, the DEC-1077 computer of the National Centre for Software Development and Computing Techniques.

The communication infrastructure of India is still not suitable for extensive on-line information facilities; the telephone system is not reliable enough to support an effective network facility. Software problems arise because programmes must be developed in terms of the machine on which they are to operate. Therefore, the incompatibility of equipment tends to make the software incompatible as well, especially when programmes are written in machine or assembly language. While using languages which are not machine-bound, such as FORTRAN, COBOL, ALGOL, etc., may seem like a solution, in actual practice such languages cannot be interchanged without suitable modifications.

A software package developed for the IBM 360 model 30 would require many changes not only in the programme but also in the programming language if it were to run on any other computer. Development of a programme suitable for the available machine is therefore preferable to acceptance of a package programme. This makes the development and use of package programmes difficult and leads to a lack of standardisation in programming language as well as in output. Machine-readable data bases are byproducts of international information network systems and are available on magnetic tapes.

These are useful in building information resources and for retrospective search and current awareness services. Again, however, the tape service is expensive and suitably sophisticated computers are scarce. The data bases have a standard format which requires extensive changes to fit existing hardware and other system requirements. Also, relevant bibliographic information has to be selected from the data base and stored. Often this storage space is scarce and expensive.

ECONOMIC PROBLEMS

The major obstacle for any innovations in developing countries is the lack of resources. The initial cost of establishing a computer system is beyond the reach of most organisations and institutions. Library and information processing is done either with spare computer capacity made available by the institution itself, or with computer time hired from another institution. The cost of hiring computer time and storage space is very high and often cannot be justified at the management level by cost-benefit analysis. At IIT, for example, CPU time per hour costs ₹ 1000 for educational purposes and ₹.2000 for business and industrial use.

Moreover, the computer provides only paper printout, and the paper often costs more than the processing. Few developing countries can afford the machine-readable data bases, either. The tapes are very expensive and because foreign exchange is involved in subscribing to them, it is even more difficult for most organisations in India and other developing countries to afford them. The annual subscription rate of one data base is now $8000. Library tasks often overlap and their peculiar nature seldom makes the advantages of computerisation seem very convincing in the light of cost-benefit analysis.

In India, libraries and information centres are attached to government organisations or research institutions, so library services cannot be calculated on a profit/loss basis. Long-term benefits have to be kept in mind while justifying such services. The libraries that have computerised some of their services or operations often have not taken such steps as a result of serious thought. Computerisation has a glamour of its own in the minds of many librarians. Overly enthusiastic librarians often run uneconomical programmes, producing lengthy listings, for instance, in the name of computerised service.

Often the manual method is used concurrently with the computerised system because of a lack of faith on the part of staff and users. The duplication of work and the cost involved in these cases is obviously unjustifiable; the librarian should know which aspects of service should be mechanised. An example of an economically viable computerised library activity is the centralised acquisition of periodicals in operation at INSDOC. This facility serves thirty laboratories, which not only frees the facilities from the tedious task of periodical acquisitions but also eliminates the cost of duplicate purchasing.

ATTITUDINAL PROBLEMS

Computers appear very awesome to developing countries. They are powerful machines which can perform many functions and therefore offer a solution to the many types of manual inefficiency which often plague the developing countries. Among librarians there are two different attitudes towards computerised facilities. One group is taken in by the glamour of modern technology and believes that computers can perform miracles. Members of this group often give insufficient thought to the real value of the computer to the organisation/institution and make uneconomical, haphazard use of the facility.

The other group, still the majority in developing countries, lacks knowledge of the potential and consequences of library automation. There is constant tension between this traditional librarian group and the 'new-wave' librarians. Professionals of the majority group do not realise that computers cannot replace human intelligence. Due to the accuracy essential for data input in library services, the librarian/information scientist is indispensable. The National Library of Calcutta conducted an experiment to computerise the Indian National Bibliography in 1968.

The scheme failed, however, because labour unions opposed it fearing retrenchment of library staff. Among developing countries, the attitudes of India's librarians are typical. They are not confident about automated services. Library staffs should therefore be trained in programming and thus be made aware of the work involved in automation. They will then realise that automation will not take away their jobs. They will also realise that computers are machines which have their limitations as well as their advantages. The communication gap between the librarian and the computer specialist is another major hindrance in establishing any effective automated system in a library.

There is often disagreement among the librarian, the programmer and the systems analyst. Librarians should be trained in computer programming and computer specialists should be versed in the special needs of library automation. Only then can a common language evolve among the three and a project be started. Administrative personnel assume a very important role in decisionmaking. Their enthusiasm, support and conviction can help realise any new plan, just as their apathy and lack of understanding of the need for accurate and speedy information can jeopardise any effort. Although many things have taken a favourable turn in India, the majority of those at the management level unfortunately are not conversant with the development of information science and are unaware of the important role of information in all areas of national development.

This very often results in insufficient planning, which in turn curbs the enthusiasm of imaginative information scientists and librarians. Due to this lack of appreciation, priorities are poorly ordered and funds are not well allocated. Administrators also have a tendency to underestimate or overestimate the capacity of automation. Any information system or service is planned for the best possible benefit to its users. Unless the users are mentally prepared to accept a new system, however, it cannot be effective. Indian users are still unfamiliar and overawed by computers, so computer awareness and interest has to be fostered to enable proper utilizaton of a system.

They should neither overestimate computer capabilities nor be afriad of interacting with the computer systems. Another obstacle is that, because batch processing systems are still in use in India, there are bulky printouts in monotonous type faces and formats which prove to be a headache not only for the librarian, but also for the user. There is no dearth of manpower in systems analysis and computer programming in India. We are already exporting software packages to countries that find them less expensive than developing their own. Library automation is still neglected, however; it is an area which has not attracted young people with appropriate expertise. Training should be given to both the librarian and the computer specialist about each other's functions and possibilities. Both INSDOC and DRTC conduct courses on automated systems in libraries. Under the forthcoming NISSAT plan, steps are being taken to build the requisite technical manpower.

Moreover, the Indian government's Department of Electronics is developing training programmes for the National Informatics Centre. There are two main objectives in training for library automation: to orient the programmers and system analysts to writing programmes suitable for automating library facilities, and to persuade librarians to accept the utility of automation and teach them to prepare accurate inputs to make the system worthwhile.

AUTOMATEDCATALOGI

Descriptive cataloging is an intellectual activity requiring considerable decision-making and one that is time-consuming. As a result, many libraries experience cataloging backlogs which impede the flow of materials into circulating and reference collections thereby preventing library catalogs from representing those collections fully and accurately. Recognizing that the cost of descriptive cataloging can approach or even exceed the value of certain materials, many libraries do not catalog paperbound books, low-cost government publications, or other relatively inexpensive items. In some research libraries, materials of presumably limited interest may be placed in off-site storage facilities with only an abbreviated catalog record created. In most libraries, conventional descriptive cataloging is not even considered for individual titles in large microform sets, even though such materials may significantly augment a library's resources in particular subject areas, and the failure to catalog them impairs their utility. To simplify decision-making, to save time, and to reduce costs associated with descriptive cataloging, libraries have historically relied on cataloging copy, ,*i.e.*, , descriptive cataloging information prepared by other libraries, especially the Library of Congress.

The automation of descriptive cataloging depends on the availability of such cataloging copy in computer-processible form. In the late 1960s, the Library of Congress developed the MARC format for the communication of bibliographic data on magnetic tape and began distributing machine- readable cataloging copy through its MARC Distribution Service. Since the late 1960s, MARC formats have been developed for various types of library materials, and the scope of the MARC Progamme-once limited to English-language monographs-has broadened steadily and significantly. The LC MARC database-the accumulation of Library of Congress cataloging data in machine-readable form-now contains more than 2.5 million records, most of them cataloged since the inception of the MARC Progamme. Although MARC tapes can be purchased from the Library of Congress for input to local computer systems, most libraries obtain access to MARC data through products and services developed by publishers, computer system developers, time-sharing services, and other intermediaries. Among the earliest of these MARC-derivative products were computer-generated micro publications such as MARCFICHE, produced by MARC Applied Research, and Books in English produced by the British Library. Created by computer-output microfilm (COM) technology, both products provided more timely and varied access to LC cataloging data than could be obtained through the conventionally printed National Union Catalog, which was itself discontinued in Favour of a COM implementation in the early 1980s.As an equally timely and flexible alter- native, several search services, including DIALOG and WILSONLINE, offer online access to the LCMARC database.

A growing number of vendors supply the MARC database on CD-ROM disks or digital optical videodiscs accompanied by software which supports the retrieval of specific cataloging records and the printing of card sets. Examples include the BIBLIOFILE system from the Library Corporation in Washington, D.C., the LASERSEARCH system from General Pesearch Corporation, and the MINI MARC I1 system from Library Systems and Services Incorporated. Although these products and services are important, most libraries obtain access to machine-readable cataloging records through one of the bibliographic utilities-organizations which maintain large databases of cataloging records and offer online access and other services to subscribing libraries.

Examples include the Online Union Catalog implemented by the Online Computer Library Center (OCLC), the Research Libraries Information Network (RLIN) operated by the Research Libraries Group, the cataloging support service operated by the Western Library Network (WLN), the Cataloging Support System (CATSS) offered by Utlas International, the LIONS system operated by the New York Public Library, the AGILE I1 service offered by Auto- Graphics Incorporated, and Brodart's Interactive Access System (IAS). While they differ in database size and composition, the number and nature of their subscribers, and the specific capabilities they support, these bibliographic utilities each maintain a database of MARC records obtained from the Library of Congress and other sources, supplemented by original MARC-format cataloging contributed by subscribing libraries. Working at local terminals, participating libraries can retrieve cataloging copy, modify it to meet local requirements, and order printed card sets, machine-readable cataloging records on magnetic tape, and other bibliographic products. Local workstations are also used to input original cataloging records for use by other subscribers. Supporting thousands of online terminals accessing millions of machine-readable records, the bibliographic utilities are among the world's largest and most intensively utilized computer-based information services.

PROBLEMS OF LIBRARY AUTOMATION

In old civilizations like India and other Asian countries, libraries have been in existence since, early times. Recent political and economic developments which have brought about various types of changes in these countries are also reflected in the evolution of information systems. India's educational system had a definite elitist slant in mediaeval times and the legacy of feudalism during the British period nurtured this trend. Libraries with very rich collections of manuscripts and other rare reading material were mainly the property of the elite. The infrastructure of the country was, moreover, not congenial for the kind of wide-ranged library system which one can envisage today. Library development has shown a marked change since, 1947. It is estimated that India now has approximately 90,000 libraries of different types. The Indian library system can be divided into four broad categories: public, academic, special and national libraries.

TECHNOLOGICAL PROBLEMS

Technological problems include both the hardware, *i.e.*, the computer as an instrument for information processing, and the software, *i.e.*, the methodology which is applied. The major problems faced today in terms of the hardware are due to the variety of computers being used in different types of research and business institutions. The computers, manufactured by various firms are not compatible. Developing countries sometimes receive sophisticated technology like computers as gifts from more developed countries; these often become obsolete from the manufacturer's point of view.

Such machines are not only unsuitable for most complex work but any technical problems which come up cannot be repaired. Information retrieval work requires machines more sophisticated than those manufactured indigenously, and few imported machines are capable of handling information retrieval applications. The random access facility and disks large enough for storage of bibliographic information are not readily available.

In most institutions, organisational goals receive priority over the library's requirements, meaning that the librarian must use the computer available rather than what is actually required according to specifications. Library activities in all institutions are done through sharing disk space as well as computer time. Therefore, when the storage capacity is not large enough to accommodate various types of data, bibliographic data are given the lowest priority. On-line facilities are rare in India. In fact, only TIFR's library has access to an on-line terminal for bibliographic data, the DEC-1077 computer of the National Centre for Software Development and Computing Techniques.

The communication infrastructure of India is still not suitable for extensive on-line information facilities; the telephone system is not reliable enough to support an effective network facility. Software problems arise because programmes must be developed in terms of the machine on which they are to operate. Therefore, the incompatibility of equipment tends to make the software incompatible as well, especially when programmes are written in machine or assembly language. While using languages which are not machine-bound, such as FORTRAN, COBOL, ALGOL, etc., may seem like a solution, in actual practice such languages cannot be interchanged without suitable modifications.

A software package developed for the IBM 360 model 30 would require many changes not only in the programme but also in the programming language if it were to run on any other computer. Development of a programme suitable for the available machine is therefore preferable to acceptance of a package programme. This makes the development and use of package programmes difficult and leads to a lack of standardisation in programming language as well as in output. Machine-readable data bases are byproducts of international information network systems and are available on magnetic tapes.

These are useful in building information resources and for retrospective search and current awareness services. Again, however, the tape service is expensive and suitably sophisticated computers are scarce. The data bases have a standard format which requires extensive changes to fit existing hardware and other system requirements. Also, relevant bibliographic information has to be selected from the data base and stored. Often this storage space is scarce and expensive.

ECONOMIC PROBLEMS

The major obstacle for any innovations in developing countries is the lack of resources. The initial cost of establishing a computer system is beyond the reach of most organisations and institutions. Library and information processing is done either with spare computer capacity made available by the institution itself, or with computer time hired from another institution. The cost of hiring computer time and storage space is very high and often cannot be justified at the management level by cost-benefit analysis. At IIT, for example, CPU time per hour costs ₹ 1000 for educational purposes and ₹.2000 for business and industrial use.

Moreover, the computer provides only paper printout, and the paper often costs more than the processing. Few developing countries can afford the machine-readable data bases, either. The tapes are very expensive and because foreign exchange is involved in subscribing to them, it is even more difficult for most organisations in India and other developing countries to afford them. The annual subscription rate of one data base is now $8000. Library tasks often overlap and their peculiar nature seldom makes the advantages of computerisation seem very convincing in the light of cost-benefit analysis.

In India, libraries and information centres are attached to government organisations or research institutions, so library services cannot be calculated on a profit/loss basis. Long-term benefits have to be kept in mind while justifying such services. The libraries that have computerised some of their services or operations often have not taken such steps as a result of serious thought. Computerisation has a glamour of its own in the minds of many librarians. Overly enthusiastic librarians often run uneconomical programmes, producing lengthy listings, for instance, in the name of computerised service. Often the manual method is used concurrently with the computerised system because of a lack of faith on the part of staff and users.

The duplication of work and the cost involved in these cases is obviously unjustifiable; the librarian should know which aspects of service should be mechanised. An example of an economically viable computerised library activity is the centralised acquisition of periodicals in operation at INSDOC. This facility serves thirty laboratories, which not only frees the facilities from the tedious task of periodical acquisitions but also eliminates the cost of duplicate purchasing.

ATTITUDINAL PROBLEMS

Computers appear very awesome to developing countries. They are powerful machines which can perform many functions and therefore offer a solution to the many types of manual inefficiency which often plague the developing countries. Among librarians there are two different attitudes towards computerised facilities. One group is taken in by the glamour of modern technology and believes that computers can perform miracles. Members of this group often give insufficient thought to the real value of the computer to the organisation/institution and make uneconomical, haphazard use of the facility.

The other group, still the majority in developing countries, lacks knowledge of the potential and consequences of library automation. There is constant tension between this traditional librarian group and the 'new-wave' librarians. Professionals of the majority group do not realise that computers cannot replace human intelligence. Due to the accuracy essential for data input in library services, the librarian/information scientist is indispensable. The National Library of Calcutta conducted an experiment to computerise the Indian National Bibliography in 1968.

The scheme failed, however, because labour unions opposed it fearing retrenchment of library staff. Among developing countries, the attitudes of India's librarians are typical. They are not confident about automated services. Library staffs should therefore be trained in programming and thus be made aware of the work involved in automation. They will then realise that automation will not take away their jobs. They will also realise that computers are machines which have their limitations as well as their advantages. The communication gap between the librarian and the computer specialist is another major hindrance in establishing any effective automated system in a library.

There is often disagreement among the librarian, the programmer and the systems analyst. Librarians should be trained in computer programming and computer specialists should be versed in the special needs of library automation. Only then can a common language evolve among the three and a project be started. Administrative personnel assume a very important role in decisionmaking. Their enthusiasm, support and conviction can help realise any new plan, just as their apathy and lack of understanding of the need for accurate and speedy information can jeopardise any effort. Although many things have taken a favourable turn in India, the majority of those at the management level unfortunately are not conversant with the development of information science and are unaware of the important role of information in all areas of national development.

This very often results in insufficient planning, which in turn curbs the enthusiasm of imaginative information scientists and librarians. Due to this lack of appreciation, priorities are poorly ordered and funds are not well allocated. Administrators also have a tendency to underestimate or overestimate the capacity of automation. Any information system or service is planned for the best possible benefit to its users. Unless the users are mentally prepared to accept a new system, however, it cannot be effective. Indian users are still unfamiliar and overawed by computers, so computer awareness and interest has to be fostered to enable proper utilizaton of a system.

They should neither overestimate computer capabilities nor be afriad of interacting with the computer systems. Another obstacle is that, because batch processing systems are still in use in India, there are bulky printouts in monotonous type faces and formats which prove to be a headache not only for the librarian, but also for the user. There is no dearth of manpower in systems analysis and computer programming in India. We are already exporting software packages to countries that find them less expensive than developing their own. Library automation is still neglected, however; it is an area which has not attracted young people with appropriate expertise. Training should be given to both the librarian and the computer specialist about each other's functions and possibilities. Both INSDOC and DRTC conduct courses on automated systems in libraries. Under the forthcoming NISSAT plan, steps are being taken to build the requisite technical manpower.

Moreover, the Indian government's Department of Electronics is developing training programmes for the National Informatics Centre. There are two main objectives in training for library automation: to orient the programmers and system analysts to writing programmes suitable for automating library facilities, and to persuade librarians to accept the utility of automation and teach them to prepare accurate inputs to make the system worthwhile.

RECOMMENDED IMPROVEMENTS

- The computers used in India should not vary so widely. Production of computers with special capacity for library automation should be taken into consideration.
- Government policy has taken a positive step in establishing large computer systems, with one sophisticated central computer capable of handling complex information to be connected to indigenous

minicomputers. The National Informatics Centre project dealing with agricultural and other governmental data processing is designed along similar lines. Such plans should be pursued.

- Indigenous, inexpensive library package programmes are very necessary. These should be usable on a large variety of machines and be capable of handling different activities in the library. The MARC format would be ideal if it could be adapted for the smaller indigenous computers. DRTC is currently involved in preparing software packages for information retrieval.
- The international data bases are being used by some organisations. However, these are expensive and often not applicable to Indian research needs. Indigenous data bases with our specific requirements should be prepared. Core periodicals in each subject relevant to India, and litreature from important Indian periodicals, should be used as input for such data bases.
- A national standard or common language for bibliographic information exchange is necessary. Efforts are being made to achieve a standard language compatible with any international standard.
- Training of personnel, *i.e.*, proper communication among the librarian, computer programmer and systems analyst is very important. Courses offering training in library automation are being taught, but there is a general need for better understanding among these three architects of library automation.
- User awareness and orientation is very much needed. The users comprise managerial policy-makers as well as the research scholars and regular clientele of a library. The need for, as well as the possibilities of, automated library facilities have to be highlighted by professionals and experts in this area. A few seminars and workshops have been conducted at New Delhi and Bangalore, namely the UNISIST workshop in August 1975 and the Indo-U.S., seminar in 1977; however, little else has been accomplished in this area.

PUBLIC LIBRARIES

India is divided into states, union territories, districts, sub districts and villages. The state central libraries serve as public libraries. There are also district central libraries, but village libraries are few and far between. Libraries and library development are included in the broad category of education which, under India's constitution, is considered the responsibility of each state.

Some states, namely Tamil Nadu, Karnataka, Andhra and Maharashtra, have very progressive library legislator! which provides the necessary framework and finances for developing good state public library systems. Despite this, only a very small percentage of the total population of India has access to public libraries.

ACADEMIC LIBRARIES

There has been some improvement in the standards and status of university and college libraries in recent years. At present there are more than 100 universities and 8000 colleges throughout the country. Most of these have library facilities which are in different stages of evolution. School libraries, however, have not been given sufficient attention. Primary and middle-level schools rarely have library facilities, and barely 20 per cent of the secondary schools have adequate library facilities.

SPECIAL LIBRARIES

These are mainly the boon of the post-independence period. Government departments, research institutions, business and industrial houses have established libraries for their own research and development programmes. Currently there are approximately 1500 of these special libraries in India; they are also at different stages of development.

NATIONAL LIBRARIES

Under the national library system, the National Library of India is situated in Calcutta. There are regional libraries of national stature at Bombay and Madras. Some libraries on special subjects are now being given the status of national libraries, *e.g.*, the National Medical Library and the Indian Agricultural Research Institute Library. The major activites of the different categories of Indian libraries are mainly routine work, such as acquisition, circulation, management, processing, reference and bibliographic service, periodical holdings, information retrieval, inventory, and so on.

The services and techniques utilised in the different libraries, however, tend to make these activities very cumbersome and slow. The acquisitions of most libraries are done independently, and involve unnecessary duplication of work and lengthy procedures. Cataloguing and classification methods differ from one library to another and are generally time-consuming and labour-oriented. This is very confusing for the users as they must thus switch from one classification and cataloguing system to another when using more than one library.

There is also a lack of bibliographic control at the national level. The Indian National Bibliography suffers from a large time lag. Almost all library activities involve long hours of manual work, tending to make library service very unpopular. Therefore, users still cannot envisage a librarian as a giver of information but consider him or her a custodian of books. In order to improve the services of libraries, application of newer methods, such as information, computer and communication technologies, will be needed. I am only concerned here with computer applications in libraries and believe that for efficient functioning of our library systems, as suggested, need automated services at some point. But serious thought must first be given to which areas will be automated, while keeping in mind the national need.

NATIONAL SCENE ON LIBRARY AUTOMATION

Elaborate automated library systems are still far off in the context of any developing country. The priorities of each country may vary, but the emphasis is mainly on providing the basic necessities of life to its people. The use of computers started in India with the establishment of computer centres at the Indian Institute of Technology and the Tata Institute of Fundamental Research during 1963-64. At present, there are about 400 computers installed at different places. The size and variety range from a Honeywell 400 to the large IBM 370/155 and DEC-1077.These computers are used mainly for scientific calculations, business applications and data processing for decision-making. Computerised library activities are found in very few organisations, and consist primarily of the use of spare capacity of available computer facilities suitable for off-line use. Although the number of institutions which have computerised library applications is still very small, the awareness of quickly and easily available information is gradually increasing.

I conducted a short survey in this connection through a questionnaire and personal letters sent to different institutions and business houses outside Delhi which have automated library facilities. Like most questionnaire surveys, this one did not prove very successful, although the personal letters I received from some heads of institutions were encouraging. I then visited some of these major institutions in and around Delhi, and interviewed many of those who work with computerised systems or have plans to do so in the future. The institutions visited were: Indian National Scientific Documentation Centre (INSDOC) and National Informatics Centre, New Delhi; Bhabha Atomic Research Centre (BARC) and Tata Institute of Fundamental Research (TIFR), both in Bombay; Documentation Research Training Centre (DRTC), Hindustan Machine Tools, Ltd. (HMT) and Central Machine Tools of India (CMTI), all in Bangalore; and Small Industries Extension Training (SIET) Institute and the Administrative Staff College of India in Hyderabad.Altogether, twenty-five organisations were contacted. While this survey may not have been comprehensive in its coverage, the extensive discussions gave a good picture of the problems facing Indian organisations using library automation.

INSDOC, NEW DELHI

Automation is used for indexes, a union catalogue of serial publications, data processing of Indian periodicals on science and technology, directory compilation, and the centralised acquisition of periodicals for thirty laboratories. The IBM 360 model 44 and IBM 1620 are used on a rental basis.

TIFR, BOMBAY

Automated operations include recent additions list, cumulative classified catalogue of books, weekly list of preprints/reports of TIFR, catalogues of progress serials and periodical holdings, and evaluations of journals from the user's point of view. The CDC 3600/160-A and DEC- 1077 computers are available in-house.

NATIONAL INFORMATICS CENTRE, NEW DELHI

Bibliographic citations are available so far only for books in its library; periodical articles are to be added. The centre is a member of INSPEC tape service and a subscriber to a patent bibliographic information system since, 1978. The HP 2 I/MX is used.

INDIAN INSTITUTE OF TECHNOLOGY (IIT), MADRAS

In collaboration with INSDOC, IIT handled the CHEM/SDI project, a computer-based SDI system using the IBM 370 model 155 system and the CA Condensates data base. The CHEM/SDI uses a subset of CAN/SDI software made available by CISTI through UNESCO for its regional pilot project. The project was also handled by NISSAT during 1976-77. The project has been upgraded into a national SDI service using CAC, INSPEC and Compendex data bases; there are more than 500 users.

DRTC, BANGALORE

This group provides education and training, and researches methods for designing and developing computer-based information systems and services. A set of fourteen programmes have been developed in COBOL for creation and updating of the data base, retrieval of bibliographical references in response to specific queries, provision of current awareness and SDI services, retrieval of factual data, provision of a referral service, the semi-automatic generation of a microthesaurus, indexing, and so on.

BARC, BOMBAY

The computer unit of the Library and Information Services of BARC uses the in-house computer Honeywell 400 and BESM 6 for information processing. Computerisation activities include: preparation of a monthly current awareness bulletin, Bibliography of Current Reports; an SDI service offered regularly to some seventy-five users since, May 1972; retrospective litreature searches based on stored data on request from BARC scientists; subject bibliographies; documentation lists; compilation of periodical holdings; loan and issue system of the library; and inventory. An SDI service using the DEC-1077 computer of the National Centre for Software Development and Computing Techniques and TIFR and the magnetic tape output of the International Nuclear Information System is being developed and will be in operation shortly.

SIET, HYDERABAD

This group has automated its Index to Product Profile, which is a list of literature available in the library to April 1976. A TDC 12 is used on a rental basis.

CMTI, BANGALORE

Here work is being done on automating an in-depth index of periodical articles to compile a data base. They have a PDF/ 11 in-house. Future plans include classifying the trade catalogue.

HMT, BANGALORE

Currently under consideration is computerisation of the comparative product profile and the issue system. The computer used is ICL 1903.

PHYSICAL RESEARCH LABORATORY, AHMEDABAD

This laboratory has a mechanised catalogue of its publications holdings and information retrieval facilities. They have discontinued CAS and plan to start SDL In use is the IBM 360 model.

OTHERS

Some industrial units, such as Asian Paints India, Ltd., Hindustan Zinc, Ltd., and Institute of Armament Technology have automated catalogues of holdings. Along with all these ventures in automated library services, a weeklong on-line demonstration of the ESRIN/RECON data base system used at Frascati, Italy was arranged at TIFR during September 1976, with the assistance of UNESCO and the European Space Agency. The Frascati centre had 10 data bases and provided access to about 7.5 million references at the time.

COMPUTER-PRODUCED CATALOGS

The automation of descriptive cataloging addresses only one part of the cataloging activity. In addition to using computers to facilitate access to cataloging copy, libraries are interested in computer-based solutions to the much discussed problems of card catalogs. The most frequently cited of such problems include substantial space consumption; the purchase of expensive cabinets and supporting furniture; Labour-intensive and time-consuming catalog maintenance routines which are intensified by changes in cataloging rules affecting the choice and form of entries; and limited convenience and retrieval capabilities. These problems can be minimized or eliminated by the replacement of card catalogs with computer-based book-form or online catalogs. Broadly defined, a book-form catalog contains successive bibliographic records listed in a page format on paper or microforms. Among the earliest applications of library automation, computer preparation of book-form catalogs can lower production time and costs while eliminating the Labour-intensive file maintenance routines associated with card catalogs. As an alternative to computer printed or typeset catalogs, computer-output microfilm catalogs have been widely implemented by libraries and library systems since the early 1970s. A number of service bureaus, book jobbers, bibliographic utilities, and other vendors have developed software to produce COM catalogs from library-supplied data, thereby eliminating the need for in-house COM recorders and customized programming catalogs. Broadly defined, an online catalog is an organized, machine-readable accumulation of bibliographic records which are maintained on disks or other direct-access computer storage media for retrieval by library users and staff members working at inter- active terminals or appropriately configured microcomputer workstations. In addition to saving space and automating file maintenance, online catalogs permit remote access by authorized persons equipped with compatible terminals, and they can support information retrieval operations-such as keyword searching of titles and series names- which are not conveniently possible with card or book-form catalogs.

Online catalogs may be custom-developed for specific library installations or purchased as prewritten software packages or turnkey systems. Examples of custom-developed online catalogs include the Library of Congress Computerized Catalog, the MELVYL system at the University of California, the LIAS system at Pennsylvania State University, the Library Computer System (LCS) at Ohio State University, and the Dartmouth College Online Catalog. Prewritten software packages suitable for online catalog implementations include BRS/SEARCH from BRS Information Technologies, a powerful information retrieval Progamme that is available in mainframe, minicomputer, and microcomputer versions; INMAGIC, a versatile data management Progamme for dominated by integrated library systems which combine database management and catalog access capabilities with circulation control, acquisitions, serials control, and other operations. Such systems may be implemented as complete turnkey configurations of hard-ware and software or as prewritten software packages designed to operate on a library owned mainframe, minicomputer, or microcomputer. Vendors include CLSI, Geac, Notis, Dynix, OCLC, Virginia Tech, Data Research Associates, Carlyle, Comstow Information Systems, Universal Library Systems, Sobeco, Sigma Data/Centel, George- town Medical Library, Washington University, IBM, Inlex, Sirsi, Utlas, Innovative Interfaces, Eyring Research Institute, Easy Data, Data Trek, and Unisys. Among the newest and most widely publicized approaches to online catalog implementation, a growing number of vendors offer public access catalog systems which employ CD-ROM storage technology. Examples include the IMPACT system from Auto-Graphics, LASERGUIDE from General Research, THE INTELLIGENT CATALOG from the Library Corporation, and the LEPAC system from Brodart. In such implementations, the library provides a machine- readable version of its catalog, typically consisting of MARC format records on magnetic tapes obtained from bibliographic utilities or other sources, to a CD-ROM system vendor who indexes and otherwise pre- pares it for conversion to one or more CD-ROM disks.

The disks themselves are created by a mastering process in special manufacturing facilities, and the library receives a specified number of disk copies plus menu-driven software designed for public catalog access at microcomputer-based workstations. Updated by periodic replacement in the manner of book-form catalogs, such CD-ROM catalogs are increasingly mentioned as an alternative to computer output microfilm for union catalogs and similar implementations.

ATTITUDE AND INITIATIVE OF THE MANAGEMENT

Attitude and initiative on the part of the management has played major role in library automation in Indian University Libraries. The management here includes both the university management and the librarian as a secretary of the management whose task is to carry out the decisions taken by the executive bodies of the university, such as Syndicate, Executive Council, etc. If the Librarian had the initiative then he was able to convince the authorities about this emergent need. In some of the cases, the initiative also came from top and the Librarian was forced (or bypassed) to do it. But the best blend was when the initiative of both the Librarian and University Authorities was synergised. If there was no initiative on both the ends than there was no progress.

Attitude and Initiative of the Uses

A library may be as smart as its readers. If the readers are smart and well aware they may force the authorities to work towards library automation. If the readers are knowledgeable about the development being taking place in the information technology, they have influenced the use of computers in library to a great extent. This is more true about faculty as they are the people who participate in decision making process. The good examples are the libraries of IITs and other higher engineering educational institutions.

Resources Available

The third important factor is the resources available with the university libraries. The resources include both financial as well as human resources. In most of the universities, the librarians are given funds only for books and journals. Some libraries do not want to or are not allowed the funds received for books and journals to be used for any other purpose, even though the University Grants Commission (UGC) guidelines permit the use of a certain percentage towards such activities (In VIII Plan it was 15 per cent and in IX plan 10 per cent).

Most of the libraries depend on the funds provided by the UGC under Inflibnet project. The distribution of the money under this project was not done logically. Big and small libraries were equated at par and as a result while some libraries remained fund starved some were not able to use the funds. Before distributing funds to libraries there should have been a survey of the requirement and certain guidelines laid down. Besides this there are no other financial resources available with the university libraries.

In order to save the university libraries from going further down UGC must do something in this direction. Another very serious problem, may be more serious than the financial one, is the lack of trained manpower.

Many of our library science schools have not based their curricula on the automation requirement of the university libraries. Some of them are even teaching today what was designed thirty or forty years back although that has become totally outdated. Not many library schools produce a candidate who can straight away go the Automation Department of a University Library and can independently work without any further training. The bifurcation of the library science schools from libraries are perhaps the one of the main important reasons for that.As a result our profession became the only profession where practice went far ahead of the teaching.

In the country people are talking about digital libraries and web-OPACs and we are teaching fundamental of computers in our library schools. This is the only profession where getting a professional degree does not require any professional training. Can you imagine a doctor without hospital training or an engineer without a training in Industry.

Non-availability of Suitable Software

Non-availability of suitable software has also played an important role. Though there are a number of software available for library management but most of them are non- standard.

The main reason behind is that most of the software have been developed without the help of a qualified librarian. As a result there were a stream of non-standard software. Some of these softwares have been developed by big corporations like CMC but have not been proved very successful. The software developed by institutions (for example DESIDOC, INSDOC, etc.,) could not be successful as they were lacking in marketing and after sales service. The librarian is confused as he is not in a position to decide what to select.

Level of Skill of Library Staff

The level of skill of library staff also played a very important role. In our country there are no standard for level of subordinate staff to be recruited in academic libraries. There educational and professional qualification vary from state to state. In some of the cases the library assistants are recruited with 12th pass and a six months certificate in library science while in Central institutions like IITs and Central Universities it is minimum graduation and degree in library science.

The institutions having better stuff went far ahead (though there are exceptions to that). The better qualified staff was better oriented towards progressive thinking which could move the things fast. This point emphasises the requirement of a uniform qualification policy for the recruitment of staff in academic institutions.

Geographical Location

Geographical location of an institution also played a very important role. The institutions near to a metro city were benefited by the availability of the resources. They were having better approach to hardware and software market and also the manpower for data entry. They were having approach to better training facilities. Hyderabad is a good example which can be cited.

LIBRARY AUTOMATION IN DEVELOPING COUNTRIES

When Information Development was launched in 1984, library automation was, looked at from today's perspective, very much in its infancy. The largest libraries in the world such as the Library of Congress and the British Library had sizeable databases of catalogue records. University library catalogues were available on-line within their institutional four walls and library circulation was also automated, but data was generally confined to the institution that held it since, there was no network resembling the internet. In 1983 the JANET network had begun to connect the universities in the United Kingdom, and some catalogues were beginning to be available online from other institutions.

The most common way of accessing remote data if there was a possibility at all was by dial-up modem using ordinary phone lines and a modem or an acoustic coupler in which the phone handset was pushed into a rubber holder to ensure no extraneous noise seeped into the phone line when it was transferring electronic signals between computers. Businesses including libraries were also connected by dedicated phone lines to locations where their computers were located when they were remote. But most automation was firmly confined to the institution where it was based. Twenty five years ago was also the beginning of the period when computers were being introduced as desk top computers, with IBM PCs and subsequently IBM PC lookalikes. Personal computers were about to make a huge impact on automation in libraries as no longer was it necessary to have a dedicated air-conditioned room to house computers.

In the early days cataloguers had to have terminals on their desks to enable access to the catalogue but eventually all staff had PCs for general administration so no longer was it was the responsibility of the library budget to purchase desk-top computers. Modems were in fact used to access remotely catalogues for bibliographical purposes, to search databases like Medline. It was already possible to dial up databases such as the British Library's BLAISE database or the US National Library of Medicine's Medline. But these facilities required good phone lines and were not available outside Western Europe and the United States.

There was no such thing as 'full text' then. Computers did not have the capacity to store so much data and data stored was often coded to ensure that it did not take up more space than was necessary. 25 years ago, while most libraries in industrialised countries had not only computerised their catalogues but also computerised their circulation, in developing countries there was very little library automation outside that organised by the United Nations agencies such as FAO's AGRIS and IAEA's INIS and these were very much in their infancy or in their planning stages.

To return to the situation in industrialised countries. In the early 1990's catalogues began to be accessible on the internet but were not web-based and required the catalogue software to be run interactively across the Internet using various different protocols. By the end of the decade, true web-based catalogues using the power of hypertext were available. Libraries began to include in their catalogues digital resources internally held and externally held (predominantly external). MARC formats thenceforward incorporated a field 856 used to link to an external resource by means of a URL (the internet address).

Users of the catalogue could click on a link and go straight to a digital resource that could be anywhere in the world. Subscriptions were possible to electronic journals but they were often not available in developing countries or if they were available the bandwidth of tehinternet in those countries was not enough to enable the materials to be read. Digital library software became available and UNESCO encouraged its implementation in developing countries by making Greenstone available free-of-charge, a digital library software package developed at Waikatu in New Zealand. Links could be made from a library catalogue to material in such a digital library. Material available on the internet which might not be easily accessible in institutions in developing countries with low bandwidth could be downloaded or sent on CD-ROM to the digital libraries and hosted locally.

The Soros Foundation set up eIFL (Electronic Information for Libraries) with the aim of creating national purchasing consortia. They have since, become involved in supporting other activities such as promoting library automation systems, mindful of the fact that without a catalogue of print and digital materials the library user cannot easily find out what is accessible. eIFL supported the European Union funded project to implement NewGenLib, a system under development in India, in Aleppo and Al Baath university libraries in Syria alongside providing them with licences at a reasonable price to access electronic resources. INASP, the International Network for the Availability of Scientific Publications, was set up by the International Council of Scientific Unions (ICSU) in 1992. Aware of the need to establish good catalogues in order to access scientific litreature, they have also participated in some library automation projects. The Andrew W. Mellon Foundation, well known for philanthropic projects in developing countries, is also supporting the development of a new library automation system at Duke University, the Open Library Environment (OLE). Although there is no participation from developing countries at this stage it is likely that any open source package developed would be supported with necessary tailoring in line with the needs of developing countries wherever they might be different.

The main feature in the last 25 years then has been in the expansion of computers into every aspect of libraries. Possibly the biggest change has been the development of digital libraries, acquiring, transforming or accessing data in digital format. In developing countries this methods of digitisation has taken place to a certain extent.

TRENDS IN THE INDUSTRIALISED WORLD

Library systems in developing countries have obviously developed alongside systems in the industrialised world. First we should look at systems for large institutions. The majority of library systems have been developed in the United States. Many commercially available integrated library systems were developed by universities for their own use and later made available to a wider audience. Dynix was one such, developed for a university library and later sold around the world to universities, public libraries and special libraries. Other systems were based from the outset on cooperatives, such as TALIS which originated as BLS, the system of BLCMP (Birmingham Libraries Cooperative Management Project) which was a cooperative set up with government funding in the 1960s.

This project was one of two established from the beginning by OSTI, the UK Office of Scientific and Technological Information, to support cooperative cataloguing. They had less incentive to expand outside their country of origin as it was their aim to serve a cooperative all of whose members were equal. In 1967, the Ohio Colleges Library Centre was established to bring library automation to Ohio academic institutions by sharing costs. OCLC as it is now has developed from being a cooperative between libraries in Ohio to being an international cooperative, and at one time promoted a library management system.

Then they ceased to support it returning eventually to the market by acquiring OLIB, an Oracle based library system. Its vision is to connect libraries of the world. Originally, as with BLCMP, it was a shared cataloguing system receiving records from participating libraries and adding them to a database which in turn could be used by member libraries to populate their own catalogues. Records were transferred between computers initially by sending large magnetic tapes, a thing of the past, from the Centre to the remote libraries. Later they were transferred by telephone lines and subsequently the transfer was done by a client computer, a PC in a remote institution, accessing the Centre's servers by the Internet. Jumping to the present, OCLC have established Worldcat which could act as a large union catalogue for the world if every library in the world added its holdings.

This concept is called Cloud Computing, on the basis that the computer is somewhere remote and no one knows or cares where exactly it is! To return to library systems established in individual institutions, VTLS (Virginia Tech Library System), another large library automation system, always had an interest in working with developing countries and have a large number of installations in the Third World after having expanded into Eastern Europe as well. Another popular system, Aleph, is based in Jerusalem surrounded by a number of developing countries some of which have considered installation though by far the largest share of the market is in Europe.

As for cooperatives like OCLC, there has existed for many years in former Yugoslavia a miniature version of OCLC, COBISS (Co-operative Online Bibliographic System and Service), which since, the break-up of Yugoslavia has expanded to include Albania and Bulgaria on the same basis as other ex-Yugoslav states. They act as a cooperative cataloguing agency but they also keep data on research projects. This institution would be a good model for other regions to adopt. Now and again a commercial library system has been licenced to a developing country institution which has subsequently found it difficult to pay the maintenance fees. Maintenance in any case is often more expensive in a developing country because of economies of scale and distance from the supplier. Additionally there may be problems caused by shortages of foreign exchange.

Now the internet reaches much of the world, distance is not so important. But there have been many instances of institutions retaining a package but not paying maintenance fees and therefore not updating it. Marshall Breeding keeps records of as many library automation packages and the sites where they are used as he can find the information. He publishes the results each year in Library Journal. The latest was published on the web in January 2009. He reviews the market as well as providing statistics about library automation suppliers.

This is a useful guide to make comparisons with developing countries. Unfortunately in his tables he makes only the distinction between the US and the rest of the world. However he also includes a general review and this year he reported that the use of Open Source packages is increasing mainly bring provided by third parties. For example, a company called Equinox provides support for the Open Source package Evergreen.

PACKAGES WHICH HAVE HAD AN IMPACT IN DEVELOPING COUNTRIES

Large libraries in developing countries had always had a certain amount of access to library automation systems. For example, the National Library of Venezuela had a system found in many US academic libraries called NOTIS. However this library's catalogue is still not available on the web. A number of countries in the former Soviet Union use IRBIS, the CDS/ISIS clone developed by the Russian National Library for Science and Technology. But ordinary libraries, public and academic, in developing countries have always lacked a wealth of possibilities for library automation. Hardware used to be expensive, and relatively speaking is still expensive for developing countries. Other problems raised by writers on the subject range from the power supply to the problems of training staff. Another issue not often raised is the need for collaboration both within and between institutions to get library automation project off the ground and then maintain it.This is a much more complex activity than a pre-automation situation where there is a library card catalogue maintained by cataloguers and used manually by staff and library patrons. Smaller systems than the ones developed for universities or networks have been developed which could be regarded as being similar sized to CDS/ISIS, for instance Inmagic and Tinlib. Some of these were not very easy to use and were not well maintained. Others were adopted by consortia or organisations in the industrialised world with branches in developing countries such as the British Council.

The main problem in developing countries has been support because of their remoteness and so those packages offering less support would be more attractive as they would be less expensive overall. This may well change in the future with the increase in the power of the internet and the next 25 years will surely see a difference in the availability of and the charges for support.

CDS/ISIS

CDS/ISIS has undoubtedly had a huge influence on library automation in developing countries. This author reviewed the package onits twentieth anniversary. Time and again, libraries have begun automation. There is even a reference to a library which began with Tinlib and has migrated to CDS/ISIS. Since, CDS/ISIS is well mentioned in the litreature, concerning library automation in developing countries, it will not be covered here. However the most interesting feature which has become available over the last five years in CDS/ISIS is a Z39.50 import facility which is available as part of IsisMARC, and which enables MARC records from external sources to be downloaded into a CDS/ISIS database compatible with the version of MARC of the records. CDS/ISIS is not essentially a library management system, rather a database management system aimed at bibliographic records which by their very nature are variable length (with for example book titles being of indeterminate length) rather than fixed length which is the case for most data processing systems. Because it is attractive to small institutions with little funding and because of its parentage (UNESCO), it has attracted a certain kind of institution, for example those in the development community. UNESCO developed a DOS version in 1985 and a Windows version which was available for many years as a beta test version but was eventually released around 1998.

However libraries were already requiring to place their catalogues on the web and a number of organisations began to develop compatible web-based systems which could be used by institutions which were developing databases for in-house use on Windows or DOS versions of CDS/ISIS. The main developer of the official version was BIREME with WWWISIS but already others were available such as Webisis. CDS/ISIS is no longer being developed by UNESCO but BIREME in cooperation with UNESCO is leading the development of ABCD on an Open Source basis.

Tinlib

Tinlib was a package which was used extensively in British Council libraries. In Ilorin Nigeria it was used from 1996 as reported by Adewoye. The library had by 2001 almost replaced its card catalogue by the OPAC. The chapter was optimistic about the future and reporting on the use of other electronic resources. However e-mail and the internet were not then available. However, TINLIB had its problems. It was not an easy system to use and contracts for it dwindled outside developing countries and it ceased to be supported. Adeyoyin describes in 2004 how the Development Policy Centre Library in Ibadan migrated their catalogue from Tinlib to CDS/ISIS.

DEVELOPING COUNTRY SCENARIOS

It is of course a fallacy to make assumptions that all developing countries will have approached and will approach library automation in the same way. The wealth of the country the distribution of that wealth and the culture of the residents will make a difference.

Nigeria and other African Countries

Nigeria has oil money and had automation early, being one of the first users of CDS/ISIS for mainframe computers. Already in1989 Eyitayo could write a paper on the attitude of automated library system vendors to investing in Nigeria. Many respondents hoped to open an office and increase their marketing. Enakrire describes a few instances in Africa where automation has been implemented, indicating that, except for branches of international organisations, it depends on the generosity of donors.

In Makerere University in Uganda, the library has benefited from donor funding through the African Virtual University Library Initiative of the World Bank to equip the library with computers and installed Internet connectivity. Other university libraries are developing their information service as they are also benefiting from the Programme for the Enhancement of Research of (PERI) under the sponsorship of the International Network for the Availability of Scientific Publications (INASP).

Through PERI, donors have paid subscriptions on behalf of libraries in Africa to access web-based journals. The University of Ibadan had a long history of automation, having begun in 1979. Georgina D. Ekpenyong wrote in 1997 about the history so far. The University of Ibadan Library was already seen as a leader in Nigeria. At that time they used CD-Rom extensively to provide bibliographic data. They took training seriously but did not yet have an OPAC.

In 2008, the John D. and Catherine T. MacArthur Foundation in Chicago awarded grants totalling US $7.1 million to expand academic and research programme and strengthen staff development at two Nigerian universities as part of the Foundation's efforts to improve higher education in Africa. The result is that they signed up to VTLS, Virginia Tech Library System, a commercially available package developed originally as Virginia Tech's own system.

Thailand

In Thailand there were efforts in the 1990s to computerise the libraries with foreign-based systems being purchased. Thammasat University library had Dynix, supported from Ameritech's Australia office, and planned to move to Ameritech's new system Horizon. In 1997 the university library sent three cataloguers to Middlesex University to learn to use Horizon. Since, then they have implemented Horizon and exchange of experience took place between Middlesex University and Thammasat University until the Systems librarian at Thammasat moved to a different post around 2006. Many universities in Thailand are able to purchase these systems often through local distributors of international or American packages. Early on though, CDS/ISIS was used and at Thammasat University they used it for databases of journal articles.

OPTIONS FOR DEVELOPING COUNTRIES

Developing countries depend on developments in the industrialised world but they do not necessarily benefit from the same options as the industrialised world can use. Moreover, some of the options may be much more attractive in developing countries or at least may seem to be so.

Developing a Library System

One solution for organisations in developing countries which might have problems with paying organisations in foreign currency but which have good local technical staff is to develop their own software system. One interesting example of this is the University of Colombo in Sri Lanka. They had begun to automate in 1991 by using CDS/ISIS and then later adopted CDS/ISIS for Windows when it became available. In 2002, Seneviratne and Amaraweera reported in Information Development that in Sri Lanka there was discussion on developing a library automation system to bridge the gap between CDS/ISIS and what commercial software was able to provide, such as Alice for Windows (UK commercial) and LibSys (Indian).

In 1997 the National Agency for Research Energy, Science and Agriculture (NARESA) now the National Science Foundation, used the CDS/ISIS DOS version to handler acquisitions, cataloguing, serials management, Current Awareness Services as well as cataloguing and indexing; this package called PURNA was then used in 34 special and academic libraries. AGRIS using CDS/ISIS was widely influencing libraries in the agricultural sector and the Windows version was then used in the National Library of Sri Lanka for its union catalogue.

Now they are using Genisis, a package to make it easy to implement BIREME's WWWISIS on the web, development of which was undertaken in

France by Pierre Chabet but for which a manual was written in Sri Lanka (partially a translation from the documentation in French) by Ms. Deepali Talagala Director/Information of the Sri Lanka Scientific and Technical Information Centre based at the National Science Foundation in Colombo Seneviratne and Amaraweera discussed in their paper the features a system would need and the platforms, hardware and operating system, most used and as a result decided to make a prototype using MS Access on Windows. Development took two phases.

Firstly a web-based interface to physically dispersed databases with a user-friendly front-end reported by Kumara et al in 1998, and a library automation system described in a BSc dissertation by DMS Dilrukshi, 1999 NetLib—a library management system through the Internet. In 2002 a prototype had been developed and the system was due to be maintained by the Computing Service Centre of the University of Colombo. Unfortunately there is a high overhead in developing and maintaining systems especially for a small client base.

In the UK all university libraries have commercial systems. Newcastle, used to have their own system in the 1980s but only Lancaster remained, eventually contracting with Ex Libris to take Aleph in 2001. By 2008 both the University of Colombo and the National Library of Sri Lanka had signed up to Softlink Europe's Alice system, a system used by the British Council worldwide (for example in Oman, Jordan and Sudan: the catalogue of the British Council in Sudan is available on the internet) and so has proven maintenance in developing countries.

So developing one's own system is not to be recommended: Eyitayo noted that despite the availability of numerous off-the-shelf systems, most libraries in Nigeria that have attempted automation have chosen to commission expensive and time-consuming in-house projects, most of which have suffered severe set-backs and in most cases are not adequate for library work and often lack the capability for sharing information and interconnection with other systems.

Open Source

In the context of moving towards commercially supported systems, it is interesting to see that CDS/ISIS was attractive to libraries in developing countries. It was available without charge and so there was no danger of not being able to pay for it. Of course it was supported by an organisation with as much prestige though not so much turnover as many industrial companies. It also operated on a legal footing. Institutions had to sign a licence agreement to use the software. No doubt many institutions obtained the software illegally but the software was protected in law by the licence agreement. UNESCO were more concerned with illegal copies being made and sold for illegal profit than with institutions using the software without being officially licenced since, the spirit of the software following the ethos of the developer Giampaolo Delbigio was that it should enable institutions to participate in worldwide record sharing at many different levels. Nevertheless there was established a network of distributors which is still in place. Some acted merely as local distributors sending out the software on diskettes by post and thereby easing the burden of the hard-pressed office in UNESCO dealing with this. Other distributors were able to provide support usually of a limited nature though sometimes of a more extensive nature akin to the commercial support that is found in the large-scale library automation systems. The shareware movement was in place when CDS/ISIS was released in 1985.

In 1984, Andrew Fluegleman programmed a communications software package, PC-Talk and Jim Knopf a file management application called PC-File a year before the IBM PC was released and called it Freeware. The developers wanted to avoid commercial distribution networks and distribute the software over the now seemingly primitive and slow dial up systems whereby PC users could transfer programmes by dialling up a central computer using a modem and phone lines. The idea was that users would download the software, test it and if they liked it make a small contribution to the developer to support further development. Knopf established the term freeware as his own and no one else could use it.

There were other microcomputers around at the time, most notably the Apple Macintosh and others which are only part of history such as the BBC Microcomputer, though none ever reached the level of popularity that the IBM PC with the Microsoft Windows operating system has now reached. Incidentally Fluegleman distributed his software with the source code which led to many other developers producing their own versions and PC-Talk was improved and sold on by other developers such that Fluegleman lost control of it. Knopf however established a multi-million dollar company on the basis of PC-File.

In 1983 Bob Wallace created PC-Write which became a well used word processor and was used extensively in developing countries. Because the word freeware was reserved he called it shareware. The concept was pretty much the same. Over the years, freeware and shareware became less used as concepts probably because the most used programmes for business purposes were monopolised by Microsoft with the operating system and Microsoft Office applications. Shareware was in a sense reborn with the open source movement. It is difficult to see any difference between Open Source and shareware but the Open Source Movement has been supported from the outset by large foundations such as the Soros Foundation which founded the Open Society Initiative.

In English 'Open Source' means freely available source software which developers can use to advance the software in question. In all these cases, software developed is free though usually developers ask for a voluntary contribution. They cannot be sold on. Open Source does not necessarily mean free-of-charge but there is an implication that the availability of the source code will enable organisations to acquire and develop it for free. CDS/ISIS was no shareware or open source but many of the features of open source and shareware were responsible for the popularity of CDS/ISIS. For example, Open Source has the possibility for users with access to programming skills to make their own developments. CDS/ISIS has a feature of being able to write programme exits which enable further development. Unlike open source the source code was not made widely available but UNESCO did make it available to BIREME in Brazil where further developments have taken place. Moreover, in the Soviet Union the Russian National Library for Science and Technology developed with permission from UNESCO IRBIS, a functionally equivalent package copied from the DOS version of ISIS.

The Open Source movement gained much greater political credibility than the earlier movements did and UNESCO came under pressure to support the movement. They now have on their web site a Free and Open Source software portal. Because of UNESCO's lead in this concept, CDS/ISIS came under pressure to be declared open source in the early 2000s. But the source code is still not available.

This author believes it would lead to many different versions of the software that could generate records in databases that were no longer compatible with each other. Moreover, Open Source is seen by some as the solution to some of the problems facing the library software industry. Is Open Source all it promises to be? Over the last few years there has been a spate of mergers in the library systems industry led by the equity market resulting in a trend to discontinue the development if not the support of library systems when a company has acquired more than one such package. This severely inconveniences the using institutions which have to migrate from one system to another. Would open source be a protection against this? Open Source has become so much a fashionable option for library software that the International Federation of Library Associations and Institutions held a meeting in Senegal prior to the annual conference's meeting in Durban South Africa.

The proceedings are illustrative of the views on Open Source. The argument in Savard's introduction goes that Open Source may help to smooth out the inequalities between industrialised and developing countries. The connection with commerce is weaker than with commercial software but it is not non-existent. In industrialised countries libraries often use third-party services to support Open Source. This means the connection with the commercial world strengthens. There is no way put from paying for support. The question is who pays and there is not much difference between paying a developer or a third party.

In the conclusion of these proceedings, Diop feels there are clearly economic advantages to adopting an open source software solution but agrees that mastering open source software can take a lot of time and effort because library and information professionals are often isolated. User communities need to be built up to provide mutual help. However it remains to be seen what will be the impact of open source on library automation, particularly integrated library systems in the industrialised world. A pessimistic outcome might be that the institutions using such software feel no differently being supported by the commercial open source support companies than by the current range of commercial companies who promote systems they themselves own.

THE CURRENT SITUATION AND FUTURE PROSPECTS

Making predictions is a very hazardous occupation in anything to do with computers since, the future only tends to bring surprises. Developments in many developing countries are not as advanced as might be expected and in some places there is still a problem with electric supply: Adebibo reporting on usage of catalogues by students at the University of Ilorin in Nigeria stated: "Most respondents claimed to know how to use the card catalogues and OPAC but only a few use them. The possible reason for this low level use of the OPAC is power outages, which have become the rule in Nigeria rather than an exception. Overall, as the power of the internet increases, particularly its bandwidth and its reliability, library automation in developing countries will have the same capabilities as the industrialised world, but not the finance to support it.

In developed countries it is felt by some that the future of library automation lies in open source (outside the control of commercial suppliers) or 'Cloud Computing' (very much controlled by commercial suppliers who provide software on their own hardware and the clients access the data via the Internet). However if solutions to library automation are hosted services in the industrialised world, the suppliers of the service would be able to charge developing countries as little as they wish on the basis that every amount, however little, is profit. This has happened with hosted electronic journals where deals have been made by publishers to cover entire countries which are less than the licence fee required for a university in the west. As suggested, see if this happens. As with e-journals, it needs a champion like eIFL to promote to the suppliers the benefits of their working with developing institutions in what may be perceived as an altruistic way.

INFORMATION TECHNOLOGY-BASED LIBRARY SERVICES

New information technology can potentially support a range of traditional and Non-traditional library services. Most of the library services generated using information technology resemble closely to those generated manually with improvements and modifications to suit the requirements of automated services.

OPAC AND WEBPAC

Remote access to the Library catalogues (OPAC) was possible only through a telnet connection before the Web was launched. The web-based interfaces are now available for most of the integrated library software packages including Libsys. Web sites are increasingly providing links to their webPAC instead of telnet links to their Library OPAC.

Exploiting the provisions of hyperlinking that the web provides, various searchable elements of a bibliographic record in a webPAC are hyperlinks to other records in the database. For example, an author is a hyperlink to all records in the database for that author, a series is an hyperlink to all serial title under that series; a keyword for a record is a link to all records in database having that keyword, ,etc. In effect, a web PAC adds softwarebased functionality to a conventional OPAC. A user has additional incentives to visit the library web page hosting webPAC.

With web-based resources and services in place, many libraries are phasing out their dumb terminals. The library web sites are increasingly becoming a more logical gateway to the catalogue and other web-based library resources. The acceptability of web-based interfaces to the Library OPAC is much greater because web interfaces are familiar to the users with its graphical and navigational interfaces. The users can click complex subjects instead of typing them or remembering complex commands.

INFORMATION ALERTING SERVICES

As the name implies, information alerting services or Current Awareness Services (CAS) are produced by the libraries for their users to alert them about new developments in a given field of study. Information alerting services are issues periodically by the libraries either for internal distribution amongst staff and employees or externally to other users.

The alerting service may be issued as a newsletter reporting new developments, programmes, forthcoming seminars and conferences, events, training programmes, ,etc. It may also consist of recent additions of books and other documents in the library for a specified time period. Most library integrated system facilitate generation of such a service organised according to subject category for a given time period.

Alerting service may also consist of an indexing service issued by a library or a commercial publisher or a society that regularly indexes the contents of periodicals and some other publications systematically in a specified subject field. Such indexing services are issued at a regular interval. Abstracting services are essentially indexing services wherein an abstract of articles are included in addition to its bibliographic details. Index India and Reader's Guide to Periodical Literature are examples of indexing services. Biological Abstracts, Chemical Abstracts and Index Medicus are example of abstracting services. Most indexing and abstracting services are now available as web-based databases with sophisticated search interface.

Selective dissemination of information (SDI) is a personal form of Current Awareness Service (CAS). It refers to the mechanism of selectively directing new items of information from primary or secondary sources to individuals based on their current interests in a particular subject. SDI is delivered based on a user interest profile which is matched with updates on databases for finding the items of interest for a given user. Push technology or personalisation are more recent terms that are used in place of SDI.

DIGITAL REFERENCE SERVICE

Reference service and imparting instructional training to the library users are key areas of activities for any library. The technology now allows reference librarians to reach out to the users using the network instead of waiting at the reference desk for users to come by. Besides, imparting instructions on mechanisms of using a library, a reference librarian is also involved in delivering reference service that require deep intellectual understanding of subject.

Although automated libraries are not yet sufficiently advanced to offer interactive reference services, electronically-mediated reference services are increasingly available through libraries and information centres. Digital reference service, also called 'Ask-An-Expert' or 'Ask-A-Librarian' services are Internet-based question and answer service that connect users with individuals who possess specialised subject knowledge and skill in conducting precision searches. As opposed to static web pages, digital reference services use the Internet to place people in contact with people who can answer specific question and instruct users on developing certain skills. The people who serve as digital reference experts (also called volunteers or mentors) are most of the time information specialists, affiliated to various libraries.

LIBRARY CHAT ROOMS

Several libraries have started experimenting with offering real time digital reference service, using chat software, live interactive communication activities, call counter management software, web contact software, bulletin board services, interactive customer assistance system or related technologies. Many libraries are experimenting with Internet chat technology as an innovative method to extend and enhance traditional and remote reference service. While digital reference service is asynchronous method of information delivery, the Internet chat providing the benefit of synchronous communication between a user and a reference librarian (or mentor). Interactive reference services facilitate a user to talk to a real, live reference librarian at any time of day or night from anywhere in the world. Unlike with e-mail reference, the librarian can perform a reference interview of a sort by seeking clarifications from the user. The librarian can conduct Internet searches and push Web sites onto the patron's browser, and can receive immediate feedback from the patron as to whether his or her question has been answered to his satisfaction. Most libraries currently involved in real-time reference service are part of a collaborative network so that they can share staffing and work around the clock to truly provide reference service any time. Library of Congress Collaborative Digital Reference Service is one of such services.

Several institutions including Cornell University, Internet Public Library, Michigan State University and North Carolina University are offering Internet chat-based services using software like LivePerson, AOL Instant Messenger, Conference Room and Netscape Chat. The librarians have observed that their relatively new chat-based service logged significantly more questions in a relatively short time than their well-established e-mail digital reference service. LiveRef(sm) maintains an online registry of real-time digital reference services.

ELECTRONIC DOCUMENT DELIVERY SERVICES

The term 'electronic document delivery systems' implies delivery of electronic version of a document that might involve reproduction of an electronic copy of a document if it is not available in electronic format. The libraries had been using fax machines for immediate delivery of photocopies of articles via telephone lines.

The first use of electronic document delivery was based on scanning technology. With maturity of scanning equipment and technology, document supply services started scanning the documents as bitmap page images. Applications are built in such a way so as to automatically produce a hard copy together with a header page containing the address of the applicant which can again be send by snail mail or facsimile. A software package known as 'Ariel' is used in several libraries in developed countries for delivery of scanned articles via Internet.

The Ariel software is loaded on an Internet-enabled computer, can receive and send electronic information to other libraries which have installed Ariel. Availability of most of the peer reviewed research journals in electronic format, inexpensive technology to scan articles and improved electronic delivery mechanisms are some of the enabling factors that have contributed to well-established electronic document delivery system now available commercially. More recently most of the secondary services that were available on CD ROM or through online search services are now available on the Internet where the bibliographic references are linked to their full-text on the publisher's site.

The technology has now been perfected and there are several electronic document delivery services that allow a user to download an article in full-text from their site or deliver them electronically as attachment to e-mails. Most electronic publishers and aggregators like OCLC, OVID ,etc., are offering full-text of articles through their web sites. Different vendors have various payment options; some charge each time the journal is used, whereas others provide open access for a set annual fee. A user who wishes to have the item delivered can enter a credit card number and specify a delivery method (postal, UPS, fax, e mail, ,etc.,) and indicate whether it is a rush item (with a rush order fee attached.) The ADONIS (Article Delivery Over Network information Systems) can be considered as a landmark development in electronic document delivery system. The project was launched by a consortium of five major publishers - Academic Press, Blackwell's Scientific Publications (merged with Wiley InterScience), Elsevier Science Publications, and Springer Verlag.

The project uses combination of laser scanning, printing and digital optical storage technology for storage and retrieval of complete pages of over 650 scientific, technical and medical journal articles. The issues of journals are available on CD ROM with weekly updates for distribution to each centre in various countries licensed to use the system for document delivery.

LIBRARY WEB SITES

Libraries are using web technology to create home pages as starting points or as gateways for searching information about the library. A home page reflects characteristics of an academic institution.

It provides an opportunity to the library to propagate its services and facilities to the academic community worldwide. The home pages of libraries are increasingly used as an integrated interface designed to deliver detailed information about a library as well as to provide access to all computer-based services offered by a library.

Several library web sites facilitate virtual guide to the physical facilities including collections, services and infrastructure available in the library through their web sites. Most library web sites provide library layouts and floor plans to guide users to physical location of facilities and services along with link to relevant information. Besides offering information, the library web sites of academic institutions invariably hosts subject gateways or subject portals that contains links to web resources for subjects of interest to the institution. Most of the IT-based library services mentioned in this article are offered through the web sites of libraries. The library web sites can have features like have Frequently Asked Questions (FAQ) along with their answers, library calendar listing events or show information for forthcoming events, Web forms for inviting feedback. Moreover, libraries may also use bulletin boards, threaded discussion forum and listservs to help promote and evolve web-based library services.

WEB-BASED USER EDUCATION

The www provides a dynamic environment for distributing information over a large network and web-based instructions is a suitable tool to do so. Web-based guides and teaching tools can be easily updated, accessed, and printed on demand. They may include colour graphics and screenshots. The web-based user education provides a high degree of interactivity and flexibility to the users offering them the benefit of self-pace, graduated to teach from basic to highly advanced levels and designed in a wide range of formats that accommodate diverse learning styles.

The proliferation of digital resources will generate greater demands on reference and instructional services. With availability of digital resources that can be used anywhere at any time, requirement for instructional and reference services would also grow. Failure to develop both the technological aspects and required service components would lead to under utilisation of digital resources. The library web sites can use web-based user education for imparting training to users in the following areas:

- Basic library skills along with glossary of library terms;
- Using Library OPAC/ webPAC, locating books, magazines and other library materials;
- Instructions for searching CD ROM and web-based databases and other electronic resources; and
- Instructions on subject searching training, using Boolean operators and searching Internet resources through search engines.

The web technology provides for incorporating both synchronous and asynchronous interactivity in the web-based user education.

RELEVANCE OF AUTOMATED SYNTACTIC ANALYSIS TO LIBRARY

The relevance of automated syntactic analysis to library pro-cognitive systems lies in machine processing, and in eventual machine 'understanding,' of natural language text. There is no thought that syntactic analysis alone - whether by man or machine - is sufficient to provide a useful approximation to understanding. On the other hand, there is no doubt that appreciation of the syntactic structure of natural-language text is a part, and an important part, of the over-all problem. Bobrow surveyed the work that has been done, and is being done, towards automation of syntactic analysis of English.

The efforts to automate syntactic analysis have been, essentially, efforts to implement various theories of grammar through the preparation of computer programmes that operate on natural-language text in the form of strings of encoded alphanumeric characters. The output of a successful syntactic-analysis programme is one or more sets of.assignments of the words of a sentence to grammatical categories plus, for each set of assignments, a representation of the grammatical structure of the sentence.

The grammars that have been used as bases for syntactic-analysis programmes include dependency grammars, phrase-structure grammars with continuous and with discontinuous constituents, predictive grammars, string transformation grammars, and phrase-structure transformational grammars. The main characteristics of, and differences among, these grammars are set forth in Bobrow's report.

Although it is too early to say with assurance which of them is best for our purposes much expert intuition favours the phrase-structure, transformational approach. Many of the programmes that have been successful in making syntactic analyses have depended upon a distinction between 'function words' and 'content words.' The distinction is a simple and familiar one.

Function words are words such as 'and', 'or', 'to', 'from', 'a', 'an', 'the', 'neither', 'nor', 'if', and 'whether'. Content words are words such as 'grammar', 'equivalent', 'structural', 'diagram', 'sentence', 'minimum', 'weekly', 'accept', and 'develop'. There are, of course, many more types of content words than of function words. It is therefore reasonable to store in a computer memory very detailed descriptions of the functions, characteristics, idiomatic uses, and so forth, of the function words. The successful analytic programmes have, in addition, employed dictionaries containing, for each content word, the grammatical categories into which it is normally expected to fall. It is the intention here, not to give a complete summary of Bobrow's report, but rather to relate the idea of syntactic analysis by computer to the over-all picture set forth in Part 1. Perhaps the best way to do that is to show in diagrammatic form some of the analyses that are described in detail by Bobrow.

This second sentence will be used to illustrate other grammars also, in order to display similarities and differences. Computer programmes capable of implementing dependency analysis have been developed or described by Hays of the RAND Corporation, by Kelly of the RAND Corporation, by Gross of M.LT., by Klein and Simmons of the System Development Corporation, and by several Russian workers, including Moloshnava and Andreyev. In a phrase-structure analysis that assumes continuous, immediate constituents, t the diagrammatic representation is again treelike, but the nodes of the branching structure are, at all levels except the lowest, syntactic or grammatical categories. At the lowest level, the actual words of the sentence appear.

The analysis starts at the bottom of the diagram with the string of words and proceeds to discover a superstructure consistent with their grammatical class memberships. However, the analysis may involve trial-and-error differentiation downward from assumed categories to strings of words. The analysis substitutes for 'Sentence' the two category names, 'Noun Phrase' and 'Verb Phrase.' It then substitutes for 'Noun Phrase' the category names 'Definite Article' and 'Noun.'

For 'Verb Phrase' it substitutes 'Verb' and 'Noun Phrase.' It is then in a position to substitute actual words for three of the category names. 'Noun Phrase,' however, has to be passed through one more stage of analysis before the substitution of actual words can be made. The result of the analysis—the diagram—displays the roles of the individual words of the sentence and, in addition, shows how the several roles are interrelated. In the foregoing example, the analysis proceeded in a succession of binary branchings. An alternative formulation makes use of multiple branching to produce coordinate structures with fewer levels. Bobrow compares binary structure and coordinate structure in the phrase, 'the old black heavy stone.'

Computer programmes capable of making immediate constituent analyses have been developed or described by Robinson of the RAND Corporation, Cocke of the International Business Machines Corporation, and Klein of the System Development Corporation. Kuno and Oettinger of Harvard have developed extensively the technique of predictive analysis advocated by Rhodes of the

National Bureau of Standards. Predictive analysis takes advantage of the fact that, once he has heard the beginning of a sentence, the listener can rule out many of the myriad syntactic patterns into which sentences are, a priori, capable of falling. Predictive analyses keep track only of the alternative interpretations that are consistent with the part of the sentence that has already been analysed. At the very beginning, there are usually but few alternatives, for then the interpretations are not differentiated.

In the midcourse of an analysis, there may be many possible ways in which the sentence can go. At the end, however, the analysis should converge upon one pattern of grammatical categories, or, at any rate, upon a set of patterns among which a choice can be made on the basis of semantic interpretation of the sentence itself and of its context. The Kuno Oettinger programmes determine all the alternatives. Related programmes developed by Lindsay of the University of Texas find only one syntactic pattern but provide diagnostic information on the basis of which it is possible to clear up misinterpretation through 'postediting.' A minor problem for machine analysis is introduced by the fact that two words may together fill a grammatical category without being contiguous in text. This problem is not faced squarely by immediate-constituent grammars. In discontinuous-constituent grammars, however, the problem is recognised, and a special linkage is introduced to connect the separated parts. The diagram illustrates an analysis of 'He called her up.'

The linkage from 'Verb' to 'Particle' connects 'up' to 'called,' from which it has been separated by 'her.' The diagram shows a discontinuous-constituent analysis of the standard sentence, 'The man at the door turned the light out.' For the purposes of library pro cognitive systems, the most important problem in this subject area may well be one raised by Chomsky. Chomsky was concerned that two expressions of the same idea, such as 'The man drives the car' and 'The car is driven by the man' do not have similar phrase structures and do not yield similar diagrams when analysed in the ways we have been discussing. Chomsky handled this problem by setting up 'transformation rules' that transform one sentence into another, or combine *n* sentences into one, or subdivide one sentence into *n* sentences. For example, one transformation takes a sentence from active voice to passive voice. Another transformation combines two single clause sentences into a compound sentence. With transformation rules, one can build up complex syntactic structures from simple ones or analyse complex syntactic structures into simple ones. Bobrow gives an example in which the simple statements are derived from the question, 'What are the airfields in Ohio having runways longer than two miles?' Analysis and synthesis based on such transformations will surely be important for machine-aided organisation of the body of knowledge.

- X's are the airfields
- The airfields are in Ohio
- The airfields have runways

- The runways are long
- Two miles is long

The transformational-grammar approach handles the discontinuous-constituent problem neatly. A transformation changes 'turned the light out' into 'turned out the light.' As the diagram shows, the analysis then proceeds without any difficulty.

Walker and Bartlett of the Mitre Corporation are developing a parsing programme based on a transformational grammar. Harris and his associates at the University of Pennsylvania have developed a method of syntactic analysis that is intermediate between constituent analysis and transformational analysis. Although their method does not lend itself to representation by a tree diagram, a rough idea of its approach is conveyed by relating some of its terms to our standard sentence.In the sentence, the 'string center' is. . . man . . . turned out . . . light.' One 'the' is the 'left adjunct' of 'man,' and the other is the 'left adjunct' of 'light'. 'At the door' is the 'right adjunct' of 'man.' This 'string-transformational grammar' has been implemented in the form of computer programmes. The 'Baseball' programme developed by Green and associates at the Lincoln Laboratory - a programme capable of answering questions about the outcomes of the baseball games played in the major leagues during one season - has a methodological kinship to the Pennsylvania work.

From Bobrow's survey, it is clear that automation of syntactic analysis is possible. Indeed, there are several operating syntactic-analysis programmes. It is equally clear, however, that syntactic analysis is only a part - and perhaps, relatively, only a small part - of the over-all problem. The fact is that even the best analysis programmes produce discouragingly many alternative patterns. Selection among the alternatives has to be made on non-syntactic grounds, and there has not been much progress towards automation of that selection.

Furthermore, it is evident that one is a very long way from understanding what is being said when all he knows is the pattern or structure of syntactic categories into which the words of the message fit. The question was raised in Part I, whether it is desirable, in formulating the basic concepts of this field, to separate syntactic and semantic factors into the two insulated bins of a rigid dichotomy, or whether, as subtler and subtler distinctions are made in the process now called syntactic analysis, that process will start to become semantic as well as syntactic. Although we are not in a position to decide, one way or the other, on that question, we have an intuitive feeling that the latter is more promising as a line of development. We should, in this connection, refer to work that we regard as extremely promising, work being carried out by F.B. Thompson and his colleagues.

SAVING LIBRARIES WITH TECHNOLOGY

There has never been a harder time for libraries: unprecedented public funding cuts, required to cope with a deep economic downturn; the challenge of keeping abreast of rapid change in the technologies of content and search and discovery; and the quiet but insistent questioning of what role there is for public libraries in the modern world. Responses have been varied but predictable. In one camp are those people who cling to the values which led to the development of the modern library service – books, education, self-advancement and personal development – and in the other those bureaucrats who argue that if money has to be saved libraries must be sacrificed in order to divert funds to more pressing social problems. Of course not everyone takes such extreme views, and many feel there is a middle way to be found which protects the best of the library tradition, exploits the existing network of buildings, and doesn't put pressure on rapidly dwindling funds.

Book Industry Communication (BIC) is firmly of this view. BIC is partially a creature of the library sector, having been set up in 1991 by the British Library, the – then – Library Association, the Booksellers Association and the Publishers Association to develop and promote standards for electronic communication in what we now call the supply chain. Its first chairman was Tony Hall, managing director of what is now Capita Software Services but was then BLCMP and subsequently Talis. Its original focus was to bring EDI (electronic data interchange) to the wider book world, but it quickly broadened its outlook to include bar code technology, product metadata, identification standards and subject classification. Much of the book trade – and a significant part of the library supply chain – runs on standards that BIC has developed over the past twenty years.We believe that, unlike the book trade, the library sector has never been able to leverage available technology sufficiently to gain real cost savings from its deployment. The savings are there to be had, but only a comparatively small number of libraries have taken advantage of the opportunities. There are various reasons for this. One is the lack of the commercial drivers which galvanise interest from the book trade. Another is the lack of technical expertise in libraries themselves. Another is the huge diversity that comes from multiple library authorities making independent investment decisions on the basis of their own needs.

Perhaps the most telling, though, is the fact that the companies which exist to serve the library sector – LMS providers, RFID suppliers, stock suppliers and others – have made too good a living from the non-standard environment which these other factors have allowed to develop. Stock suppliers have made their money from servicing books to the specific needs of their customers rather than from the books themselves; LMS and RFID suppliers have been only too glad to tailor systems to individual needs rather than sell a standard product. These are the costs which BIC believes can be saved; and we are encouraged in this by the growing realisation by the companies involved that better delivery of standard products is in the end a more realistic and appropriate policy to adopt.

BIC's remit is about standards, collaboration and consensus. We believe there are huge wins to be made from eliminating waste in the library supply chain, by using technology and standards in a judicious way to cut away at the cost structures that have been allowed to exist in the public library sector because of its fragmented structure.

WHAT ARE THE KEY COMPONENTS OF THIS STRATEGY

EDI is one. Though the BIC standards are widely adopted by libraries and their suppliers, only a minority of libraries has implemented the full cycle of EDI messages – quotes, orders, delivery notes, invoices – and reaped the benefits of error avoidance, once-only keying and paperless transactions. Fewer still have been able or willing to create electronic links between library and corporate finance offices, so that invoices can flow electronically between approval and payment. EDI may be a little complicated to set up, but all the major library suppliers have invested heavily in standards-based electronic communication, and transaction costs are a fraction of any alternative and repay the investment many times over when it is in place.

RFID is another. This technology is hardly new, having been widely adopted by libraries, primarily as a more sophisticated alternative to bar codes for self-service applications, and where it has been implemented it has been universally acclaimed as a way to enable the more productive deployment of staff, facilitate longer opening hours, and provide a more welcoming environment for users. Now, with the help of the BIC/CILIP RFID in Libraries Group and its support for the new ISO 28560 standard, RFID is expanding its potential beyond self-service to stock management and other functions in the library, reducing workloads and providing ongoing cost reductions.

What is more, the standard enables libraries to invest in the technology, confident that they are not locked in to any specific vendor's software or hardware. BIC has published a UK profile for the standard, which has the acceptance and support of all the major RFID suppliers.

The work BIC has done on RFID has spawned other things too. For many years the required communication between self-service devices and LMSs has been handled by 3M's SIP2 protocol. In response to growing dissatisfaction from LMS providers, BIC has commissioned an entirely new communication framework which both extends the functionality of SIP2 but also defines web services as a mechanism for the transfer of information.

6

Automated Library Stock Verification with Barcode and Library System

INTRODUCTION

The modern technology has enabled automation and integration of the various processes of libraries and information centres to reduce or avoid human intervention and to increase the efficiency and speed. As the libraries provide open access service to make the holdings available to the users, the loss, damage, and misplacement of books are inevitable. To know and replace the lost books, and to maintain balance between various subjects, and to take adequate precautionary measures, it is necessary to do periodical inventory and accounting of the library collection of the library.

The term stock verification thus came into existance with regard to libraries. It is also referred as stock taking, physical verification or checking, stock inspection, and inventory, taking meaning physical checkup of any article on record.

Libraries of Govt. of India and its other organisations has to do a mandatory physical verification of all their holdings as per the following guidelines:

- Complete annual physical verification of books should be done every year in the case of libraries having not more than 20,000 holdings and not fewer than one qualified library staff. In case there is only one qualified staff, the verification may be done as per sub-para.
- Complete physical verification at intervals of not more than three years should be done in the case of libraries having more than 20,000 but not more than 50,000 volumes.
- Sample physical verification at intervals of not more than five years may be done in the case of libraries having more than 50,000 volumes. If such sample verification reveals unusual or unreasonable shortage, complete verification shall be done.

Libraries traditionally perform the periodic stock verification by adopting any one of the following methods: Verification by accession register; using a separate register with accession numbers; slips containing accession numbers;

numerical counting; and shelf register cards or shelf list cards. The methods are cumbersome, time-consuming, and error prone as these are done manually.

The automated stock verification procedure adopted at Raja Ramanna Centre for Advanced Technology (RRCAT) library by employing barcode and LibSys facilities library stock verification could be performed easily with less manpower; one person scanned the barcode label (accession number) of documents and other person marked the documents by putting month and year stamp at the inside back cover to ensure that the document was physically verified. Besides, identification of damaged and worn out documents for repair, binding of obsolete volumes, and rearrangement and cleaning can also be done simultaneously. During the stock verification period, the returned (check-in) documents were also verified before shelving. Once the data capturing was over, the verification and generation of report with LibSys could also be done in a short period of time.

BARCODE DATA TRANSFER

The information that can be encoded on the barcodes is rather limited and hence, it is up to the individual libraries to decide what information they need to barcode for efficient handling of collection and for better operation of services. Libraries can use accession numbers of books, the unique information that distinguish their collection, as the vital information entity to barcode their collection. Similarly, the identification number of a user stands distinct for each member, which can be used to barcode the user's cards. Accession number/ borrower number exported from the library database/borrower database is converted to a series of black and white lines by the barcode software.

This can be printed by a dot-matrix/laser printer and pasted on all books and borrower cards. The light beam flashed from the barcode scanner on the barcode label undergoes reflection at the white lines and absorption on the dark bands. This reflected light is collected back and is converted into electric pulses by the photoelectric circuitry of the scanner. Further, these pulses are converted into binary information by the interface circuitry of the scanner before they are fed to the computer, for further processing. So, the information read from barcode acts as a substitute for the same information entered through keyboard, to handle circulation/other routines of the library database.

The barcode technology is essentially a data transfer device and hence, it works in perfect harmony with any of the computerised database systems. Any customisation needed at the user end can be done either by the in-house system personnel or by local solution providers. The barcoding setup includes the barcode scanner to read the barcoded information, its interfacing with the library computer, the software to convert the requisite information to barcodes, and the printer.

The barcode scanners may be classified into different groups like:

- As per design (handheld and fixed-mount).
- As per light source (infrared or visible).

Hand-held scanners contain no moving parts. They are compact, light and cheaper as compared to fixed-mount models. Hence, they are of interest to libraries desiring to optimise their budgetary resources. Infrared scanners can read mutilated labels; however, they need special printers. But recent times saw the dominant categorisation, as per technology, into CCD and laser scanners. In CCD scanners, light from the LEDs is used to read the barcode information, whereas laser light is used in the latter. Accordingly, laser scanners have increased scan width and range (distance from which the labels are scanned), but they are comparatively expensive. The vendors used to offer requisite software to generate barcodes from suggested fields of library database. Since, materials and readers are added only in prescribed number in a library, it will be better to avoid commercial printing of barcode labels.

All required lables can be printed either on normal paper or on purchased blank labels on a dot-matrixllaser printer, as per their availability in the library. While generating lables, provision may also be made to print some other fields like author/title/user riame in normal text to identify the labels easily, as one is more comfortable with text than numbers like accession/identification number. The user cards are normally laminated and to ensure long life of the labels on books (defective labels always lead to wrong/no reading of data), transparent cellotape can be pasted over these.

CODING FORMATS/ SYMBOLOGIES

The different code formats and how the information is encoded in bars is available in the litreature4. The same information can be encoded by different schemes; however, at the user and application level, it doesn't make much distinction and the user may use any of the schemes. The same information can be encoded to and satisfactorily decoded from more than one scheme without hampering efficiency or time. Limitations are imposed by the barcoding software one uses, and it is better to consult the individual operational manual for such information.

Some of the common formats are:

- *Universal Product Code (UPC)*: US standard to encode only digits, UPC-A to encode 12 digits or UPC-E to encode 6 digits.
- *European Article Number (EAN)*: European code to encode digits, available in two variations:. EAN-8 to encode 8 digits and EAN-13 to encode 13 digits.
- *Interleaved 2 of 5. (ITF)*: Supports only numeric characters but can be used for variable length.
- *Code-39*: Encodes capital alphabets, numerical and few special characters like $, +, per cent. Asterisk (*) must be used as the start and stop character. Lowercase alphabets cannot be encoded.
- *Code-1 28*: Encodes both the lower and the upper case letters, numeric and special characters found on the keyboard.

- *Codabar*: Encodes only numeric and few special characters and is the most widely used coding format. Generally, libraries use this symbology to encode books and borrower cards.

BARCODING AT THE IIT KHARAGPUR CENTRAL LIBRARY

The Central Library of the Indian Institute of Technology, Kharagpur, is one of the few libraries in the country to have a huge database of their entire collections.

Initially, the computerised issue return of books6 was done by keying in the accession number of books and identification number of borrower, but this mechanism was prone to errors and. also resulted in long queues at the circulation grant desk. Out of the project of ₹ 10 lakh received from AICTE in 1994 for the conversion of the conventional central library into the electronic library, the Library procured 5 CCD barcode scanners and one HP-5Si Mx Laser Printer. It was decided to barcode books and hence, the details of books brought for issue/return were exported from the library database for generating barcode labels with accession number as the key field and the labels were printed on the laser printer using 'Softbar vl' software supplied by the vendor.

The Library also received a consignment of 'Nashua Laser Labels' in 30 labels per page format as gift from one of its alumni settled in US. The system generates three labels for each book to be pasted on the back of title page, secret page and last page. To fasten the process, personnel were given honorarium and encouraged to work overtime/on holidays to barcode the entire book collection. Side by side, new books processed by the technical processing section were also barcoded before release. Out of a special operating fund of ₹ 1 lakh received from the Institute in 1998, all the pending old books were also barcoded.

Now, the entire collection of over 2 lakh books is barcoded. From the academic year 1998-99, all B.Tech and M.Tech students were given a laminated barcoded library identity card and the practice of issuing separate borrower cards as per the entitlement was discontinued.

This facility will be further extended to faculty, researchers, and other staff in near future. This practice not only resulted in saving a large amount of stationery for printing numerous borrower cards but also a total saving of staff time which would have otherwise been spent for filing those cards. The user can have a book in one third of the pre-barcode issue time. The faculty, students and the personnel manning the circulation desk find the barcode technology user-friendly, efficient and fast.

ADOPTION IN OTHER LIBRARIES IN INDIA

Few of the computerised libraries in the country like American Centre, British Council, other ITs, some RandD libraries have already started barcoded circulation. With an investment of less than a lakh, the computerised libraries can procure barcode related hardware and software. A CCD scanner can be purchased for ₹ 15,000 and a laser scanner for ₹ 25,000 with comparable costs for relevant software. It is always better to have a feedback from the nearby libraries who use this technology before procuring one. Also, the potential vendors may be called to give a demonstration of this technology.

The procurement may be carried out in one go or in stages, so that those required for barcoding active collection may be purchased first and on completion of that work, more scanners may be bought. The accrued savings for the first few years will be more than what has been invested. Further, it will also improve the status of the library which will move one step closer to realise the fourth law of library science.

APPLICATIONS OF BARCODING

Barcoding offers a lot of comfort and ease to handle bulk routine tasks efficiently. The application of this technology for issue/return of books is widely identified and practiced in the developed countries of the world. A few of the computerised libraries in our country have also started experiencing the fruits of this technology. It is important to emphasise that this technology is not limited to circulation work. Newnham describes the barcoding of DNA samples in Britain. It is not out of place to ponder over future barcoding applications in a library. With the help of a data gathering device, the barcodes can be used to verify stock, as libraries have to resort to stock verification, at intervals.

If the provision for multiple barcodes or multidimensional barcoding is incorporated to handle call number information also, wrong shelving of books can be autodetected which would help the staff to rectify the same. The individual journal volumes are handled in a library with lots of intricacies. Many a time these issues have to be taken out of the display area for Xerox work. There are also chances of their shelving in wrong cabinets.

These problems are tackled by using a control number for the current journal issues and barcoding them accordingly. A database of journal issues can thus be generated so that their management through cards can be avoided. If the parent institution also has a computerised accounting system, all the bills can be routed after barcoding so that their follow up and processing are done efficiently. Barcoding has come a long way and it is here to stay for faster and efficient library work.

IMPLEMENTATION OF BARCODE TECHNOLOGY AND LIBSYS AT RRCAT LIBRARY

To improve the library service and to have an efficient control over the entire operation, the LibSys, which is a commercially available integrated multi-user library automation package, was implemented at RRCAT in 1995. To improve the services further, the barcode technology (print-related automatic identification technology) was implemented in 2000. The hardware installed to implement these technologies at RRCAT are: Laser barcode scanner for reading labels (at circulation counter); portable data capturing terminal with build-in laser scanner for inventory (stock verification); and accessories such as cradle, cable, battery and other items. The softwares for interfacing the data capturing terminal with computer are: PowerGen, SysTools and Label Works for Windows for label designing.

BARCODE AND BARCODE SCANNER

The barcodes are being used effectively to speed up, avoid human error, and automate the processes in industry for production planning control, materials management, purchase/ sale, and inventory control. In libraries, barcode is being used to automate the data-capturing process, for stock verification, and in the circulation counter for issue/return of documents.

A barcode is a sequence of dark bars on a light background or the equivalent of this with respect to the light-reflecting properties of the surface. The coding comprises in the relative widths or spacing of the dark bars and light spaces. A barcode scanner is an optical device that reads the code by scanning a focussed beam of light, generally a laser beam, across the barcode and detecting the variations in reflected light. The scanner converts these light variations into electrical variations, which are subsequently digitised and fed into the decoding unit programmed to convert the relative widths of the digitised dark/light spacings into numbers and/or letters.

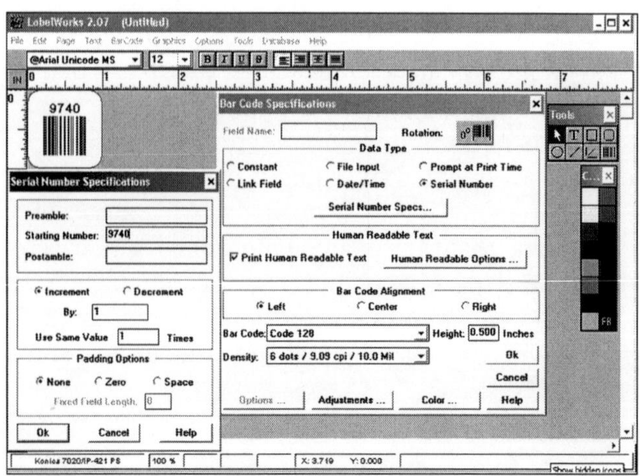

Fig. Barcode Label Design SpecificationsBarcode Labelling

Each document in a library should be uniquely identified for barcode labelling purpose. Most of the libraries in India use accession number for this purpose. RRCAT has also used the same for printing barcode labels. The labels designed using Label Works for Windows, which supports major barcode symbologies. Code 128, a high density linear symbology that can encode text, numbers, several functions and the entire 128 ASCII character set was selected for designing the labels. Figure shows the barcode label design specifications.

DATA CAPTURING, MODIFICATION AND UPLOADING

The datalogic formula 732 wizard terminal was used to capture the data. The portable data collection laser scanner terminal scans the encoded data and automatically decodes and stores up to 128 KB of data in the memory. As the accession number differs from one to other, the terminal stores approx. 2500 accession numbers. The data was downloaded into the PC using Systool's (software utility for data exchange) and was saved in a data file (*.dat). Later downloads were also appended to the same file. The PowerGen was the other software utility used to build personalised settings as per the requirements.

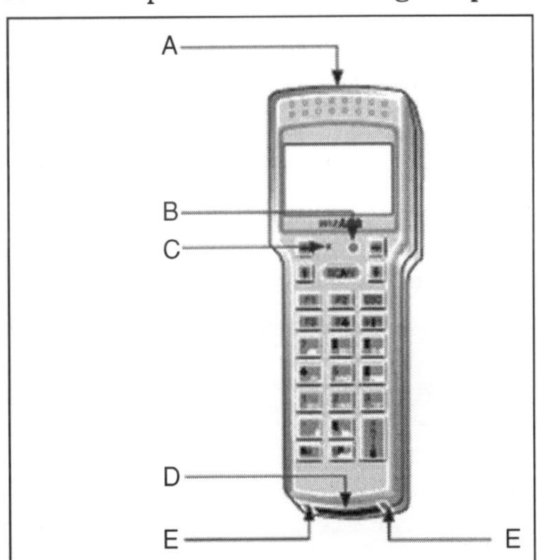

Fig. Datalogic Formula 732 Wizard Terminal.

Notes:

A. Laser beam output window

B. Two colour LED

C. Reset key (shielded)

D. Cradle communications window

E. Contacts for battery recharging

Each document was scanned and stamped (month and year) manually at the inside back cover to avoid duplication. During scanning, the terminal stores the accession number of each document and automatically displays the document number for a moment. If a data scanned is wrong, it can be manually updated or rescanned, and if a document has been inadvertantly scanned multiple times, the terminal simply stores the documents with duplicate accession numbers. The downloaded data in the PC shows a vertical bar '|' (pipe) character after each accession number. The '|' characters were manually removed from the file using the windows text editor. The comprehensive file was then moved to LibSys work file ('wfilexx' directory).

DATA PROCESSING

As the entire collection of RRCAT was catalogued in the LibSys, the data analyses and report generation was carried out through the LibSys cataloguing stock verification module. The initiation of stock verification function is executed at once. This operation sets the system for the big exercise on inventory entails.

Data Analysis

The LibSys provides data verification in two ways; accession numbers one by one, and list of accession numbers in a file. All accession numbers are stored in a file. The system registers accession numbers for verification in the database. After matching the accession number from the file, the LibSys automatically generates an exception case file with extension '*. exp' and saves it in the work file path, , *i.e.*, , in the wfilexx directory. This file enlists the list of mis-matching accession numbers and wrongly scanned numbers.

Report Generation

As the term stock verification implies only on stock, a list of missing accession numbers is generated against the captured data file. After several cross checkings, the final verification report is prepared in a text (*.txt) file. The flow chart is presented in figure.

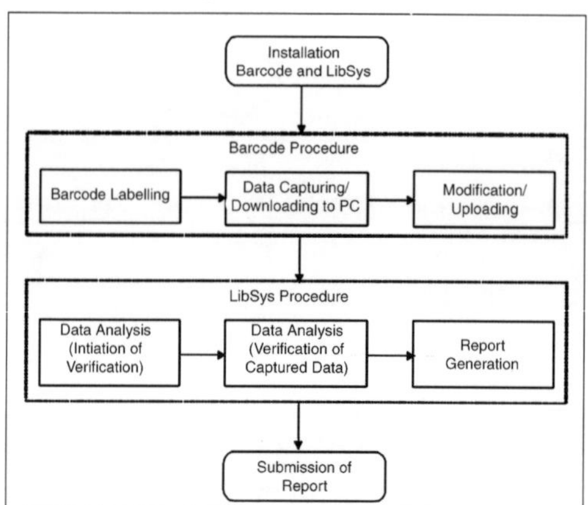

Fig 10.3 Flow Chart of Automated Stock Verification

7

Information Technology and Digital Library

INTRODUCTION

Although digital libraries are intended to support education and knowledge work, current digital library interfaces are narrowly focused on retrieval. Furthermore, they are designed for desktop computers with keyboards, mice, and high-speed network connections. Desktop computers fail to support many key aspects of knowledge work, including active reading, free form ink annotation, fluid movement among document activities, and physical mobility.

This chapter proposes portable computers specialized for knowledge work, or *digital library information appliances*, as a new platform for accessing digital libraries. We present a number of ways that knowledge work can be augmented and transformed by the use of such appliances.

These insights are based on our implementation of two research prototype systems: XLibris, an "active reading machine," and Tele- Web, a mobile World Wide Web browser. The standard platform for accessing today's digital libraries is a desktop computer with a keyboard, a mouse, information retrieval software, and a network connection. Unfortunately, desktop computers are not suitable for many types of knowledge work.

Studies of people using electronic and paper documents show that desktop systems fail to support four important activities:

- Active reading
- Free form ink annotation
- Fluid movement among document activities
- Physical mobility

As a result of focusing on the desktop, today's interfaces for accessing digital libraries support retrieval in isolation, without addressing these broader work practices. We propose a new platform for accessing digital libraries: specialized portable computers designed for knowledge work, or *digital library information appliances.*

In this paper, we draw on our experience designing and building two research prototype information appliances— the XLibris "active reading machine" and the TeleWeb mobile Web browser— to show how these devices can support a broad range of activities in the digital library.

INFORMATION SCIENCE

What is information science? The question, while seemin-gly simple, begs another, more complex one: *How is information science, or for that matter any field, to be defined?* This is a complex problem dealt with at length in philosophy and in other fields. Lexical definitions are necessary for providing a broad description and boundaries of the subjects covered by a field, but they cannot provide for a deeper understanding. Webster does not a field define. This is not to reject clear lexical definitions—not at all—just to establish their limitations.

In approaching the discussion of information science, I am taking the problem point of view as elaborated by Popper who argued that:

- [S]ubject matter or kind of things do not, I hold, constitute a basis for distinguishing disciplines. . . .*We are not students of some subject matter, but students of problems*. Any problem may cut right across the border of any subject matter or discipline.

Our emphasis is on problems addressed by information science. Although we provide definitions of information science and other fields in interdisciplinary relations with information science later in the chapter, we are doing this solely to advance the understanding of problems addressed by different fields and their relation to information science problems. Debates over the "proper" definition of information science, as of any field, are fruitless, and in expectations naive. Information science, as a science and as a profession, is defined by the problems it has addressed and the methods it has used for their solutions over time.

Any advances in information science depend on whether the field is indeed progressing in relation to problems addressed and methods used. Any "fixing," if in order, will have to be approached by redefining or refocusing either the problems addressed, or the methods for their solutions, or both. Information science has three general characteristics that are the leitmotif of its evolution and existence. These are shared with many modern fields.

They can also be viewed as problem areas with which infor-mation science has to deal on a general level:

- First, information science is interdisciplinary in nature; however, the relations with various disciplines are changing. The interdisciplinary evolution is far from over.
- Second, information science is inexorably connected to information technology. A technological imperative is compelling and constraining the evolution of information science, as is the evolution of a number of other fields, and moreover, of the information society as a whole.
- Third, information science is, with many other fields, an active participant in the evolution of the infor-mation society. Information

science has a strong social and human dimension, above and beyond technology.

A number of works that I freely consulted dealt with various historical aspects of information science.

Among those works are:

- Shera and Cleveland,
- Bourne,
- Herner,
- Salton,
- Cleverdon,
- Swanson,
- Lilley and Trice,
- Farkas-Conn,
- Buckland and Liu, and
- Rayward.

Still, a comprehensive history of information science is a project for a future historian of science. As yet only historical pieces and different perspectives of pieces exist. A history of any field is a history of a few powerful ideas. I suggest that information science has three such powerful ideas, so far. These ideas deal with processing of information in a radically different way than was done previously or elsewhere. The first and the original idea, emerging in 1950s, is *information retrieval*, providing for processing of information based on formal logic. The second, emerging shortly thereafter, is *relevance*, directly orienting and associating the process with human information needs and assessments.

The third, derived from elsewhere some two decades later, is *interaction*, enabling direct exchanges and feedback between systems and people engaged in IR processes. So far, no powerful ideas have emerged about *information*, as the underlying phenomenon, or *"literature"*, as the object of processing.

However, one can argue that the idea of mapping of "literature," that started with exploitation of citation indexes in 1960s, may also qualify as a powerful idea. In a non-historical sense this stage deals with these powerful ideas and with leitmotifs. They form a framework for understanding the past, present, and future of information science.

ORIGIN AND SOCIAL CONTEXT IN INFORMATION SCIENCE

Information science is a field that emerged in the after-math of the Second World War (WW II), along with a number of new fields, with computer science being but one example. The rapid pace of scientific and technical advances that were accumu-lating since the start of the 20th century, produced by mid-century a scientific and technical revolution. A most visible manifestation of this revolution was the phenomenon of "information explosion," referring to the exponential and unabated growth of scientific and technical publications and information records of all kinds, so masterfully synthesized and illuminated by de Solla Price.

In a remarkable turn of events, the impetus for the development of information science, and even for its very origin and agenda, a respected MIT scientist and, even more importantly, the head of the U.S. scientific effort during WW II.

Bush did two things:

- He succinctly defined a critical and strategic problem that was on the minds of many, and
- Proposed a solution that was a "technological fix", and thus in tune with the spirit of the times.

Both had wide appeal and Bush was listened to because of his stature. He defined the problem in almost poetic terms as "the massive task of making more accessible a bewildering store of knowledge". In other words, Bush addressed the problem of information explosion. The problem is still with us. His solution was to use the emerging computing and other information technology to combat the problem. But he went even further. He proposed a machine named Memex, incorporating a capability for "association of ideas," and duplication of "mental processes artificially." A prescient anticipation of information science and artificial intelligence is evident.

Memex, needless to say, was never built, but to this day is an ideal, a wish list, an agenda, and, some think, a utopia. We are still challenged by the ever-worsening problem of the information explosion, now universal and in a variety of digital formats. We are still trying to fix things techno-logically. We are still aspiring to incorporate Memex's basic ideas in our solutions. A number of scientists and professi-onals in many fields around the globe listened and took up Bush's challenge.

Governments listened as well and provided funding. The reasoning went something like this: Because science and technology are strategically important for society, efforts that help them, information activities in particular, are also important and need support. In the U.S., the *National Science Foundation* (NSF) Act of 1950 established NSF and provided a number of mandates, among them "to foster the interchange of scientific information among scientists in the U.S. and foreign countries" and "to further the full dissemination of information of scientific value consistent with the national interest".

The 1958 National Defence Education Act enlarged the mandate:

"The National Science Foundation shall..undertake programme to develop new or improved methods, including mechanized systems, for making scientific information available".

By those mandates, an NSF division, which after a number of name and direction changes is now called the Division of *Information and Intelligent Systems* (IIS), has supported research in these areas since the 1950s. Importantly, the field-defining studies that NSF supported included, among others, Cranfield IR evaluation studies in the 1950s and 1960s, large chunks of SMART studies from the 1960s to 1990s, and now the Digital Libraries

Initiatives. In the U.S., information science developed and began flourishing on its own in a large part due to government support by a host of agencies, as did many other fields.

Historically, the support was a success—it was instrumental in creation of the whole enterprise of information science and even of the information online industry based on IR. But to the credit of information science it kept growing on its own even after government support slackened substantially. This cannot be said of a number of other fields or areas that floundered after government stopped being their main source and resource.

SOCIAL CONTEXT

It is a truism to state that information was always important for any society in any historical period. But the role of information and its degree of importance differed. With the evolution of the social order to a "post-industrial" society, or "post-capitalist" society or what we now commonly also call "information society," knowledge and information is assuming an increasing central role in every aspect of life. The classic study by Machlup, followed by a number of similar studies, documented the startling structural changes in the economy and society as driven by the growth of information and knowledge production and processing.

Popularly, they were summarized by Drucker:

> The change in the meaning of knowledge that began two hundred fifty years ago has transformed society and economy. Formal knowledge is seen as both the key personal and the key economic resource. . . [K]nowledge proves itself in action. What we now mean by knowledge is information effective in action, information focused on results.... The actual products of the pharmaceutical industry is knowledge; pill and prescription ointment are no more than packaging for knowledge.

Addressing the problem of information explosion, information science found a niche within the broader context in the evolution of the information society. In its various manifestations and attempted solutions, the niche is getting broader and bigger. But by no means does information science hold a monopoly in that niche. As the importance of infor-mation is increasing in society, more and more resources and expenditures are channeled into various information-related activities. More and more research funds, projects, and initia-tives are devoted to information in various disguises. It is not surprising then that more and more fields, researchers, professionals, and businesses are turning to information, and even "discovering" information. There is gold in information. Information science has many competitors—it may be even swamped by them.

CHALLENGES AND OPPORTUNITIES IN LIBRARY SERVICES

E-learners are frequently silent and invisible as they search and explore a library's online resources, and they do not have the same access that on-campus learners have to formal library instruction sessions. With the array of digital resources available to them, the multiplicity of interfaces and search tools, and the need for evaluation and critical thinking when using the Internet for research, "information literacy" skills are a must-have for e-learners. Information literacy refers to competencies with information sources in a variety of formats. According to the Association of College and Research Libraries, an information literate individual is able to:

- Determine the extent of information needed
- Access the needed information effectively and efficiently
- Evaluate information and its sources critically
- Incorporate selected information into one's knowledge base
- Use information effectively to accomplish a specific purpose
- Understand the economic, legal, and social issues surrounding the use of information, and access and use information ethically and legally

Supporting the integration of information literacy skills training into the core curriculum has become an important issue for libraries. As an extension of their traditional role of providing library instruction sessions and developing instructional materials, librarians are designing online tutorials and courses that promote information literacy and encourage active learning. Particularly fine examples are the University of Texas System Digital Library's *TILT—Texas Information Literacy Tutorial*; and Utah Academic Library Consortium's *Internet Navigator*, a multi-institutional online course developed by a team of librarians and Web developers.

The British Open University Library has developed *SAFARI*, a freely available interactive tutorial, as well as an information literacy course called *MOSAIC (Making Sense of Information in the Connected Age)*.

Many libraries provide instruction to e-learners by making information available on their Web pages, including frequently asked questions, library glossaries, research guides, and "how-to" pages.

Athabasca University Library's Digital Reference Centre integrates resources with contextual instruction and provides links to instructional resources, including a detailed guide to Internet searching that encourages e-learners to think critically about Internet resources, and library research guides such as the *AU Library Guide to Researching Topics in Women's Studies*. Online tutorials usually operate on a model in which the e-learner interacts in isolation with a computer.

Their effectiveness can be enhanced by the addition of more interactive forms of instruction. The librarians at the Florida Distance Learning Reference and Referral Center, for example, have experimented with chat software to simulate a virtual classroom and open up "live" group instruction to e-learners. Librarians can also work with faculty to develop a library thread in a course discussion area, or to open a discussion forum on the library Web pages.

REFERENCE

E-learners require more than access to e-resources. Traditionally, a reference librarian acts as an additional type of resource, one who can be counted upon to provide expertise in making sense of library systems and research tools, and to offer a helping hand along that often slippery path known as the research process. Virtual library users face additional challenges in mining relevant information out of a computer system that "obstinately" returns zero hits in response to a query that does not match the character strings in its database files. The most common means of providing electronic reference services to remote users has been e-mail, the advantages and disadvantages of which have been well documented in the literature.

The around-the-clock and around-the-world accessibility of e-mail allows users to connect with librarians beyond the walls of library buildings and outside the usual hours of operation. E-mail provides a written record of requests and responses, permits the electronic transmission of search results, and allows librarians time to reflect on requests. One of the most serious concerns about e-mail reference services is their impact on the traditional face-to-face reference interview, particularly the absence of the verbal and non-verbal cues that typically assist a librarian in effectively responding to a question. Hulshof identifies three issues related to the use of electronic communication in serving virtual patrons: immediacy, intricacy, and interaction. Because it is so easy for a learner to send a request electronically and have it arrive at the library instantly, there is a perception that the librarian's response will be as immediate.

The learner may become frustrated, not realising that the process of locating information and developing a response takes the librarian just as long when the request is made electronically as when it is made in person or in any other way. The more intricate or complex the request, the longer it will take for the librarian to clarify it and respond appropriately: a series of e-mail messages may be required, which will further reduce the immediacy of the e-mail request.

Immediacy and intricacy relate to the lack of interaction: the opportunity to discuss and clarify enquiries that occurs in person or over the telephone is not so easily accommodated by e-mail. There are ways to deal with some of these issues. A welldesigned reference Web form, such as that provided on the Ask AU Library: Ask about a Research Topic Web page, which encourages elearners to include full identifying and course information, to describe clearly their research problem and search terminology, and to state the parameters of the assignment, can clarify requests for librarians and reduce the need to e-mail back and forth.

Automated replies, which are sent out by the e-mail programme in response to the receipt of a message, can be used to reassure e-learners that their messages are being received, and can let them know what to expect in terms of service. E-mail reference service can be enhanced and supplemented with additional technologies that raise the level of interaction with realtime or live communication.Chat technology allows e-learners and librarians to send text messages back and forth instantly, using a form of communication that is familiar to most Internet users. There have been a number of library experiments with Web contact center software, which is modeled on the private sector's online solution to providing customer support. Web contact center software provides a higher level of interaction than does basic chat software, allowing for queuing and routing of messages, as well as enabling librarians to "push" Web pages to users. Providing e-learners with a toll-free telephone number remains an effective and convenient reference services strategy, particularly for intricate enquiries. The telephone reference interview works best when both librarian and e-learner are working in front of computers connected to the Internet.

AIMS OF THE DIGITAL LIBRARY

The main aim, considering our hugely rich heritage, is and remains an eminently cultural one. The cultural aim is and remains in any case the main one also in all the other countries in the world, both where the Digital Library is used to create a support to academic studies and where the intention of documentation of historical memory prevails.

Actually, as is clearly seen from the international account which is widely summarised below, the two aims are complementary and the problem shifts to the choice to be made at the start, so that the Digital Library can be developed in a coherent and uniform way in both directions.

In the case of Italy, the attention to local memory and the support for research might be the two ideal boundaries within which Digital Library initiatives should be directed and maintained.

It should also be pointed out that this cultural aim is seen as the cog-wheel for the creation of new work, professional growth and recognition of national culture at an international level.

THE TECHNICAL/LIBRARIANSHIP FRAMEWORK

Both from the definition and from indications deriving from the models analysed, the Digital Library undoubtedly presents itself as an extraordinarily complex structure. This complexity is analysed from various points of view, both the purely technical and the specifically librarianship ones.

Given the implications that the latter more than any other has in our view on the success of any project, we will focus on these themes in the summary and omit others for which we will simply refer to the main study.

Organisational Aspects

On the basis of the proposed analysis, the Digital Library is seen to be a "complex Library" and as a new information system in terms of:

- Objects to be handled
- Format of data
- Means of description (metadata)
- Organisation of research (search engines)
- Interfaces (informatics and/or human)
- Production activities (Workflow, Budgeting)
- Integration of different types of applications and systems
- Complex and distributed system

The Digital Library which organises production activities needs to define the methodologies for the treatment of the various materials in the context of a project (Workflow) and consequently the investment policies (Budgeting) both for the moment of production and for the subsequent conservational maintenance. A functional profile of the Digital Library is outlined with indication of the following functions:

Net infrastructures	Pac/web opac
Database bibliographic/metadata	Ocument management system
Digital repository	Maging
Storage	Raphics
Interface	Tatistics
Safety	

For each of these the functional requirements to be fulfilled in the Digital Library are specified. In particular it is stressed that in a Digital Library the objects to be handled are very different in nature:

- They can integrate metadata for description and management
- They can be local and remote
- They can concern other information data (online courses, Web pages)
- They can be multi-format (text, audio, video, images,....)
- They can be original digital objects: electronic publications

Evolution of Services and the Profession

The evolution of the potentialities of the services generated by the Digital Library and the parallel evolution of the profession are among the most significant and complex aspects of the Digital Library.

With the greater availability of information, the Digital Library still presents itself as a service structure. Some of the many statements and definitions indicated and analysed strongly stress the function of service-provider in relation to other similar institutions.

For example:

- The appeal for cooperation ("the Digital Library is not a separate entity")
- The appeal to the particular use of technologies ("the Digital Library needs technologies for connecting the resources of different libraries with information services")

- The appeal relative to access ("the aim of the Digital Library is universal access to its collections and services").

The characteristics of the service also change because of the changed attitude of the user and the different interaction between user and intermediary. This leads to a careful consideration of the qualitative evolution of the reference services, in which this mediation will be a strategic element in the development of the Digital Library.

Undoubtedly the problem of professionalism is one of the most significant of those related to the Digital Library, both because of how this professionalism is defined and how it is changing with the new services and the new skills which are required.

It is agreed that we are in the face of a true revolution, mostly brought about by facts which are outside the librarianship field in the strictest sense, but have evident repercussions on the functions and the very nature of the library, hence of the librarian. The librarian's work is the fruit of different, complementary kinds of know-how which mean that he/she operates as a:

- Professional handigital libraryer of digital information
- Producer of digital information
- Communicator of digital knowledge to provide this type of service the librarian of the digital library
- To know the users with whom he/she is in contact better in order to adapt adequate tools and products to specific demands
- To adapt the procedures for presenting data- interface and not to propose them according to a single standard procedure
- To give access also to non-bibliographical inform-ation available on the Web From the analysis it emerges that there will be an affirmation of professional figures who are able to unite the more classic principles of librarianship with the prospects offered to the profession by digital technologies and telematic connections. The most substantial changes will be seen in the most classic areas of the librarian's profession, ,*i.e.*,:
- *In the description of resources*: With the advent of metadata and the implications dictated by the reflections deriving from the debate on Functional Requirements for Bibliographic Records;
- *In the services*: With particular regard to the sector of Reference and Document Delivery;
- *In conservation*: Where simple conservation is united with production and extended access to resources which were once inaccessible.

These changes are inevitably translated into practice by the emergence of new qualifications and new professional figures. At the basis we can identify a strong demand for entrepreneurship on the part of the managerial class, as has already been noted in the illustration of the model proposed by EFQM. In this regard it appears that the prevailing librarian will be a professional with the ability to combine different solutions, different public and private operators within and outside the structure: a sort of professional who moves between the classic principles of the profession and the new technological possibilities and suggestions, a professional who is able to unite opportunities and risks in a productive way.

The Italian scene does not favour great optimism in this sense. In many libraries we perceive a widespread situation of unawareness of the change in progress and a growing gap between those who know and those who do not, with the growing risk of a sort of "returning illiteracy".

This phenomenon seems particularly present in the large Italian libraries which are mainly government-run, and which are seriously behind as regards basic training, continuous updating and the retraining of the managerial class. Attending to basic and continuous training, also taking advantage of the possibilities offered nowadays by distance learning technologies, is becoming more and more a priority goal.

Thorough study of digital themes reveals that, though technology is important, it is more than ever an instrumental fact and hence secondary to that of giving staff the means for dominating the change.

Technologies and Standards

Undoubtedly the technological component is the factor through which a Digital Library is set up. The same can be said of the attention necessary for the application of descriptive standards (metadata) for access to the resources and their sharing, as well as for their fruition.

However, although the study reserves a significant part for these themes, it seems to us correct to emphasise here that technology presents itself above all as an instrumental and not a priority fact, due to its continual evolution.

In fact within a precise cultural and organisational reference framework, and with the availability of adequate skills, we should be careful to adopt market standards and move towards solutions which are technologically open to continual evolution. The study deals with the following themes under a series of sections:

- Digital supports (Text, Audio, Images, onwards: a comprehensive survey of the "objects" of the Digital Library.
- Telematic infrastructures and Internet onwards: an analysis of web demands and of the current range of offers in our country. The services offered by Infostrada, Albacom, I-net, Telecom, Garr and Rupa are examined.
- Automated management systems: a survey of to what extent and how the present library automation systems are being adapted to the advent of the digital. With a brief examination also of the Italian scene and of the features of SBN (servizio bibliotecario nazionale), which at the present time does not seem to be prepared for any kind of digital function.

Among the most innovative services is the ASP: "A further evolution, which may significantly influence the market in the years to come, is the starting-up of the so-called ASP (Application Service Provider). In practice, ASP is a service for library management which is completely entrusted to the outside.

The only thing which the library has to manage locally is the connection to Internet. All the functions, from research to data input to the management of all the other functions are the concern of the system provider." It seems to us useful to recall this particular solution since it is proposed as one of the services that could be offered by the Digital Library., although with a different significance.

- Data Storage on the function of storage. It should be pointed out that in the face of a continually changing situation from both the technological viewpoint and that of competitiveness of the offer, a continual updating on each of these themes is crucial.

Digitisation

One of the most important technical aspects is that of acquiring a mastery of the materials and modes of treatment for digitisation. "The project of setting up a digital library needs thoroughly to evaluate the different types of document which are involved in the scanning process, whether it be a question of books, archive documents or more specifically museum documents, since also the latter are involved in the process of technological transformation of conservation and of fruition through informatics and telematic instruments".

The theme of hybridism is dealt with. "(...) a theme which is closely related to the conservation of the library document at the moment when we are planning the setting-up of digital library. The demands of a conservation system are, in fact, better fulfilled by a combination of technologies".

"The practice of hybridism thus consists of combining the two technologies: converting into digital and producing microfilms from the digital or viceversa producing microfilms and converting them into digital". For each type of material, technical and methodological indications are provided in the second part. Indications are given in particular for the following materials:

- Supports of vegetable origin (papyri)
- Cloth supports
- Wooden supports
- Paper supports (with particular regard to manu-scripts [illuminated, illuminated with close binding, loose binding or loose-leaf, monochromatic], printed books, postcards and prints in general, tissue paper)
- Supports of animal origin (parchments)
- Supports of mineral origin
- Supports of chemical origin (microfilms, slides) Indications are given regarding the general criteria to apply for photographic and digital resolution.

The Organisation of a Project

Granted that each project has a separate story, a general reference scheme for the typical operations of a digitisation project is however proposed on the basis of what is offered by the professional literature.

Description of the Resources

In the Digital Library the problems of description take on more and more importance and a large part of the study is dedicated to these. What determines special attention to the problem is the need to understand all the different features of the digital object.

The various categories of Metadata necessary for identifying the object for its conservation and transmissability in time are analysed.

A survey of the standards of description and their evolution, directly influenced by the nature of the objects to which they will be applied, is proposed. Mention is made of ISBD (ER), of bibliographical formats such as MARC and Unimarc, of the problem of resource identifiers URN, DOI, URL, PURL, and finally a part is dedicated to the most significant standard so far developed for the purpose, ,*i.e.,* Dublin Core.

The debate on description also regards environments other than the library, in particular archives and museums; the EAD and CRM developed standards take this debate into account. Some international projects dedicated to this theme are of great importance. Some of these also include Italian participants.

The problems of the standards and Metadata return in the second part within a series of operational proposals and recommendations.

"The importance is underlined that some specific applications of projects for a digital library should start up the experimentation of the model IFLA FRBR because of its potential for analysing and documenting in a precise way the work, the expression, the manifestation, the copy, connections among them and respectively to the intellectual responsibility and the concepts treated.

This model is suitable for the treatment of electronic resources in their multiple versions, allowing documentation of critical editions, versions, new editions, translations, transpositions and revisions on similar or different supports.

This could be adequately applied in the treatment of prestigious collections which boast a rich literary history, thus furnishing a precious, rich access to which the function of digital conservation can be associated". And " metadata are necessary for the management of transactions which require the precise identification of the users of the objects treated, of the use that is to be made of them".

The initiatives of the digital library cannot ignore this function; they must define the parties involved and their role, the object of the transactions, the action to be carried out on the requested objects (*e.g.* read, listen, see, save, transfer), the parameters which limit it (in terms of place, time, amount, repeatability, hence the number of times in which the action may be repeated), and also the action of whoever uses the service in exchange for acquired rights".

For conservation: "Regardless of the technique used to guarantee conservation and the future use of the digital resources, it is necessary to document clearly how to put these functions into practice and hence to define the features of the format of the software and of the instruments in order to use a certain resource over time".

"Besides the previously-expressed recommendations relative to the features of the metadata for the functions of identification and access, management of rights and conservation of the digital resources, some proposals are put forwards which cover on the one hand the activity of support to the description and management of the digital resources, on the other the actions of coordination which are necessary at an institutional and interinstitutional level, on both a national and an international scale".

Legal Problems (Copyright) in Italy

In this as in other cases, uncertainty prevails as to the behaviour to be adopted in the face of laws which are still mainly orientated towards traditional documentation. "The reference norms for copyright in a digital environment derive from the interpretation of the existing norms, from analogical application and from the appeal to the general principles of the law. In general there is even a lack of a consolidated jurisprudential doctrine and practice.

In view of the particular nature of the new technologies and the many different possibilities that they offer in comparison with traditional supports (paper, videocassettes, photographs etc.), the recourse to analogy and to interpretation of the existing norms is sometimes difficult.

Thus for a more complete protection, contractual solutions are often used to clarify the conditions of use of digital material, either through contracts (or licenses) or through regulations of access (or general conditions)."

Regarding services:

"In offering services to the users of a databank we must necessarily follow the legislation established for that type of support or negotiate with copyright-holders. If we wish to offer certain paid services on material which is still protected by copyright, we must necessarily negotiate the procedure to be adopted with the author, since he/she has all rights over the work".

Concerning the protection of the rights of a database: "In this case we can establish services, conditions of access to the database, limitations of liability, guarantees, applicable legislation and so on.

The contractual solution has undoubted advantages since the creator of the database defines his own liabilities and the conditions of access within a legislative picture which is not always clear and complete".

Even in the case of copyright we are faced with a situation which is continuously changing. "the legislation on this matter is still evolving, and there is very little jurisprudential doctrine and practice; despite this some guidelines can be already identified in current legislation or in analogical application. There are numerous problems regarding the possibility of offering paid services, in that obligations deriving from legislation on copyright, as well as some regulations about electronic trading, would emerge.

While the offering of "traditional" non-profit-making services on material not protected by copyright (public property) in any case seems to be easier, even if a clear legal framework is lacking ". In this as in other cases, the need for constant observation of the evolution of the law remains open.

There is a similarly strong need to acquire the necessary skills in the case of negotiation for the acquisition of original digital resources. This is possible both by means of an internal process (special training as required), and thanks to the activation of external references (outsourcing) which are specifically dedicated to negotiation.

Examination of the Existing Situation

One of the fundamental elements in the setting-up of Digital Library in the world (but also in Italy for few but significant examples) is cooperation in terms of sharing of experience, knowledge and programmes. This assumption can clearly be drawn from the observation of what has actually happened and is in progress, above all outside our country.

A significant part of the study is that dedicated to an inventory of what has been created in Italy and abroad from all the previously-mentioned points of view. It is from this survey that the most significant part of the proposals arise; they are outlined concretely in the second section of the study.

PROBLEMS USING DIGITAL LIBRARIES

The digital libraries outlined in the previous section all differ in their coverage, access, and features, but the abstract process of using them is more standard.

Figure shows an abstract workflow for using any given digital library.

We do not propose this as a universal model, which every user will follow, but provide it to illustrate some of the problems with managing data and metadata in the libraries described in the previous section on digital libraries.

Tasks represented by white nodes are normally performed exclusively by humans, while tasks shown in blue nodes can be performed wholly or partly by machines of some kind.

The main problematic tasks that make digital libraries difficult to use for both machines and humans are "GET" (publication) and "GET METADATA". These are shown in bold and discussed further in the Identity Crisis section of this paper.

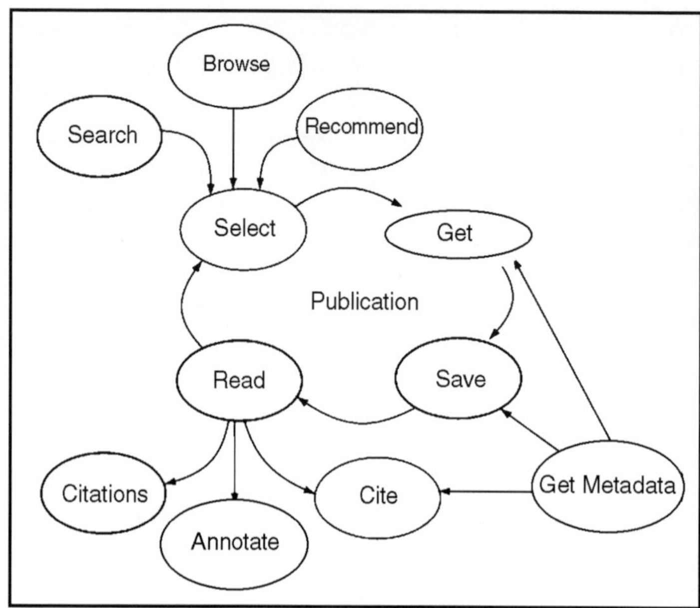

Fig. A Typical Workflow for Using a Digital Library Representing a Subset of the Literature.

To begin with, a user selects a paper, which will have come proximately from one of four sources:

- Searching some digital library, "SEARCH" in Figure;
- Browsing some digital library ("BROWSE");
- A personal recommendation, word-of-mouth from colleague, etc., ("RECOMMEND");
- Referred to by reading another paper, and thus cited in its reference list ("READ").

Once a paper of interest is selected, the user:

- Retrieves the abstract and then the paper (i.e., the actual paper itself as a file), "GET" in Figure)
- They save the paper, for example by bookmarking it, storing on a hard-drive, printing off, etc., ("SAVE"). Saving often involves getting the metadata, too, ("GET METADATA"). By metadata, we again mean the basic metadata about a publication, such as the author, date, journal, volume, page number, publisher, etc. In practice, this means any information typically found in an EndNote or BibTeX entry;
- They read the paper, "READ" in Figure;
- They may annotate the paper, ("ANNOTATE");
- Finally, they may cite the paper ("CITE"). Citing requires retrieving the metadata, if these have not been retrieved already.

This abstract workflow is idealized, but highlights some problems with using current digital libraries, for both humans and machines.

- *Identity Crisis*: There is no universal method to retrieve a given paper, because there is no single way of identifying publications across all digital libraries on the Web. Although various identification schemes such as the PubMed identifier (PMID), Digital Object Identifier (DOI), ISBN, and many others, exist, there is not yet one identity system to "rule them all."
- *Get Metadata*: Publication metadata often gets "divorced" from the data it is about, and this forces users to manage each independently, a cumbersome and error-prone process. Most PDF files, for example, do not contain embedded metadata that can be easily extracted. Likewise, for publications on the Web there is no universal method to retrieve metadata. For any given publication, it is not possible for a machine or human to retrieve metadata using a standard method. Instead there are many inadequate options to choose from, which add unnecessary complexity to obtaining accurate metadata.
- *Which metadata*? There is no single way of representing metadata, and without adherence to common standards (which largely already exist, but in a plurality) there never will be. EndNote (RIS) and BibTeX are common, but again, neither format is used universally across all libraries.

We describe each of these issues more fully in the following sections.

Identity Crisis

We are suffering from an acute identity crisis in the life sciences. Just as sequence databases have trouble managing the multiple identities of sequences, digital libraries also suffer from being unable to identify individual publications and their authors.

These are essential pieces of information that make libraries easy to use, and also help to track citations, but in the present implementation they create considerable barriers to users and machines. Any single publication or author is identified by numerous different URIs.

An important task for managing these disparate collections involves reconciling and normalizing these different identity schemes, that is, calculating if two different URIs identify the same resource or not.

For example, a human can fairly easily determine that each of these URIs identify the same publication, but writing a generic programme to automate this for arbitrary URIs is more challenging: http://nar.oxfordjournals.org/cgi/conten t/full/36/suppl_1/D13; http://www.ncbi.nlm.nih.gov/pubmed/18045 790; http://www.pubmedcentral.nih.gov/article render.fcgiartid1781113; and http://dx.doi.org/10.1093/nar/gkm1000.

Where DOIs exist, they are supposed to be the definitive URI. This kind of automated disambiguation, of publications and authors, is a common requirement for building better digital libraries. Unlike the traditional paper library, machines play a much more important role in managing information. They come in many forms, typically search-engine bots and spiders such as Googlebot, but also screen-scrapers, feed-readers workflows programs, Web services,, and ad hoc scripts, as well as semantic Web agents and reasoners. They are obviously of great importance for text-mining, –, where computer algorithms plus immense computing power can outperform human intelligence on at least some tasks.

Publication metadata are essential for machines and humans in many tasks, not just the disambiguation described above. Despite their importance, metadata can be frustratingly difficult to obtain.

Metadata: You can't Always GET What you Want.

As well as the problem of extracting metadata from PDFs, getting metadata for any given URI which identifies a publication is also problematic. Although the semantic Web has been proposed as a general solution to this –, it is currently a largely unrealised vision of the future.

The Open Archives Initiative mentioned previously provides a solution to this problem, though it is not adopted by all publishers.

So, given an arbitrary URI, there are only two guaranteed options for getting any metadata associated with it. Using http, it is possible to for a human (or machine) to do the following.

- *Http GET the URI*: Getting any URIs described in the previous section Digital Libraries, URIs, and DOIs will usually return the entire HTML representation of the resource. This then has to be scraped or parsed for metadata, which could appear anywhere in the file and in any format. This technique works, but is not particularly robust or scalable because every time the style of a particular Web site changes, the screen-scraper will probably break as well. Some Web sites such as PubMed Central make this easier, by clearly identifying metadata in files, so they can easily be parsed by tools and machines.
- *Http HEAD the URI:* This returns metadata only, not the whole resource. These metadata will not include the author, journal, title, date, etc., of the publication but basic information such as the MIME type which indicates what the resource is (text, image, video, etc.), Last-Modified date, and so on.

The lack of an adequate method for retrieving metadata has led to proposals such as the Life Sciences Identifier (LSID), and BioGUID (Biological Globally Unique IDentifier).These may be useful in the future if they become more widely adopted, but do not change the current state of the digital library.

As it stands, it is not possible to perform mundane and seemingly simple tasks such as, "get me all publications that fulfill some criteria and for which I have licensed access as PDF" to save locally, or "get me a specific publication and all those it immediately references".

Metadata for Publications

Even if there were a standard way to retrieve metadata for publications, there is still the problem of how to represent and describe them. In addition to EndNote (RIS) and BibTeX, there are also various XML schemas such as the U.S. Library of Congress Metadata Object Description Schema (MODS) format and RDF vocabularies, such as the Dublin Core mentioned earlier.

Having all these different metadata standards would not be a problem if they could easily be converted to and from each other, a process known as "round-tripping". However, some conversions gain or lose information along the way. Lossy and irreversible conversions create dead-ends for metadata, and many of these mappings are non-trivial, *e.g.*, XML to RDF and back again.

In addition to basic metadata found in EndNote and BibTeX, there are also more complex metadata such as the inbound and outbound citations, related articles, and "supplementary" information.

The identity crisis, inability to get metadata easily, and proliferation of metadata standards are three of the main reasons that libraries are particularly difficult to use and search as automatically as one would wish. These are challenging problems to overcome, and the tools we describe in the next section tackle these problems in different ways.

Some Tools for Defrosting Libraries

Although libraries can be cold, the tools described in this section could potentially make them much warmer. They do this in two main ways. Personalization allows users to say this is my library, the sources I am interested in, my collection of references, as well as literature I have authored or co-authored.

Socialization allows users to share their personal collections and see who else is reading the same publications, including added information such as related papers with the same keyword (or "tag") and what notes other people have written about a given publication. The ability to share data and metadata in this way is becoming increasingly important as more and more science is done by larger and more distributed teams rather than by individuals.

Such social bookmarking is already available on the Web site of publications such as the Proceedings of the National Academy of Sciences (http://www.pnas.org) and the journals published by Oxford University Press.The result of personalization and socialization is integration of a kind that cannot be achieved by machines alone. First, we look at personalization-only style tools, then we examine tools that also allow socialization of the library through sharing.

Zotero.org and Mendeley

Zotero is an extension for the Firefox browser that enables users to manage references directly from the Web browser. As with most Web-based tools,

Zotero can recognise and extract data and metadata from a range of different digital libraries. Users can bookmark publications, and then add their own personal tags and notes. Currently, Zotero does not allow users to share their tags in the same way that more "sociable" tools such as CiteULike and Connotea do, although enhancements to the current 1.0 version of Zotero may include this feature. Zotero bookmarks cannot be identified using URIs, so it is not possible to link in from external sources to these personal collections.

Mendeley is a similar application that helps to manage and share research papers, although as well as having a Web-based browser version it is possible to store bibliographies using a more powerful desktop-based client that automatically extracts metadata from PDF files, but it can only do this where metadata is available in an amenable format.

MyNCBI

MyNCBI allows users to save PubMed searches and to customise search results. It also features an option to update and e-mail search results automatically from saved searches. MyNCBI includes extra features for highlighting search terms, filtering search results, and setting LinkOut, document delivery, and external tool preferences.

Like Zotero, MyNCBI currently allows personalization only, with no socialization features. It is also limited to publications in PubMed. As we have previously seen, computational biologists frequently require access to many publications outside PubMed, so they cannot capture their entire library in MyNCBI alone. Like Zotero, it is currently not possible to link to personal collections created in MyNCBI.

Mekentosj Papers

Papers, is an application for managing electronic publications, originally designed by Alexander Griekspoor and Tom Groothuis. Although it is not a typical browser-based Web application, it can be closely integrated with several services on the Web-like Google Scholar, PubMed, ISI Web of Knowledge, and Scopus mentioned in the Digital Libraries section of this paper. The Papers application demonstrates how large collections of PDF files can be managed more easily. Papers provides a simple and intuitive interface shown in Figure to a collection of PDF files stored on a personal hard drive.

It looks and behaves much like Apple's iTunes, an application for managing music files, because the user does not have to know where the data (PDF file) is stored on their hard drive. Unfortunately, Papers is only available for Apple Macintosh users, and there is no version for Windows, which limits its uptake by scientists.

It looks and feels much like the popular iTunes application, allowing users to manage their digital libraries by categories shown at the top. It is presently available only under Mac OS/X.

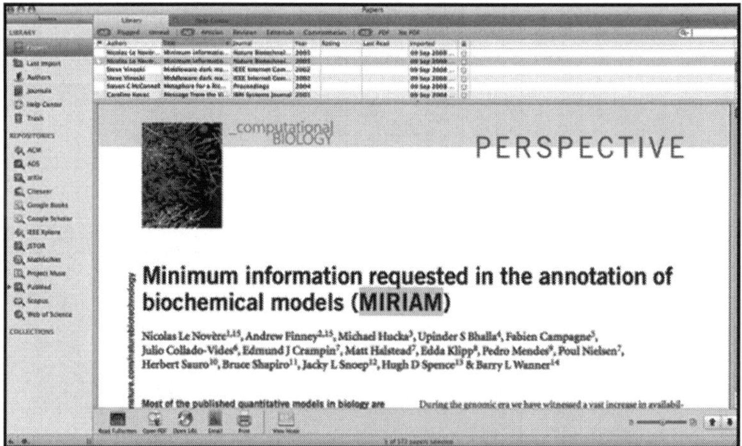

Fig. Mekentosj Papers can Organize Large Collections of Locally Stored PDF files, with their Metadata.

The personalization of libraries is nothing especially new or groundbreaking, and scientists have been creating personal libraries for years, for example by having their own EndNote library or BibTeX file. Tools such as Zotero, MyNCBI, and Papers just make the process of personalization simpler.

However, socialization of digital libraries *is* relatively new, in particular the ability of *multiple* users to associate arbitrary tags with URIs that represent scientific publications. This is what CiteULike, Connotea, and HubMed all allow, thereby capturing some of the supposed "wisdom of crowds" in classifying information.

CiteULike.org

CiteULike is a free online service to organize academic publications, now run by Oversity. It has been on the Web since October 2004 when its originator was attached to the University of Manchester, and was the first Web-based social bookmarking tool designed specifically for the needs of scientists and scholars.

In the style of other popular social bookmarking sites such as delicious.com it allows users to bookmark or "tag" URIs with personal metadata using a Web browser; these bookmarks can then be shared using simple links such as those shown below.

The number of articles bookmarked in CiteULike is approaching 2 million, indicated by the roughly incremental numbering used. While the CiteULike software is not open source, part of the dataset it collects is currently in the public domain. Publication URIs are simple: http://www.citeulike.org/article/1708098.

CiteULike normalizes bookmarks before adding them to its database, which means it calculates whether each URI bookmarked identifies an identical publication added by another user, with an equivalent URI. This is important for social tagging applications, because part of their value is the ability to see how many people (and who) have bookmarked a given publication. CiteULike also captures another important bibliometric, viz how many users have potentially *read* a publication, not just cited it. It seems likely that the number of readers considerably exceeds the number of citers and this can be valuable information. Time lags matter, too.

This is particularly the case with Open Access, where the "most-accessed" *Journal of Biology* paper of 2007 had in June 2008 been accessed in excess of 12,000 times, but has been cited just nine times (note that early access statistics can provide good predictors for later citations).

CiteULike provides metadata for all publications in RIS (EndNote) and BibTeX, providing a solution to the "Get Metadata" problem described in the previous section Metadata: You Can't Always GET What You Want, because every CiteULike URI for a publication has metadata associated with it in exactly the same way.

Connotea.org

Connotea is run by Nature Publishing Group and provides a similar set of features to CiteULike with some differences. It has been available on the Web since November 2004. Connotea uses MD5 hashes to store URIs that users bookmark, and normalizes them after adding them to its database, rather than before.

This post-normalization means Connotea does not always currently recognize when different URIs (such as the examples in the section Identity Crisis) identify the same publication, a bug known as "buggotea", which also affects CiteULike to a lesser extent. Like CiteULike, URIs in Connotea are simple.

A publication about Connotea, for example, is identified by the URI http:/ /www.connotea.org/uri/685b90ae66cf bc3fc8ebeed0a5def571. Metadata are available from Connotea in a wider variety of formats than from CiteULike, including RIS, BibTeX, MODS, Word 2007 bibliography, and RDF, but these have to be downloaded in bulk only, rather than individually per publication URI.

The source code for Connotea is available, and there is an API that allows software engineers to build extra functionality around Connnotea, for example the Entity Describer.

HubMed.org

HubMed is a "rewired" version of PubMed, and provides an alternative interface with extra features, such as standard metadata and Web feeds which can be subscribed to using a feed reader. This allows users to subscribe to a particular journal and receive updates when new content (*e.g.*, a new issue) becomes available.

An example URI for a publication on HubMed is http://www.hubmed.org/display.cgiuids168 45111. Like CiteULike, HubMed also solves the "Get Metadata" problem because metadata are available from each HubMed URI in a wide variety of formats not offered by NCBI. This is one of HubMed's most useful features. At the time of writing, HubMed provides metadata in RIS (for EndNote), BibTeX, RDF, and MODS style XML. Users can also log in to HubMed to use various personalized features such as tagging.

Advantages of using CiteULike and Connotea

Both CiteULike and Connotea require users to invest time and effort learning how to use them, and importing or entering bibliographic information. Why should they bother? Managing bibliographic metadata using these tools has several advantages over the common scenario of storing un-indexed PDF files locally on a personal computer.Both CiteULike and Connotea provide a single place (a Web server) where data (PDFs) and metadata can both be shared and more tightly coupled; this has the following benefits.

Searching

Easier and more sophisticated searching is possible. Conversely, given a collection of PDFs on a hard drive, it is typically difficult (or impossible) to make simple queries such as "retrieve all papers by [a given author]".

Managing

When authoring manuscripts, managing references in a Web-based repository can save some of the pain of re-typing metadata (*e.g.*, author names) for a given publication. Provided the publication has a URI that is recognized by these tools, metadata are automatically harvested on behalf of the user, saving them time.

Tagging

Tags are just keywords, but these allow both persona-lisation and socialisation of bibliographic data, see for papers cited in this Review as an example. Tagging of papers by other users allows non-expert users to explore related papers in ways that may not be possible through traditional reference lists, since exploring a subject of research in which you are not expert is made easier by following links added by other potentially more expert users.

Server-based

Hosting a bibliography on a Web server means that, if and when the user moves computer, the library is still accessible. However, keeping local and remote versions requires appropriate synchronisation, which can be problematic.

Serendipity

Many serendipitous discoveries or intellectual linkages that may be determined via co-occurrences (*e.g.*, –) exist in science, and these can be assisted by browsing links provided via social tagging.

Future Tools

The tools described here are the first wave of Web 2.0, Library 2.0, or even Science 2.0 style tools that are helping to defrost the digital library. There will certainly be plenty more in the future; for example, the Research Information Centre from the British Library is investgating innovative new tools in this area, backed by Microsoft.Some are calling it "Web 3.0", but, whatever the name, it seems likely that we will see many digital library applications that will exploit the novel social features of platforms such as Facebook, and OpenSocial. Here they can exploit the identity mechanisms already built into those systems.

Personalization and socialization of information will increasingly blur the distinction between databases and journals, and this is especially true in computational biology where contributions are particularly of a digital nature. Scientific contributions to digital knowledge on the Web often do not fit into traditional scientific publishing models. This is usually because they are either too "small" or too "big" to fit into journals. Web logs or "blogs" are beginning to fill the "too small" gap and can be used for communicating preliminary results, discussion, opinion, supplementary material, and short technical reports – in the style of a traditional laboratory notebook. Biological databases, such as those listed in the annual NAR database review, have long filled the "too big" gap in scientific publishing.

They are clearly more significant than their publications alone. As we move in biology from a focus on hypothesis-driven to data-driven science, it is increasingly recognized that databases, software models, and instrumentation are the scientific output, rather than the conventional and more discursive descriptions of experiments and their results.In the digital library, these size differences are becoming increasingly meaningless as data, information, and knowledge become more integrated, socialized, personalized, and accessible. Take Postgenomic, for example, which aggregates scientific blog posts from a wide variety of sources. These posts can contain commentary on peer-reviewed literature and links into primary database sources. Ultimately, this means that the boundaries between the different types of information and knowledge are continually blurring, and future tools seem likely to continue this trend.

FUNDAMENTAL DOCUMENT ACTIVITY IN DIGITAL LIBRARIES

READING AND DIGITAL LIBRARIES

The first and most fundamental document activity is reading. "Reading" encompasses a broad range of complex and poorly understood practices involving documents, including skimming, searching, browsing, speed-reading, surfing, reviewing, and rereading. Although we often take it for granted, reading can be hard work. We use the term *active reading* to distinguish this rich collection of activities from simply looking at words on a page.

Desktop computers do not support active reading. Once expected to create a paperless office, computers have instead produced ever-increasing quantities of paper documents. Dataquest predicts printers and copiers will generate over 1012 pages in the U.S. in 1997. This statistic suggests that people do not use computers to read. The reason for this is obvious: paper supports extended, focused, deep reading practices better. Current research on digital libraries does not address a broad range of reading activities. Instead, as David Levy points out, digital libraries support shallower, more fragmented, and less concentrated reading.

The research focus in this field is on tools for search, selection, and distillation, tools that promote identification and extraction of information fragments. Because digital library interfaces do not support active reading, people search online and then print documents to read them. This "search and print" reality contrasts with the "search and read" ideal held by researchers.

Although a dual online/paper system is not *a priori* undesirable, we will show the many advantages of an online system that enables a variety of reading practices. The XLibris active reading machine supports a broad class of reading activities by employing a "paper document metaphor" (as opposed to the desktop metaphor) that imitates the physical experience of reading and marking on paper. The paper document metaphor follows lessons learned from a number of studies comparing reading online to reading on paper, summarized below.

TANGIBILITY

Readers often move paper documents to avoid glare, to speed up handwriting, or to adjust their perspective of a text. In contrast, most computer displays are stationary while in use, so that readers must move themselves— their heads, their bodies, and their arms— rather than their display. XLibris supports paper document-like tangibility by running on tablet displays. Although XLibris has not been deployed for real use, people say that holding a page-sized display in their lap and being able to easily reposition it changes their online reading experience. The tangibility of paper documents also supports navigation. Turning paper pages seems easy and natural, and the weight and thickness of a paper document convey length and location.

In XLibris, pressure strips on the case of the device provide a tangible interface for page turning: pressing on one side of a sensor moves to the next or previous page, and holding down initiates riffling through pages. The harder you press, the faster you move. A quick animated transition indicates the direction of turning. Finally, "location guides" of varying thickness drawn in the top cor- ners of each page provide feedback about the length of the document and the reader's current location.

Multiple Displays

People often work with multiple pieces of paper simultaneously, either with several pages from one document or with several documents. Most of today's computers provide multiple virtual displays through use of a windowing system. Unfortunately, the effort of managing window layout and switching among windows can interfere with reading.

Therefore XLibris displays a single page image and does not support windows. Since limiting the digital library information appliance to a single page image is problematic, we have considered a number of ways to address the need for collateral displays.

Presenting two full-page images side by side, as in Book Emulator, makes text unreadable on current tablet displays, but may be feasible as LCD technology evolves. A form factor with multiple physical displays is another approach.

(Bush's vision of a Memex desk included multiple displays). In our case, to maintain mobility, a book (instead of a tablet or desk) with two opposable LCD panels may be appropriate. Weiser presents an enticing vision of ubiquitous computing with devices so cheap they can be scattered and used as paper.In the near term, however, a small number of pen computers in conjunction with nearby desktop displays or even paper may provide the most practical solution to the problem of collateral document work. In summary, XLibris employs tangibility, page orientation, and fixed layout to provide an online reading experience comparable, in many ways, to reading from paper.

Page Orientation and Fixed Layout

Paper documents are laid out on fixed-size pages. The page layout often communicates the type of the document (*e.g.*, business letter versus technical article) and where to find important information (*e.g.*, a return address). The fixed layout also supports spatial memory and helps readers find old information.

In these and other ways, paper pages give readers an excellent "sense of the document." This sense of the document is often lost online.Most CRT monitors cannot display a full page of text legibly, leading to awkward scrolling and zooming. Word processors and Web browsers commonly re-flow the text on a "page." And hypertext versions of paper documents can lead to disorientation and a sense of being lost. XLibris respects pages by displaying the image of a single page at a time.Because the LCD panels we use are designed for landscape viewing, XLibris rotates the image 90° to approximate the portrait orientation of a typical printed page. XLibris stores the image of each page and the underlying text; this "image + text" file format is compatible with printed and with scanned documents.

FREE FORM INK ANNOTATION

"Until we provide support for smooth integration of annotation with reading, it is likely that people will continue to annotate paper materials, even as they read materials in a digital library." – Cathy Marshall The second key document activity is annotation. Knowledge work involves reading combined with categorizing, speculating, remembering, judging, or, more broadly, critical thinking.

This active reading process is facilitated by underlining, highlighting and making notes on the text or in a separate notebook. Marking on paper helps readers "make the text their own" and is a common practice associated with deep understanding of written information. In a nutshell, readers write. Unfortunately, annotation online is quite different from its paper-based cousin. Interfaces for annotating often involve selecting a command, pointing with a mouse, and typing on a keyboard. They generally require much more effort than scribbling with a pen.

Text annotations are not as visually distinct as ink marks, and online annotations often cause changes in the layout of the document. We believe that the ability to make unstructured, free-form, idiosyncratic ink marks is a crucial feature of any interface to digital libraries.

Although such marks may not have explicit meaning to the computer, they have rich semantic meaning, supporting visual and episodic memory. An essential aspect of ink on paper is its lack of modality: users can write anything they want, anywhere on the page. In XLibris, we followed this principle by letting users scribble notes, draw figures, highlight, or annotate text, all without switching modes or applications. Readers highlight and mark-up document page images as they read or flip to a blank page in a lined notebook for more space. XLibris provides several colors of ink, several highlighter pens, and a stroke-based eraser.

FIELDS REVEAL SEVERAL INTERESTING TRENDS

Recent events in these two fields reveal several interesting trends, not only in strategic planning but also in the underlying thinking of leading commentators. Although there is considerable ferment and thus many trends underway, there are four areas where publishers and digital librarians face similar challenges. The strategic decisions that each group makes in the coming years will have significant impact on their long-term futures. First, the hurdles to publishing a well-packaged text artifact are dropping rapidly. The result has been that authors, both in the academic and popular literature spheres, now have the option of creating their own digital artifacts without publishers' assistance.

Many already manage online presences and engage in dialogue with readers. In response publishers and digital librarians are testing strategies that reinforce their own roles. Second, the disruptive nature of digital media has forced publishers and digital librarians to evaluate their own native skill sets in a new light. The library profession's core competencies - collection development, information counselling, interpretation and preservation - involve in-depth analysis of information resources. Yet librarians already format, revise, copy-edit and even print bibliographies, scholarly e-journals, festschrift, and full-scale books in many cases.

As these content-intensive roles become more important, research libraries have responded by creating senior management positions with titles such as director of digital scholarly publishing, director of digital publishing, or director of built content. These positions carry responsibility for assessing new opportunities to publish, as well as assisting research faculty in doing so themselves. Publishers also have the opportunity to review what they do well, re-evaluating existing functions to include new services such content aggregation, developing much-enlarged Web presences, taking on custodial roles and offering services for long-term preservation of their own built content. The technological hurdles to adding new services of this nature are just as low for publishers as they are for librarians who are involved in digital publishing. Both groups are limited chiefly by imagination, by perceived commitments to doing "business as usual," and by the high cost of retraining their already-well-trained workforces to take on new tasks in addition to their existing workflows.

Third, both publishers and digital librarians are looking beyond the boundaries of their own fields of expertise for new ideas and strategies. For example, new social media have carried a heavy impact on the news industry, and both librarians and publishers have studied newspapers as a cautionary tale. News media were one of the first zones where readers began "talking back" to the press and contributing substantive new content. The Blogosphere has also attracted interest, although it increasingly produces voluminous and cyclical "blooms" of creative work that are followed by inactivity and the formation of "dead zones." This pattern suggests that new media are only as vibrant as the minds that are driving them forward. However, over time the Blogosphere has become firmly established as an effective platform for commentary, news, cultural critique and debate.

The Blogosphere's experience implies that longer-term value takes time to emerge as a new technology matures. Fourth, both groups have come to realise that as digital convergence has accelerated, bold action is required. As a consequence, the pace of intellectual thought that is devoted to innovation has also accelerated. There is also greater acceptance that bold actions may succeed or fail, yet they must be attempted to gain new knowledge and expertise. Both groups show evidence of complex responses to the necessity of taking bold action, because both groups believe that they must protect legacy print programmes, whether as book sales or print collections, even as they step into new digital futures. This is a difficult balancing act, because reader and user community loyalty may be challenged as risks are taken. These four trends illustrate the turmoil, and indeed, the excitement of the times for both publishers and librarians. They also illustrate how each group is operating on the knowledge creation continuum, and how they might choose convergent or divergent strategies when compared to each other.

Divergent Strategies

There is a large common ground of shared strategies among publishers and digital librarians, derived primarily from the interactive nature of social media, and how it may be adapted for research or to enhance popular literature. However, the points of divergence between the two groups are pronounced. Divergent strategies flow directly from the history of each group. Digital librarians are working very hard to preserve and advance the role of managed knowledge resources, branded by the library, as part of the teaching process. In addition to experimentation with e-reserves and e-readers, they are now staking a large claim on the full-service teaching Web "portals." Open-source instructional portals now include a variety of added functions, including the ability at attach related files, images and simulations.

They also operate as eportfolios for students that follow them throughout their academic careers, and as information management tools for the faculty. Academic librarians perceive important new roles for information services in these learning spaces. Academic librarians are also brainstorming about ways to enhance "built" content that is created by the faculty—a key zone of knowledge creation where libraries may assume the role of digital publishers. The opportunities are vast, as pre-publication content creation encompasses the supporting information, texts and data sets that lead to finished work. Strategies to preserve this knowledge base are rapidly taking shape, and they are evidence of innovative thinking about librarian core competencies. What is more, the library profession's original core competencies—particularly collection development and classification—gain new relevance and importance as digital publishing moves to the forefront. Metadata schemes are vital tools for managing vast amounts of digital assets. The prevailing scheme, the Metadata Enhanced Technical Standard (METS), has seen heavy involvement by digital librarians; it ensures that metadata are portable and stay attached to a digital artifact, allowing the metadata and the object they describe to migrate over time. In contrast, publishers are in the early stages of harnessing XML to manage content more flexibly.

The most significant divergent characteristic between publishers and digital librarians has been librarians' willingness to enter into collaborative alliances, launching aggressive outreach to faculty authors, building political lobbying groups, and forming consortia that negotiate for better prices. They also have become software developers at their host universities, emphasising open-source computing. Ming-xing Huang envisions even more broad alliances, called

"Digital Library Alliances"—which would enable academic libraries and their partners to enhance digitisation initiatives and search capabilities in ways that mimic large commercial firms such as Google. Digital librarians have also sought explicit partnerships with publishers themselves, when a shared goal could be seen. For example, the California Digital Library (CDL) entered into an early agreement with the Berkeley Electronic Press (BePress)—a full service journal publishing solution. Conversely, publishers' efforts to form large-scale collaborations have taken more measured steps.

With respect to libraries, collaborative efforts most often take the shape of advisory committees, which meet with editors and publishers once or twice per year. This has been a useful process, contributing to several significant joint efforts, such as the Wiley Online Library. Wiley's new "learning space" includes extensive links to library services for training and other assistance in using the aggregation of content. Digital librarians could afford to choose a collaborative stance, because they have been able to draw on strong relationships with their user communities. Historically, library patrons would visit a library in person, creating opportunities for a direct, personal relationship with welltrained professional staff. Armed with very good metrics on what library patrons actually need and how they prefer to gain access to resources, digital librarians are exploring how to create "user experiences" that reinforce a bond between the library and the user. Just as important, the library profession conceptualised the digital library as a matrix of content, services and human interactions from the earliest planning process.

In essence they have argued that a digital library is far more than a content platform; it is an entire community. For example, facilitating and teaching how to use of information services, whether print or online, is a measurable core competency for librarians. They have argued that technology should enhance human connectivity, rather than replace it, and they have backed up this claim with solid e-metrics showing how people are using libraries.

This assertion of the digital library as community is not nearly as evident in the professional literature of publishing. However, publishers are beginning to reach similar realisations about digital media, and are examining different approaches. As online publishing creates new synergies between print and electronic artifacts, the book gains a broader venue for discovery: the Web itself. Publishers continue to evaluate reader responses to books and related Web sites; and while print books will continue to exist, new zones are opening up for books to grow via Web sites, as e-books, and as subjects of reader forums. If indeed these trends follow their current course, the digital or Web version of a given book may eventually become the "master copy of record."

Convergent Strategies

There is a large common ground of shared strategies among publishers and digital librarians, core competencies must now include a robust and dynamic "conversation" with their readers, collaborators and user communities. Although this may seem obvious during the Internet era, it Nonetheless symbolises a major challenge for established players on the knowledge creation continuum.

New ideas and new technologies, commonly known as "Web 2.0", currently emphasize ubiquitous interaction in a wide variety of locations and via a long list of tools, ranging from desktop computers to "smartphones." Among publishers, this interactive paradigm and the tools it has spawned have caused a seismic shift in thinking.

A book's usefulness is no longer limited to the experience of reading it; it now has a lifespan that can take many forms, involve communities in addition to solo readers, and last for years. In response publishers have launched serious attempts to enter the Web 2.0 sphere. Likewise, digital librarians have seen their print-based mission expand exponentially to include not only the finished works of scholarship and literature, but also the artifacts created by the overall process of creating scholarship, from start to finish. Library responses also include innovative combinations of digital collections and community-building features, such as allowing commentary, running newsfeeds, and adding Wikis to facilitate dialogue. Publishers continue to focus on sales and profits, and they are experimenting with social media to increase revenue.

Two strategies dominate the landscape: narrowcasting and community-subscriber services. Narrowcasting refers to the strategy of discovering discrete markets or user communities who share strong interest in very specific literature, and then offering them targeted products that are based on market analysis. This approach is greatly assisted by "viral marketing," a common term in the Internet era, which describes how news of events or products can travel very quickly, even circumnavigating the globe in a matter of hours in some instances. Narrowcasting would be paired with general marketing strategies, just as print sales would be complemented by e-book sales, still a small revenue stream. Community-subscriber based strategies also make explicit publishers' new role as their own distribution outlets, joining bookstores, libraries and online firms such as Amazon in direct consumer outreach. Direct outreach is another example of treatment substitution, as it establishes a new zone of service on the knowledge creation continuum for publishers, shifting them further into the zone of distribution and perhaps even preservation.

Recent developments in textbook publishing provide evidence of innovative approaches by publishers and digital librarians, who are exploring classroom teaching aids. It is now possible to print textbooks or sections of them on demand, use e-readers to read them, or purchase printed readers, and the entire idea of how textbooks support teaching is rapidly evolving. Publishers are now perfecting "portal" style learning zones on the Web, which are based on textbooks but include many added features, including unbundled chapters, added teaching aids and accompanying training modules. Interestingly, 55 per cent of students still prefer to buy the textbook in print as part of their study plan. Meanwhile, digital librarians are also involved in teaching portals, and they have been perfecting e-reserve systems and new formats for class e-readers. Finally, publishers are beginning to show interest in managing their backlists more along the lines of a repository or collection of resources. However, whether publishers will take up archiving and preserving content remains uncertain. Once again, networked information technologies have lowered the hurdles to creating online archives. But in practical terms, taking on an archival role would require publishing staff to learn new skills, or recruit new talent to join the firm. Early evidence suggests that publishers have not fully embraced the link between the process of acquiring, editing and selling books and the long-term value of archiving the material. This further suggests that publishers continue to regard themselves as facilitators of the early stages of a book's lifespan, but not as the custodians of its entire lifespan.

DEVELOPMENT OF TOMORROW'S DIGITAL LIBRARY

The development of tomorrow's digital library information appliances is an iterative process. Our current cycle, however, is not complete until we evaluate the ideas presented in this paper. Towards this end, we have begun a series of laboratory user interface experiments and are in the planning stage for a real-world deployment. One experiment suggests that free-form ink marks made while reading are better for query formulation than traditional relevance feedback.

People who have tried XLibris agree that our approach of taking a work practice and augmenting it— rather than redefining it— makes the system immediately accessible. Information *appliances* must be accessible. The digital library community must decide whether digital libraries should, as we propose, support users throughout the process of turning information into knowledge. If so, there are many issues that must be addressed.

One reviewer of this paper asked: "Where is the digital library?" We purposely avoided describing protocols, services, and architectures because we believe infrastructure should *support* the vision of working with a digital library information appliance, not *define* it. The next step is to understand how users of digital library information appliances should interact with external repositories. For example, should users pay authors to cache documents on their devices, even when they do not read them? How should users search repositories that are not always accessible?

How should searches be distributed between local and remote databases? These and other issues require further investigation. We have shown how information appliances based on the paper document metaphor can support active reading. Because these systems allow people to work on digital documents much as they would on paper, this provides an alternative to the standard "search and print" model of digital libraries.

Furthermore, by integrating a wide variety of document activities, and by allowing fluid movement among them, disruptive transitions between paper and digital media can be eliminated. The combination of the paper-like and the digital allows us to augment these activities without redefining them. Finally, the mobility of a digital library information appliance supports work away from the desk. With all these benefits, digital library information appliances can create a rich, universally accessible, digital library experience that improves the way we work. Clearly there is an exciting future for digital library information appliances in the digital library.

DIGITAL LIBRARIANS: PRESERVING THE PAST, LOOKING FORWARD

Throughout the same eras of upheaval and change, librarians faced similarly daunting challenges. Researcher calls heralding the imminent demise of a proud profession crowded the professional literature of every specialised sector of librarianship for decades. In response, various innovators have explored a mulitiplicity of strategies. Nancy Lemon argues that rethinking traditional roles enables librarians to climb organisational "value chains;" Researchers review the plight of news media libraries and see a history of cyclical renewal, in which existing jobs give way to new opportunities in new locations. Among corporate libraries, a wide variety of bareknuckle strategies have been put forward, urging librarians to find a competitive edge by offering services that can be demonstrated to boost profits.

In the public libary sphere, despite straitened civic budgets and the shock of new media, libraries have achieved a degree of success in staying relevant. Circulation, library card membership and on-site use of services are at an all-time high, countering the idea that community libraries are outdated during the digital era. On the contrary, they are more popular than ever. Therefore even as pessimism about the future became a standard feature in the professional literature, a parallel stream of daring and innovative thinking has run concurrently among a wide spectrum of library specialists. The resulting intellectual ferment has produced new paradigms and new energy for rethinking library goals in light of the emergence of digital technology. Rather than wait to see what would happen, librarians repeatedly took initiative with new media. They staked an early claim on the crucial issue of intellectual property and copyright, working both with and against publishers as needed to preserve the library's public service mission. As part of this process, librarians became more deeply aware of the publishing industry's travails with digital media. This awareness led to greater strategic knowledge about the marketplace.

Spanning "Online" Eras

Librarians were shaken by the rapid emergence of Web-based information resources, because they had been important players in the previous "online" economy that was dominated by firms like LEXIS/NEXIS and Dialog Information Services. This first "online" era gave librarians the opportunity to cast themselves as experts who conducted mediated searches on behalf of users such as attorneys, scientists and business leaders. As the initial "online" era faded and the Internet exploded into growth, librarians joined the first wave of Internet e-mail "conversationalists", Web content users, Web site producers, and aggregators of high quality information.

They also grasped the importance of creating stable and robust Web portals, which organised and "branded" library-hosted aggregations of databases; such activist strategies stretched scarce budgets while formalising a Web-based library presence. Similarly, the economic upheaval caused by the skyrocketing price of scholarly journals generated energetic responses on the part of research libraries, including formation of the Scholarly Publishing and Academic Resources Coalition (SPARC), as well as active congressional lobbying to protect copyright and "fair use" principles from a runaway marketplace.

The same upheaval also sparked a sustained outreach to faculty, in search of much stronger partnerships with the academy's principle content creators. In general, digital librarians have been agents for innovation over the past 15 years, and have participated in the sweeping process of rethinking scholarly communications. This lengthy process of trial and error has transformed digital librarians' self-perception. Rather than viewing digital media as a force of dislocation that would bring ruin to the profession, digital librarians have instead embraced it. Likewise, constant downward pressure on budgets forced innovative survival plans to the forefront, emphasising new technologies.

From Online Repository to Publishing Platform

The turmoil of the Internet's early years also produced solid initiatives to understand the digital library as a publisher in its own right. Thomas provides an early and comprehensive road map that offers large research libraries a template for launching high quality publishing services. She also describes the early emergence of online repositories as a new form of curated information resources. Online repositories grew quickly throughout the early years of the twenty-first century, taking much inspiration from the digital archiving efforts of the computer science and engineering fields.Librarymanaged repositories also grew up with a strong bias for interoperability, which has led to more dialogue about the need for large-scale "federations" of digital libraries, even at the international level. As these repositories became more accepted, use skyrocted. The University of California's eScholarship repository experienced more than one million downloads in its first two years of operation. "Post prints" and research reports are now also collected in online repositories, and are frequently overseen by digital librarians, or at least coordinated by them.

In late 2009, eScholarship recast itself as a full-scale "publishing platform," which drew strength from the reputation of its source - the University of California system.

Although this is not the only example of a library-sponsored publishing service with university imprimatur, it is certainly one of the most high profile experiments. The evolution of library-based online repositories and their current transformation into fullscale publishing platforms is a prime example of how contributors can expand their role and move into new "zones of progressive release". Digital librarians' publishing solutions are guided by two objectives: first, to empower authors, and second, to create robust, collaborative blocs of institutions that share expertise and improve access. These are new "treatments" that address the changing needs of academic publishing. Publishers are rushing to reinvigorate their relationships with authors, but to some degree they are playing a game of catch-up.

Metadata as Enhanced Competency

Perhaps the most significant advance on the part of digital librarians has been the profession's embrace of structured metadata and taxonomy as a reinvigorated core competency. Even as they faced the twin challenges of integrating new technologies and shrinking budgets, digital librarians participated in the formation of international metadata standards such as the Dublin Core.

Libraries became key institutional members of new groups such as the Coalition for Networked Information and the National Digital Library Federation. Academic librarians experimented with diverse forms of preservation, including digital repositories, e-journals, and increasingly, full-scale publishing initiatives that originate within the library. Many metadata platforms and languages have been explored, but Extensible Markup Language (XML) has become a dominant tool for managing digital assets.

XML is a "meta-language of languages," enabling developers to create taxonomies and metadata schema that are customisable, portable and attached to the "digital objects" they describe. The emergence of national and international standards for metadata, the ascendance of digital objects which are transferrable among collections, and a strong focus on systems interoperability have elevated the library profession to a technical status considerably higher than it enjoyed before the advent of the digital era. Although digital librarians are not the only XML developers - many computing firms and other academics are heavily involved—they have left an imprint on the development stream of XML.

XML-based systems have become accepted across many industries beyond the academy, and now play a crucial role in information management and data warehousing by large corporate firms. XML-based information architectures are essential tools for managing text, images and other artifacts, creating new workflows that are based on the principle of "one text, multiple outputs".This kind of workflow would transfer very effectively to the publishing world, yet the publishing industry has been slower to adopt XML workflows at a universal level. The opportunity to manage digital assets using XML is an important leap forward that publishers have not yet fully embraced, and forward-looking commentators have recognised this shortfall.

INFORMATION ACCESS IN DIGITAL LIBRARIES

A digital library (DL) system comprises a large, distributed information space, where the objects carrying the knowledge required by the users, live. Setting up and maintaining a DL would be entirely useless if users were not provided with the adequate tools to access the DL information contents. In defining the information access service of a DL, there are at least 3 areas of the information system field which can give significant contributions:

- *Information retrieval* (IR) can contribute content-based methods, that is methods that exploit the signal level of an information object. For textual objects, these include all classical methods based on the statistical properties of language, such as the vector-space method and the probabilistic method. For non-textual objects, in the last decade there has been a fluorishing of methods for similarity-based retrieval of images, video and audio objects.
- The *database* area can contribute all methods for attribute-based information querying, ranging from traditional databases, to semi-structured databases; the methods falling under the last category are especially useful when ad- dressing the *structure* of objects.
- *Knowledge representation* can contribute methods for accessing objects by querying descriptions of their contents; these descriptions are typically couched in terms of representations of the underlying domain of discourse, or *ontologies* as these have come to be termed lately.

Putting the techniques found in the fields all together at work, requires a conceptual schema which integrates in a unique framework the different aspects of DL objects addressed by each of them. In what follows as suggested, try to sketch such a schema.

A CONCEPTUAL SCHEMA OF INFORMATION ACCESS

We characterise the space of information access by the following, orthogonal dimensions:

- The information access model, which establishes the basic terms of the system/user interaction;
- The information access mode, which establishes the role of the user and that of the system during their interaction.

INFORMATION ACCESS MODELS

Similarly to an information retrieval model, an information access model specifies:

- A representation of the objects to be accessed;
- A representation of the user information needs; and

- A function associating a set of objects to each user information need.

Information access models can be categorised according to the options available on each one of their dimensions. For object representation, following we distinguish between simple objects and composite objects. Simple objects cannot be further decomposed, and can be represented along the following dimensions:

- *Content abstractions*: these are representations used to access objects via IR techniques. They are created by IR indexers in an automatic way, by extracting low-level features from objects, such as the number of word occurrences in a text, or the energy level in a certain region of an image); content abstractions retain that part of the information originally present in the object content that is considered sufficient to characterise the object for access purposes;
- *Content representations*: these are symbolic representations of the meaning of documents, that is descriptions formulated in some suitable knowledge representation language, spelling out the truth conditions of the object. Content representations can be constructed manually, sometimes with the assistance of some knowledge extraction tool, or automatically, for instance via object classification methods. They can be precise or uncertain, depending on whether or not the content representation formulas are expressed in an un- certain logic, such as fuzzy or probabilistic logic.

Composite objects are structured set of simple objects, thus they are typically represented as mathematical *structures*, reflecting their internal organisation. Finally, objects, whether simple or composite, can have a *profile*, that is an attribute-based description of their external properties, such as the author and the publisher of a book, or the data and time at which an image has been taken, and the like.

In the context of digital libraries, the 4 dimensions of object representation reduce to 3 only, since content representations and profiles are typically grouped together under the label of discovery metadata. The metadata associated to a DL object can therefore vary from simple records typically adhering to some standardised schema to very complex representations expressed in some knowledge representation language which must be coupled with a representation of the underlying domain of discourse, in order to be properly used for, *e.g.* information access. In summary, as suggested, therefore consider object representation as being categorised as:

- Content,
- Metadata, and
- Structure.

For information need representation, we have 2 options: formal language queries or natural language queries. For the retrieval function, we have 2 options: exact match or best match. Not all combinations of these options give rise to meaningful information access models. Considering the object representation options we have the following:

- Content is typically addressed via IR techniques, based on natural language queries and best-match retrieval function. For instance, users access the con- tent of an image base by providing as a query an image itself In so doing, users are implicitly asking the system to retrieve images which 'looks' similar to the image query, at least as far as the system can tell. For this reason, methods providing access by content are often called '*similarity-based*' access methods. An analogous pattern is found in access models for textual or for audio content. Notice that in some models of this kind, the query may not be expressed in the same medium as the sought objects. For instance, when accessing by content a video database, users may provide an image as a query, and the system is expected to retrieve the scenes sharing visual similarity with the provided image. Similarity-based access models are medium-dependent, in that different media require different techniques, and the possibility of using the same or a similar technique across different media is very limited. In addition, experience has shown that even within the same medium, the effectiveness of techniques is application-dependent: for example, retrieving by similarity sport images requires different techniques from those necessary to establish the similarity of X-ray images.
- Metadata is typically addressed via formal language queries, thus we are in the realm of databases or knowledge representation, depending from the degree of sophisticatedness of the involved representations. For instance, to query a Dublin Core scheme, one needs a very simple language allowing to state basic relational conditions on simple numeric- or string-based attribute values; instead, to query an OWL representation the ability to state conditions involving taxonomies and navigation of graph structures is required. In general, a query to metadata takes the form of a logical formula, and an exact match retrieval function is employed for query evaluation, grounded in some logical theory. We call these models *semantic* access models. Some retrieval engines allow to exploit information retrieval techniques when accessing objects via their metadata records. This is achieved by seeing metadata records as pieces of text whose words are the attribute values. Such a text is treated in the same way as textual content, and matched against a natural language query as in a similarity-based textual access method. This kind of access model is widely employed on bibliographic records, as it frees users from the necessity of knowing the meaning of meta- data attributes.
- Also object structure can be queried in two different ways:
- Via exact match retrieval functions, such as the one underlying the

query language XPath. In this case, the structural query is mostly embedded into a larger query addressing either content or metadata. We do not have therefore separate classes of access models but sophistications of similarity-based or semantic access models allowing also the specification of structural clauses in queries.

- Via best match retrieval functions, which express in a quantitative way the degree of similarity between the structure of each object and a user provided structure class. These models have been investigated in the con- text of XML, and are a structural variation of similarity-based models. We call the models falling in this class 'similar structure-based access models'.

In summary, we have the following information access model categories:

- Similarity-based access models, possibly with structural conditions;
- Semantic access models, possibly with structural conditions; and
- Similar structure-based access models.

INFORMATION ACCESS MODES

Independently from the access model, the information access modes establishes the role of the system and that of the user. Each of these two can be either passive or active. Excluding the case in which they are both passive, we have the following 3 types of information access systems:

- *Query-answering systems*: in this case the user is active, that is, poses a query, while the system is passive, that is it just evaluates the user query and returns the result.
- *Filtering systems*: In which the user is passive, that is, does not pose any query, and the system is active, that is it selects on a stream of incoming objects, those that are deemed as relevant for the user; the relevance assessment is performed by relying on a user profile.
- *Personalised query-answering systems*: in which the user is active, that is, poses a query, and the system is active too, in that it alters the query evaluation process by taking into account the user preferences, represented as a profile. Recommendation systems also fall into this category, since they propose recommendations along with the answer to the query.

DISTRIBUTED SEARCH ACROSS IN DIGITAL LIBRARIES

The peer-to-peer (P2P) approach allows handling huge amounts of data of digital libraries in a distributed and self-organising way. These characteristics offer enormous potential benefit for search capabilities powerful in terms of scalability, efficiency, and resilience to failures and dynamics. Additionally, such a search engine can potentially benefit from the intellectual input of a large user community. However, recent research on structured P2P architectures is typically limited to exact-match queries on keys. This is insufficient for text queries that consist of a variable number of keywords, and it is absolutely inappropriate for full-fledged Web search where keyword queries should return a ranked result list of the most relevant approximate matches. This stage builds upon the MINERVA system architecture presented in and brings current challenges to ultimatively making distributed search across digital libraries feasible. MINERVA provides ranked search on data and an efficient query mechanism that adheres to reasonable space and bandwidth limits. Unlike the approach criticised in, we do not spread inverted lists across the directory, but use only pointers to promising digital libraries as compact metadata and utilise these pointers to efficiently answer multiple-keyword queries. We leverage the extensive local indexes to incorporate features that are impossible in the approach studied in, such as phrase matching or proximity searches. Our bandwidth requirements are well within the postulation that a query should send no more data than the size of the documents ultimatively retrieved.

RELATED WORK

Recent research on structured P2P systems, such as Chord, CAN, Pastry, or P-Grid is typically based on various forms of distributed hash tables (DHTs) and supports mappings from keys to locations in a decentralised manner such that routing scales well with the number of peers in the system. We briefly discuss some prior and ongoing projects towards P2P Web search. Galanx is a P2P search engine implemented using the Apache HTTP server and Berkeley DB. The Web site servers are the peers of this architecture; pages are stored only where they originate from. PlanetP is a publish subscribe service for P2P communities, supporting content ranking search. PlanetP distinguishes local indexes and a global index to describe all peers and their shared information. The global index is replicated using a gossiping algorithm. The system appears to be limited to a few thousand peers. Odissea assumes a two-layered search engine architecture with a global index structure distributed over the nodes in the system. A single node holds the complete, Web-scale, index for a given text term. Query execution uses a distributed version of Fagin's threshold algorithm.

The system appears to cause high network traffic when posting document metadata into the network, and the presented query execution method seems limited to queries with at most two keywords. The paper actually advocates using a limited number of nodes, in the spirit of a server farm. The system outlined in uses a fully distributed inverted text index, in which every participant is responsible for a specific subset of terms and manages the respective index structures. Particular emphasis is put on minimising the bandwidth used during multi-keyword searches. considers content-based retrieval in hybrid P2P networks.

The peer selection for forwarding queries is based on the Kullback- Leibler divergence between peer-specific statistical models of term distributions. In addition to this recent work on P2P search, prior research on distributed IR and metasearch engines is also potentially relevant; see for overviews. However, their work has assumed a relatively small number of digital libraries or databases and a fairly static configuration.

DESCRIPTION OF THE SYSTEM DESIGN

As a detailed description of the system design has already been given in, we only present a brief overview here and refer the interested reader to this prior work. We view every library as autonomous. A conceptually global but physically distributed directory, which is layered on top of a Chord-style dynamic hash table (DHT), holds only very compact, aggregated information about the peers' local indexes and only to the extent that the individual peers are willing to disclose. Every peer is responsible for a randomised subset of the global directory.

The global directory consists of aggregated information (Posts) that contains contact information about the digital library who posted this summary together with statistics to calculate IR-style relevance measures that try to estimate the relevance of a particular digital library to a query. These measures are used to support the peer selection process, *i.e.*, determining the most promising libraries for a particular query. If, at query time, the local query result is considered unsatisfactory by the user, a library retrieves a list of potentially useful libraries. Using collection selection methods from distributed IR and metasearch, a number of promising libraries for the complete query is computed from these PeerLists. In we have studied promising and efficient techniques for this purpose. Subsequently, the query is forwarded to these libraries and executed based on their local indexes.

The results from the various libraries are combined at the querying peer into a single result list; this step is referred to as result merging. The goal of finding high-quality search results with respect to precision and recall cannot be easily reconciled with the design goal of unlimited scalability, as the best information retrieval techniques for query execution rely on large amounts of document metadata.

Posting only compact, aggregated information about local indexes and using appropriate peer selection methods to limit the number of peers involved in a query keeps the global directory manageable and reduces network traffic. We expect this approach to scale very well as more and more peers jointly maintain the moderately growing global directory.

COLLABORATIVE SEARCH ACROSS DIGITAL LIBRARIES

Our work is driven by the question of how a collaborative search across digital libraries can benefit from the unique nature of the P2P paradigm. We want to address the shortcomings of centralised search engines and further benefit from the intellectual input of a large user community.

Democratic Community Search

To overcome the danger of the infiltration of a centralised index by (commercial) interest groups we leverage the indexes from potentially thousands of digital libraries, making it harder to bias the final query results.

Implicit User Feedback

Additionally, we want to incorporate the fact that every library has its own local index, *e.g.*, by executing all queries first locally at the initiating library and using implicit-feedback techniques for automated query expansion.

User Recommendations

We want to incorporate local user bookmarks into our query execution. Bookmarks represent strong recommendations for specific documents. Also, user bookmarks can be considered as compact samples of peer indexes that describe their fields of interest. Queries could be exclusively forwarded to thematically related libraries with similarly interested users, to improve the chances of finding subjectively relevant pages.

Replication

In order to achieve service levels comparable to today's search engines and in order to actually benefit from the infrastructural advantage of a distributed system, we are going to introduce a certain degree of replication to the directory.

Currently, as dictated by the DHT-style maintenance approach, a peer gracefully leaving the system forwards its share of the global directory to another peer. Analogously, a library entering the system asks for its appropriate share of the directory.

While one approach to ensure a valid, complete, and up-todate directory is to simply rely on the libraries to regularly re-send their Posts to the directory, it is also necessary to replicate parts of the directory to avoid data loss as libraries ungracefully leave the system.

Also, replication can serve as a load-balancing measure, relieving the burden from peers that host popular parts of the directory, and increases data availability.

Adaptive, self-tuning strategies for choosing appropriate degrees of replication and placing replicas are an open issue in our ongoing work.

Caching and Proactive Dissemination

To further enhance query efficiency, statistical summaries and also the results of queries from across the network may be cached in a way that allows other peers not only to instantly benefit from the existing query results but also to benefit from click streamst that were recorded on the occasion of similar queries.

Statistical summaries may also be disseminated proactively among thematically related peers. Finding good strategies to this end is a widely open issue.

Overlap-aware Query Routing

Peer selection has been a research issue for years. Most of the existing literature estimates the expected result quality of a collection, typically using pre-computed statistics, and ranks the collections accordingly. We believe that this is insufficient if the collections overlap, *e.g.*, in the scenario of digital libraries that share an arbitrarily large fraction of documents.

We argue for the extension of existing quality measures using estimators of mutual overlap among collections. Preliminary experiments show that such a combination can outperform popular approaches based on quality estimation only, such as CORI. Taking overlap into account during collection selection in this scenario can drastically decrease the number of libraries that have to be contacted in order to reach a satisfactory level of recall, which is a great step towards the feasibility of distributed search across digital libraries.

Benefit/Cost Optimisation

Ultimatively, we want to introduce a sophisticated benefit/cost ratio when selecting remote libraries for query forwarding. For the benefit estimation, it is intuitive to consider such measures.Defining a meaningful cost measure, however, is an even more challenging issue. While there are techniques for observing and inferring network bandwidth or other infrastructural information, expected response times are changing over time. One approach is to create a distributed Quality-of-Service directory that, for all peers, holds moving averages of recent response times.

MODERN DIGITAL LIBRARY SYSTEM

Invenio is an integrated digital library system originally developed at CERN to run the CERN Document Server, currently one of the largest institutional repositories worldwide. It was started over 15 years ago and has been matured through many release cycles. Invenio is a GPL2 Open Source project based on Apache/WSGI + Python + MySQL architecture. Its modular design enables it to serve a wide variety of usages, from a multimedia digital object repository, to a web journal, to a fully functional digital library.The development strategy used to implement Invenio ensures it is flexible in any layer. Being based on open standards such as MARCXML and OAI-PMH 2.0 its interoperability with other digital libraries is guaranteed. Being originally designed to cope with the CERN requirements for digital object management, Invenio is suitable for middle-to-large scale digital repositories.

Records can be of any nature. This presentation will introduce the different features of Invenio, their usage in the CERN context and how other institutions and projects are also driving some of its development.

USAGE

Besides being used to run the CERN Document Server, Invenio has also been chosen by several other big institutions or projects. Among them it is about to be used to serve the SPIRES High Energy Physics information through the recently launched INSPIRE service, that will become the repository of reference for high energy physics. It is used by the EPFL. ADS has expressed interest to move to an Invenio-based platform, while starting a collaboration at the data level between astrophysics and high energy physics worlds. For example in Spain Invenio is already used by the *Dipòsit Digital de Documents* (DDD) and by the "Repositorio Digital de la Universidad de Zaragoza". Recently the European Commission has chosen Invenio to become part of two important projects D4ScienceII, and OpenAIRE, with the latter having the goal to set up a portal where all the EC funded research project documents will be available.

FEATURES

Let us demonstrate the key Invenio features by following the lifetime of a record in the system, from ingestion to dissemination. As an integrated digital library, Invenio is built to allow the management of digital objects and the meta-data associated with them. Meta-data are stored in the MARCXML format, which has the flexibility to store any kind of information and which can be easily converted, thanks to XML style-sheets to any other meta-data format.

INGESTING RECORDS

Data and Meta-data can enter into Invenio powered repositories through different ways. They can be manually deposited by an author, through custom and fully configurable web interfaces, backed by an equally configurable work-flow architecture, that lets the submission administrator set up any kind of procedure triggered by a deposition. Meta-data and data can as well be harvested regularly from OAI-PMH compatible repositories. Data can also be input into the system from any non-standard format by writing ad-hoc conversion scripts either in XSLT or in the proprietary BibConvert's language. Users also have the possibility to upload records by sending e-mails that will be parsed automatically. The system can be configured to accept submission by robots thanks to the availability of a simple web API.

DIGITAL OBJECT MANIPULATION

Fully fledged tools to integrate and manipulate digital objects are available. In particular Invenio can manage multiple formats for the same document, multiple revisions, automatic conversions between formats, automatic stamping of PDF documents with watermarks, creating icons, automatic text extraction to allow for full-text searching, automatic meta-data extraction and many more. Data consistency is also ensured by MD5 checksum being continuously verified.

INDEXING AND RANKING

All the new records ingested into the system and their modifications are indexed by a very fast indexing engine that has been developed in-house. All the indexing stages are configurable; which metadata fields to index, how to extract tokens, which language is expected in order to apply stemming and removing stop words, and so on. A plug-in based ranking engine takes care of creating special indexes to be used at search time for sorting results based on word similarity, citations, download statistics, and to present citation networks.

CURATING RECORDS

Curators have powerful web-based tools to manipulate records, whilst maintaining change histories, auto-completion of fields based on fully configurable knowledge bases, multi-record modification, assisted duplicate record finding and an efficient AJAX-based record merging tool, and so on. Curators can also exploit flexible tools to perform meta-data compliance checks against configurable rules. Automatic tools are also available to extract citations and references from scientific papers and to extract keywords based on a given ontology, to enrich the available meta-data. Distributed curation activities can be instantiated through integration of Invenio with RT, one of the most famous open source ticketing systems.

DISPLAYING RECORDS

Bibliographic records can be displayed in any format, thanks to an easy and fully-configurable formatting layer, which allows creation of record-based rules to choose which representation of a record to use, while each representation can be fine tuned to fit any particular need.

Thus any kind of content can be hosted and properly displayed, such as multimedia documents, books, address book contacts, and so on. Records can be organized in a flexible hierarchical structure using real and virtual collections. Each collection can in turn be customised to choose the look and feel and the kind of features enabled. The whole web appearance of Invenio can be fully customised thanks to an integrated templating system, thus facilitating integration of Invenio into an existing institutional portal. Since Invenio is being developed in an international environment it supports internationalization and comes translated already in 25 different languages.

SEARCHING AND BROWSING RECORDS

A powerful search engine resides at the core of Invenio Fig. 3.1. Supporting a Google-like syntax, it can be used to dig into the repositories in a very easy way, while allowing the more experienced users to take advantage of many advanced features such as regular expressions, range queries, selection of meta-data, and many more.

Results can be clustered by collections and ranked with respect to word similarity, number of citations, downloads based rankings, and any other pluggable algorithm. Any search query can automatically turned into an RSS feed to add to a personal news aggregator. Thanks to integrated support for MODS and UnAPI standards, search results can be stored in Zotero, a powerful Firefox plug-in useful to organize a personal digital library. The system offers users powerful citation and author analyses.

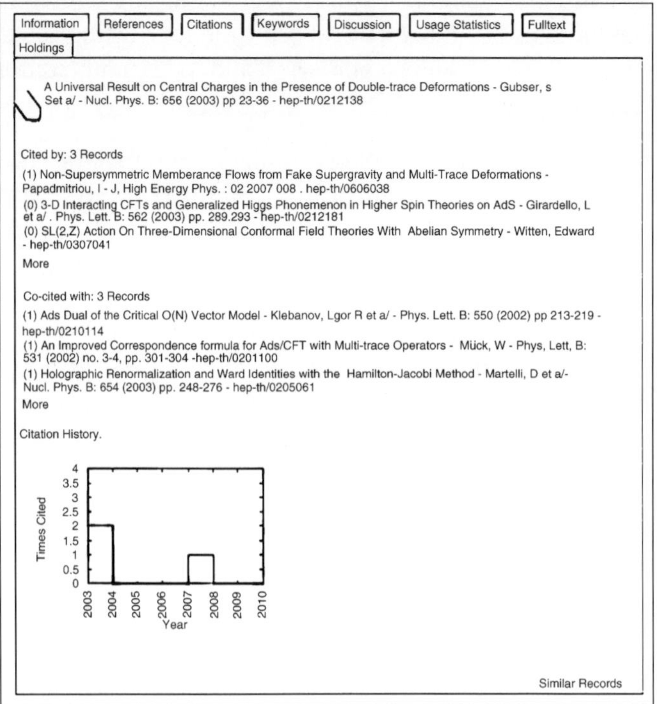

COLLABORATIVE TOOLS

Invenio integrates several collaborative and typical web 2.0 tools such as baskets, to store and share records or external resources with other users, personal e-mail notification alerts, record commenting and reviewing, internal web-based messaging tools, approval/reviewing work-flows.

EXPORTING RECORDS

Data and meta-data can be exported in several ways, the most important being through OAI-PHM protocol and by means of a pluggable exporting module.

AUTHENTICATION AND AUTHORIZATION

While offering for free local accounts management, Invenio can be integrated with institutional user databases to delegate the authentication phase and to exploit externally available user details.

Using the *role based access control* (RBAC) model of Invenio one can define a list of roles, attach users to particular roles, and grant rights to perform actions such as view-restricted-collections based on user group membership, user IP address, and more.

CIRCULATION

Invenio supports the operation of a physical library by integrating a circulation module, as well as by supporting inter library loans. Users can submit loan requests, and follow the request status, the librarians have a web interface to accept/reject loan requests, to send overdue letters, to set up sub-libraries, etc.

CREATING JOURNALS

As an example of an application that has been built on top of the core Invenio, the web journal module lets repository administrators create online web journals with regular issues built from articles stored in the repository itself. A specific appearance can be set up in order to have a layout providing journal-like reading experience. This is currently used today for producing the official CERN Bulletin, which is issued every two weeks.

8

System Design in Library Management

INTRODUCTION

The project titled Library Management System is Library management software for monitoring and controlling the transactions in a library.The project 'Library Management System' is developed in java, which mainly focuses on basic operations in a library like adding new member, new books, and updating new information, searching books and members and facility to borrow and return books.

'Library Management System' is a windows application written for 32-bit Windows operating systems, designed to help users maintain and organise library.

Our software is easy to use for both beginners and advanced users. It features a familiar and well thought-out, an attractive user interface, combined with strong searching Insertion and reporting capabilities. The report generation facility of library system helps to get a good idea of which are the books borrowed by the members, makes users possible to generate reports' hard copy. The software Library Management System has four main modules.

- *Insertion to Database Module:* User friendly input screen
- *Extracting from Database module* – Attractive Output Screen
- *Report Generation module:* Borrowed book list and Available book list
- *Search Facility system:* Search for books and members

SYSTEM ANALYSIS

EXISTING SYSTEM

System Analysis is a detailed study of the various operations performed by a system and their relationships within and outside of the system. Here the key question is- what all problems exist in the present system? What must be done to solve the problem? Analysis begins when a user or manager begins a study of the Programme using existing system. During analysis, data collected on the various files, decision points and transactions handled by the present system. The commonly used tools in the system are Data Flow Diagram, interviews, ,etc. Training, experience and common sense are required for collection of relevant information needed to develop the system. The success of the system depends largely on how clearly the problem is defined, thoroughly investigated and properly carried out through the choice of solution.

A good analysis model should provide not only the mechanisms of problem understanding but also the frame work of the solution. Thus it should be studied thoroughly by collecting data about the system. Then the proposed system should be analysed thoroughly in accordance with the needs. System analysis can be categorised into four parts.

- System planning and initial investigation
- Information Gathering
- Applying analysis tools for structured analysis
- Feasibility study
- Cost/ Benefit analysis.

In our existing system all the transaction of books are done manually, So taking more time for a transaction like borrowing a book or returning a book and also for searching of members and books.

Another major disadvantage is that to preparing the list of books borrowed and the available books in the library will take more time, currently it is doing as a one day process for verifying all records. So after conducting the feasibility study we decided to make the manual Library management system to be computerised.

PROPOSED SYSTEM

Proposed system is an automated Library Management System. Through our software user can add members, add books, search members, search books, update information, edit information, borrow and return books in quick time. Our proposed system has the following advantages.

- User friendly interface
- Fast access to database
- Less error
- More Storage Capacity
- Search facility
- Look and Feel Environment
- Quick transaction

All the manual difficulties in managing the Library have been rectified by implementing computerisation.

FEASIBILITY ANALYSIS

Whatever we think need not be feasible.It is wise to think about the feasibility of any problem we undertake. Feasibility is the study of impact, which happens in the organisation by the development of a system. The impact can be either positive or negative. When the positives nominate the negatives, then the system is considered feasible. Here the feasibility study can be performed in two ways such as technical feasibility and Economical Feasibility.

TECHNICAL FEASIBILITY

We can strongly says that it is technically feasible, Since, there will not be much difficulty in getting required resources for the development and maintaining the system as well. All the resources needed for the development of the software as well as the maintenance of the same is available in the organisation here we are utilising the resources which are available already.

ECONOMICAL FEASIBILITY

Development of this application is highly economically feasible.The organisation needed not spend much m one for the development of t he system already available. The only thing is to be done is making an environment for the development with an effective supervision. I f we are doing so, we can attain the maximum usability of the corresponding resources.Even after the development, the organisation will not be in a condition to invest more in t he organisation.There fore, the system is economically feasible.

SYSTEM REQUIREMENTS

This management system can be used in windows 98, Windows2000, Windows XP and Windows NT, supported for other platform such as Applet, Macintosh and UNIX.

The system must be running Windows 98, Windows 98 or Windows NT4.0 operating system and must meet the following hardware requirements.

- For Windows 95 based computers, a 486/ 66 MHz or higher processor with 8MB
- For Windows 98 based computers, a 500/88MHz or higher processor with 32 Mb of RAM
- For Windows NT based computers, a 488/ 66 MHz or higher processor with 16 MB of RAM
- For Windows 200 based computers, a 700/850 MHz or higher processor with 512 MB of Ram

INPUT DESIGN

Input design is the process of converting user-oriented input to a computer based format. Input design is a part of overall system design, which requires very careful attention. Often the collection of input data is the most expensive part of the system. The main objectives of the input design are:

- Produce cost effective method of input
- Achieve highest possible level of accuracy
- Ensure that the input is acceptable to and understood by the staff.

Input Data

The goal of designing input data is to make enter easy, logical and free from errors as possible. The entering data entry operators need to know the allocated space for each field; field sequence and which must match with that in the source document. The format in which the data fields are entered should be given in the input form.Here data entry is online; it makes use of processor that accepts commands and data from the operator through a key board. The input required is analysed by the processor. It is then accepted or rejected. Input stages include the following processes:

- Data Recording
- Data Transcription
- Data Conversion
- Data Verification
- Data Control
- Data Transmission
- Data Correction

One of the aims of the system analyst must be to select data capture method and devices, which reduce the number of stages so as to reduce both the changes of errors and the cost.Input types, can be characterised as:

- External
- Internal
- Operational
- Computerised
- Interactive

Input files can exist in document form before being input to the computer. Input design is rather complex Since, it involves procedures for capturing data as well as inputting it to the computer.

OUTPUT DESIGN

Outputs from computer systems are required primarily to communicate the results of processing to users. They are also used to provide a permanent copy of these result for latter consultation.Computer output is the most important and direct source of information to the users. Designing computer output should proceed in an organised well through out the manner. The right output must be available for the people who find the system easy o use. The outputs have been defined during the logical design stage. If not, they should defined at the beginning of the output designing terms of types of output connect, format, response etc,Various types of outputs are:

- External outputs
- Internal outputs
- Operational outputs
- Interactive outputs

- Turn around outputs

All screens are informative and interactive in such a way that the user can full fill his requirements through asking queries.

DATABASE DESIGN

The general theme behind a database is to handle information as an integrated whole. A database is a collection of interrelated data stored with minimum redundancy to serve many users quickly and effectively. After designing input and output, the analyst must concentrate on database design or how data should be organised around user requirements. The general objective is to make information access, easy quick, inexpensive and flexible for other users. During database design the following objectives are concerned:-

- Controlled Redundancy
- Data independence
- Accurate and integrating
- More information at low cost
- Recovery from failure
- Privacy and security
- Performance
- Ease of learning and use

SYSTEM IMPLEMENTATION

Implementation is the stage in the project where the theoretical design is turned into a working system. The implementation phase constructs, installs and operates the new system.

The most crucial stage in achieving a new successful system is that it will work efficiently and effectively. There are several activities involved while implementing a new project they are:

- End user training
- End user Education
- Training on the application software
- System Design
- Parallel Run And To New System
- Post implementation Review

END USER TRAINING

The successful implementation of the new system will purely upon the involvement of the officers working in that department. The officers will be imparted the necessary training on the new technology.

END USER EDUCATION

The education of the end user start after the implementation and testing is over. When the system is found to be more difficult to under stand and complex, more effort is put to educate the end used to make them aware of the system, giving them lectures about the new system and providing them necessary documents and materials about how the system can do this.

TRAINING OF APPLICATION SOFTWARE

After providing the necessary basic training on the computer awareness, the users will have to be trained upon the new system such as the screen flows and screen design type of help on the screen, type of errors while entering the data, the corresponding validation check at each entry and the way to correct the data entered. It should then cover information needed by the specific user or group to use the system.

POST IMPLEMENTATION VIEW

The department is planning a method to know the states of t he past implementation process. For that regular meeting will be arranged by the concerned officers about the implementation problem and success.

SOFTWARE TESTING IN LIBRARY MANAGEMENT

Is the menu bar displayed in the appropriate contested some system related features included either in menus or tools? Do pull –Down menu operation and Tool-bars work properly? Are all menu function and pull down sub function properly listed ?; Is it possible to invoke each menu function using a logical assumptions that if all parts of the system are correct, the goal will be successfully achieved? In adequate testing or Non-testing will leads to errors that may appear few months later. This create two problem:

- Time delay between the cause and appearance of the problem.
- The effect of the system errors on files and records within the system

The purpose of the system testing is to consider all the likely variations to which it will be suggested and push the systems to limits. The testing process focuses on the logical intervals of the software ensuring that all statements have been tested and on functional interval is conducting tests to uncover errors and ensure that defined input will produce actual results that agree with the required results. Programme level testing, modules level testing integrated and carried out. There are two major type of testing they are:

1 White Box Testing.
2 Black Box Testing.

WHITE BOX TESTING

White box some times called 'Glass box testing' is a test case design uses the control structure of the procedural design to drive test case.Using white box testing methods, the following tests where made on the system:

- All independent paths within a module have been exercised once. In our system, ensuring that case was selected and executed checked all case structures. The bugs that were prevailing in some part of the code where fixed

- All logical decisions were checked for the truth and falsity of the values.

BLACK BOX TESTING

Black box testing focuses on the functional requirements of the software. This is black box testing enables the software engineering to derive a set of input conditions that will fully exercise all functional requirements for a Programme.

Black box testing is not an alternative to white box testing rather it is complementary approach that is likely to uncover a different class of errors that white box methods like.

- Interface errors
- Performance in data structure
- Performance errors
- Initialising and termination errors.

GUIDES TO COMMERCIALLY AVAILABLE SOFTWARE

There are a large number of commercially available library automation software packages. Studies that enumerate, compare and highlight the salient features of these software packages are also in abundance. An effort is made here to review some such selected studies to enable one to fathom the length, breadth and depth of the problem of selecting a suitable software for one's use. Clossbrenner in his book How to buy software: The master guide to picking the right programme describes much general and specific application software but does not mention the library housekeeping or information storage and retrieval software packages. A number of software packages are mentioned which could be used for general applications and other areas related to library automation. These include packages for word processing, database management, statistical manipulation, online searching of databases, etc. The book is a comprehensive, user friendly master guide for selecting suitable software for specific purposes. Hansen in Microcomputer user's guide to information online lists more than 100 sources of information, and their access software. Rowley lists some text retrieval software for microcomputer and for mainframe/ microcomputer systems. Further, She adds a list of library house-keeping software, their features and suppliers. Mahajan surveys some 40 software packages.

SOFTWARE WITH CD-ROM DATABASES

The CD-ROM databases are usually provided with information retrieval and public access software. Valas gives a comparison of some well known CD-ROM information retrieval software packages. There are not many publications dealing with the comparison of different CD-ROM information retrieval software packages. Richards and Robinson suggest a model for evaluating CD-ROM software whereas, Harry and Oppenheim discuss the various criteiia for evaluating electronic databases. jacso describes the evaluation, selection and installation of CD-ROM software, data ware and hardware. Jasco searches for skeletons in the database cupboard to find errors of omission and commission.

McFaul comes out with a final report on consistent interface guidelines. Tian-Zhu limits his‘ formal analysis to searching capabilities and ease of use of CD-ROM user interfaces. Sieverts and others give additional programmes for testing, evaluating and comparing software for information storage and retrieval. Most of these studies are confined to user interfaces as the principle of comparison of software packages. They usually give rules on how to rank the CD-ROM publications, how to give marks for the CD-ROM databases in addition to the software. In many cases the performance factors that are most important for professional searchers are usually missing from these collection of rules. Valas emphasises the performance factors that are considered to be the most important viewpoints for a professional searcher. "A retrieval system may be as user friendly as you wish; but you will not like it if one single e search step in an intricate query may take two hours and displaying the hits may take another two; or if complicated search strategies are not possible at all."

CATEGORIES OF SOFTWARE

Computerisation of Library and information services, involves non-numeric data processing, text retrieval, manipulation of strings of characters and information retrieval, etc. Some general purpose software packages can be used for these purposes and for specific needs, special purpose software are also available in the market.

The various categories of such software and their features are:

- Basic software for data entry, validation, sorting and merging of files, and editing of data
- Word processing software to manipulate text-storage, recall, use and modify; alignment of margins, addition and deletion of string of characters, manipulate paragraphs, etc.
- Database management systems (DBMS) for creation and management of databases, file management systems, relational database management systems (RDBMS), network and hierarchical DBMS
- Text-Retrieval Packages for storage and retrieval ‘of non-numeric records (tabular or even graphics). These are self-contained software, require minimum involvement of computer specialists, records are independent of variable length for natural language text, have access to data by context, inverted file access, user interfaces which makes them simple and easy to use. Search and indexing facilities are other important features

- Software Associated with Searching Online Retrieval System and CD-ROM Databases. Major online systems have their own software usually written in command language, provide access to external databases, private or personal file facility, and permit editing of search files on micros
- *Library House Keeping Software*: These have provision for acquisition, cataloguing, circulation control, serials control and statistical report generation.

Library automation software or computer based information storage and retrieval systems cover two major functional areas, namely:

- Control and management of library resources, and
- Access to documents and information.

These two areas deal with library house-keeping systems and text retrieval systems respectively. Gradually, the distinction between them is vanishing. In latest software packages there is provision for both library house-keeping operations as well as public access for information retrieval. In addition, there are software packages for re-organising and presenting information in desired format, producing publications, arid to control and manipulate statistical and financial data.

Library automation software packages can also be grouped in four categories:

- Word processing,
- Library house-keeping operations,
- Management communications and support, and
- Text retrieval.

The type of software can be categorised based on the hardware or computer systems used. For example,

- Microcomputer-based software
- Mini computer-based software
- Large mainframe-based software

Each of these categories of software may be either In-house software that is owned and operated by the library, or shared with other libraries through a consortium arrangement-through a bibliographic information network.

DELNET DATABASES AND THEIR SIGNIFICANCE

UNION CATALOGUE OF BOOKS

DELNET provides access to more than 8 million biblio-graphic records of books in English language available with various member libraries located in and outside the country. The databases can be accessed by any of the desired fields including Title, Author, Subject, Date of Publication. The Boolean operators can also be used for refining the search queries. The sorting can be done on the searched results. The searching using Phrase searching, Any Words and includes can be used. The records can also be retrieved using the specific indexes including Title, Author, Subject, etc. The database size grows with each passing day as more and more data from the member libraries are being merged in the centralized union catalogues.

DELNET has developed its own modules on Basisplus software, an RDBMS. The member libraries availing to the Interlibrary Loan facility can place the requests online through the system itself for getting the books on loan. The Interlibrary Loan is one of the most popular services of DELNET, the resource sharing is done not only between the libraries located in India but also outside India. It is quite heartening to note that DELNET has evolved a very successful functional model of Interlibrary Loan/Document Delivery services. Through these services, the users, faculty, researchers and scholars of the member libraries are able to get and refer to the books which are not readily available in their own libraries.

At times the books are out of print and are not even available with the book publishers themselves. The Reference books are also lended out though for fewer loaning period. It is worth mentioning that certain libraries in the country which are reference libraries like Central Reference Library, Delhi University, Indian Institute of Advanced Study, Shimla does lend out books to DELNET. It is only possible due to the mutual cooperation and benefit the libraries generates from the process of resource sharing.

It demonstrates a win-win situation. DELNET charges only for the nominal courier for sending the books on loan and it is the responsibility of the borrowing Institution to return back the book at their own cost. In India wherein the users and also the libraries have the limited resources, through the resource sharing the needs of the information users are fulfilled in most economical ways. I would like to mention that DELNET also serves its member-libraries outside India. DELNET has also created a database of E-books which are available in the public domain.

Union List of Current Journals and E-journals Consortium in India

The journals are a vital source of current information for the scientific research. The information about the availability of the current journals is of great help for the document delivery services. DELNET is maintaining an online union list of current journals available in the fields of Science and Technology, Social Sciences and Humanities. This database has more than 25,000 unique titles of current journals available in member as well as the non- member libraries of DELNET. The database is updated continuously by receiving the list of currently subscribed journals and this database contains the information about the journals not only available with the member libraries but also with the major reputed libraries in India which are the Non- members.

The photocopies of journal articles are arranged from the libraries and are supplied to the requesting libraries. It is also one of the most popular services.

In India a major E-journals consortium was formed in 2000 named "INDEST (Indian National Digital Library in Science and Technology Consor-tium" with a financial contribution of ₹200 million by the Ministry of Human Resource Development (MHRD), Govern-ment of India. All India Council for Technical Education (AICTE) has also contributed ₹37.5 million to this. Thirty Eight centrally funded government institutions including the IITs, NITs and NITs and few others are the core members of INDEST.

The private Institutions are self supported. Under the consortium, an access to more than 6500 journals from various publishers and aggregators are provided. The UGC Infonet E-journals consortium covers 4453+ejournals and provides access to nearly 100 Universities of the country. It has been noticed that private institutions who are not able to afford being the member of the consortium is greatly utilizing to the DELNET Document Delivery Services.

Moreover, at times the members of the Consortium also approaches DELNET for the delivery of the journal articles since the desired journal may not be the one covered under the access or the desired specific issues are not available online. There is lot much of speculation about the extent of utilization of E-journals in the Institutions and a large number of studies have been carried out to know about the pattern of accessibility. Moreover it has been noticed that if a Institution ceases to be a member of the Consortium because of the non availability of the digital archiving, the users are deprived to browse the issues for which the Institution had paid to the consortia.

Union Catalogue of Journals

DELNET has also created a database containing the holdings data of the journals available in the member libraries besides containing the other bibliographical information about the journals. At present the database contains 19,289 records of the journals. It is a good resource for tracking down the articles from the rare, old issues of the journals dating back to late 19th and early 20th century. DELNET does receive a number of requests from the libraries for locating the journal articles from the very old issues of the journals. It is a good resource for locating the articles from the rare old issues of the published journals.

Database of Journal Articles

There are a number of libraries, though not many on the network who are involved with the articles indexing in the machine readable form. A large portion of the library budget is annually spent on subscribing to the journals, either in print or in online mode by the libraries but the libraries lack the access to the databases containing the bibliographic details about the journal articles.

For the researchers and scholars it is very essential to know about the latest articles getting published in their specific fields of discipline. This specific database contains more than 800,000 records and is growing in size.

For journal articles, the concerned users, researchers send the requests with their bibliography through e-mail and DELNET arran-ges for the full text delivery. DELNET also helps in providing the list of articles through various other networked sources and the fulltext copies of the selected articles are provided on demand.

Databases of Non-print Materials

DELNET does maintain the databases of CD-ROM, Video recordings and sound recordings available in the member libraries. The non-print materials can not be loaned out from the libraries, however the video recordings and sound recordings are being taken on loan in special cases though for a lesser period of time. The CD-ROMs are used for keyword searching and the concerned bibliography containing the abstracts are provided to the requesting libraries. There are 2,281 records of CDs available with member libraries, 748 sound recordings and more than 5,000 videorecordings listings in the respective databases.

Database of Thesis and Dissertations

This database contains around 45000, Thesis and Dissertations submitted to the various Universities and Institutions. This database contains bibliographic information and since thesis and dissertations are the reference materials available in the libraries, the researchers and scholars use this database to know about the works being carried out in their specific fields.

There has been some projects in India concerning the digitization of the Thesis and Dissertations by INFLIBNET and University of Mysore (Vidyavahini project), but the project has not taken off due to the copyright restrictions.

USEFULNESS OF DELNET UNION CATALOGUES

The access to Union Catalogues created and developed by the library networks remains the most highly used resources by the member-libraries. The locations data available in the union catalogues helps the respective users to find out the availability of the documents in their own regions, state and in different locations of the country and outside.

It is a very effective resource discovery tool and is a great boon to the scholars and researchers of the country. The survey results have highlighted the fact that 85.7 per cent of the member-libraries finds DELNET Union catalo-gues useful and 86.3 per cent of the library users are getting benefited (Fig. 5.3 and Fig. 5.4).

While 78.9 per cent of the Postgraduate students, 62.5 per cent of the faculty and 53.7 per cent of the graduate students are getting benefited from the DELNET services. The content available through the union catalogues are very selective in nature since the libraries purchase the titles through a strict selection process.

LIBRARY RESOURCE SHARING LIBRARY NETWORK

India, the largest democracy in the world with an estimated population of 114 millions has more than 1,00,000 libraries comprising academic libraries, public libraries, special libraries and libraries attached to the research and develop-ment institutions, government departments and ministries, etc. There is no denying the fact ICT has brought a paradigm change in the functionality of the libraries in the country but this technological change pattern is not seen uniformly across the wide-section of the libraries in the country.

On one hand the country is proud to have the most sophis-ticated libraries with ISO certifications and the implementation of modern tools and technologies, on the other hand, we do encounter the challenges of providing a better infrastructure in the form of PCs and Internet connectivity in the libraries that are still striving hard to get the necessary hardware and Internet connectivity in their libraries from their managements. The adoption of standards, retrospective conversion work, the adoption of suitable library software packages continues to remain as the major areas of concerns for the libraries and the library and information science professionals.

In such constraints and hostile conditions, DELNET has been able to establish itself as an effective, operational resource sharing library network in India. The network whose journey started as a city based library network in 1988, emerged as a major operational library network not only in India but in South Asia, connecting more than 1597 libraries in 30 States and UTs in India and seven other countries.

The network is growing from strength to strength, with escalating resources of union catalogues, the wider coverage of libraries from varied disciplines, the growing number of users and the horizontal and vertical expansion in its services to its members. This paper highlights the incredible and pioneering work being done by DELNET-Developing Library Network which is a non-governmental, non-profit making organisation with inputs from the Ministry of Communications and Information Technology, Government of India and located in its own building in the well-known academic environment of Jawaharlal Nehru University at New Delhi.

I would like to reiterate that DELNET do not receive any government funding and is based on a self-sustainable model, it is considered as a role model for the library networks especially of the developing nations. A survey has also been conducted by the author to assess the utilisation of DELNET resources among the member-institutions and is reported in the article. The questionnaire technique was used to get the inputs from the member-libraries. 147 libraries responded to the questionnaire.

THE GENESIS OF LIBRARY NETWORKING IN INDIA

In India during the late 1980s and 1990s there was a move-ment to establish city and regional-based library networks by NISSAT (National Information System for Science and Technology), a body under Dept of Scientific and Industrial Research (DSIR), Government of India. It provided some financial assistance for the setting up of these library networks.

This has lead to the mushrooming of various city library networks in India including:

- BONET (Bombay Library Network),
- CALIBNET (Calcutta Library Network),
- DELNET (Delhi Library Network which later became Developing Library Network in 2000),
- PUNENET (Pune Libary Network).

The University Grants Commission (UGC) has also developed INFLIBNET (Information and Library Network) in 1991 to network the University Libraries in the country. Only a few networks were able to work on the self sustainable model and continued to exist after the initial phases of implementation and functioning. DELNET, started as a project in 1988 became a national library network in India by the year 2000. UGC continued funding INFLIBNET to provide the support to the University Libraries in the country. The remaining city library networks due to the lack of planning for developing the networked resources and its functions soon perished from the networking scene of the country.

DELNET-DEVELOPING LIBRARY NETWORK

DELNET-Developing Library Network is a major operational resource sharing library network in India connecting more than 1597 libraries in 30 States and UTs in India and seven other countries. DELNET was conceived as a city based library network in Delhi in 1988 and was known as Delhi Library Network, networking the libraries of the Delhi region. It got registered as a society in 1992. With the availability of DELNET services on the World Wide Web, the accessibility soon was transformed from the local dial up connectivity for the Delhi region institutions to the global access through the Web.

This gave a great boost to DELNET and soon DELNET crossed the geographical boundaries within the country and also became accessible outside. It was on 13th September 2000 that the name of DELNET got changed from DELNET-Delhi Library Network to DELNET-Developing Library Network. The main objectives of DELNET is to promote resource sharing among the member-libraries by collecting, storing and disseminating information and by providing networked services to the researchers and scholars to supplement their research activity.

FIVE Cs-FUNCTIONAL PARAMETERS OF DELNET

We would like to mention the five Cs of the Library Networking which is essential for an operational library network and governs its functionality.

These five Cs are:

1. Connectivity;
2. Cost;
3. Computers;
4. Client; and
5. Content.

Connectivity

The connectivity is a life line for the smooth functioning of a library network. There is an availability of the leased-line, wireless, broadband, VSAT and Wifi connectivity in the libraries. The DELNET services are accessible through the World Wide Web by the registered member libraries. The DELNET databases are hosted on Basis Web server and are connected with a 11 mbps RF link offered by National Informatics Centre, Ministry of Communications and Infor-mation Technology, Government of India.

The network remains functional on 24/7 basis. The web tracking software installed at DELNET servers gives a day to day picture of the usage of the DELNET services by the member libraries. It is quite heartening to note that the access to the servers hosting the databases are being made by the researchers and scholars of the member libraries at different times starting from midnight to early morning besides the usual peak hour network access. The survey conducted among the member libraries have shown very encouraging figures regarding the availability of the dedicated links in the libraries. ninety per cent of the respondents have confirmed the availability of the dedicated Internet facility in their libraries.

The University Libraries have the largest availability of the dedicated Internet facility with 95.2 per cent affirmed the availability of the dedicated link, followed by 90.7 per cent in Institutes, 89.7 per cent in Research/Special Libraries and 86.7 per cent in the Colleges. The survey results shows that Internet has been able to penetrate well among the organisations in the country and the libraries have the Internet bandwidth availability with them. It is found that in 97.3 per cent of the organisations, the faculty has Internet facility at their own desk. It is quite essential to have the direct internet access in order to utilise the library network's resource and services to the fullest.

Cost

The cost of membership to the library network and the resources provided through them are important for the sustainability of a library network. DELNET membership charges are quite nominal, it is T 7500 per annum for the libraries in India and SAARC nations, the non-SAARC members pays USD 500 per annum. The membership fee is kept same for all Institutional Members whether it is a University, an Institution, an RandD organisation, a specialized library or a school library. The democratic approach, an unbias one, helps in promoting the resource sharing. Also it leaves an impression of being equal in their participatory roles in a network for resource sharing.It is worth reporting that some of the library networks in India could not grow and sustained themselves due to the exorbitant membership charges rates and different categori-zation of the members on the basis of their collections, etc. DELNET charges for the actual courier charges for sending the books on Interlibrary loan and the member-institutions and their researchers finds it an affordable one.

In a developing country like India, Cost of getting the desired material plays a crucial role. Herein, the researchers and scholars for higher research are not being helped financially to a reasonable extent through scholarships, grants, etc. contrary to their counterparts in the Western world.

Computers

In order to facilitate the optimum use of the library network resources and services, the researchers, scholars and faculty of the member institutions should have adequate availability of the computers.

Through the survey conducted, it was found that 43.2 per cent of the libraries have upto 10 computers in the library whereas 59.1 per cent of the University Libraries have more than 20 computers in the library and only 32.2 per cent of the respondents have more than 20 computers in their libraries.

It is quite evident that the libraries are not better equipped with the availability of the computers in their libraries though there may be separate computer labs or the computer departments but they are not the part of the libraries.

Client (Member-Libraries)

The more diverse the library network has the coverage, the more effective would be the resources of such a library network. In DELNET, the participating libraries are from various disciplines and they pool their resources together and share them across the network.

I would like to mention the fascinating scenario of resource sharing wherein a technical book required by a SandT Library will be available in a library specialising in Commerce discipline rather than being available in the best technical libraries.

The resources and the collections becomes more trans-parent for the act of resource sharing. The survey results have shown that 92 per cent of the member-libraries are aware about DELNET services and 61 per cent are the frequent users of the DELNET services.

It would like to mention that DELNET organizes one day orientation programmes in member-institutions located in various parts of the country. This enables in better promotion and spreads awareness about DELNET and helps in popularizing the services among the users, faculty and researchers of the member-libraries.

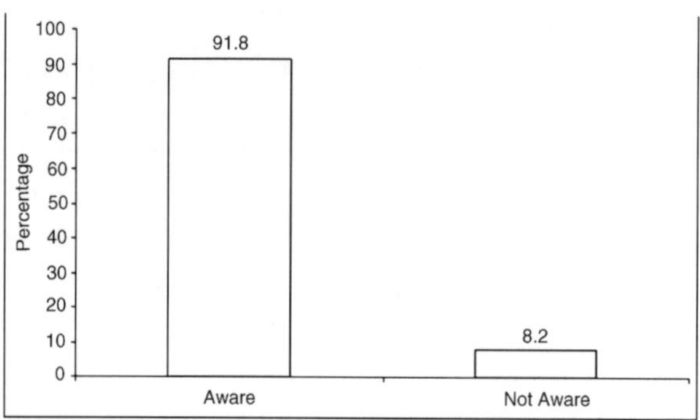

Fig. Awareness about DELNET Services among the Library Users.

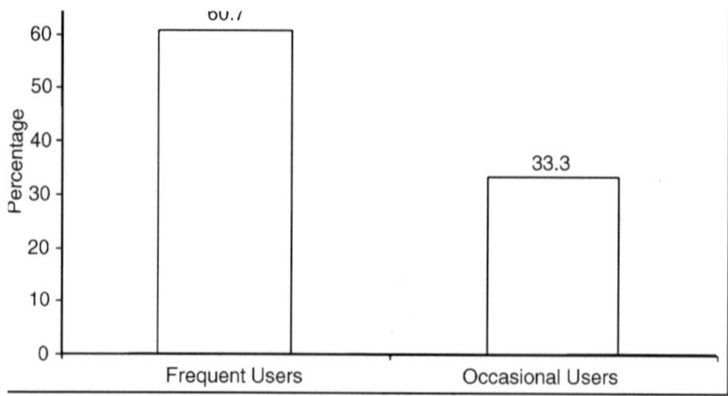

Fig. How Often do you Use DELNET Services.

Content

Content is a major resource of a library network. The greatest concern for a library network is the consolidation of the resources lying scattered across the member-libraries. This ensures a wider access to information to the information seekers. Since inception, DELNET is actively engaged in developing the union catalogues and union lists which are the major resource strength for any library network. The records in the DELNET databases are growing in size and more and more resources are becoming accessible to the member libraries. These resources are the major source for resource sharing as they carry the locations data wherein physically the information may be available.

The database are collected through the electronic transfer of the exported records through the online facility, e-mail, ftp protocols; the data is physically sent in CDs by the member libraries. I would like to mention that in a country like India, the cooperative cataloguing or cooperative collection building is still not in existence. There is a lot much of duplication efforts in the libraries for cataloguing the same titles in different libraries. The various libraries in the country are using various software packages which ranges from the commercial software packages (Libsys, Alice for Windows, Virtua, etc) which may be adhering to international standards to the inhouse developed software packages developed with the backend on SQL, Access, Excel, Oracle, Sybase, etc. DELNET collects the records from the member libraries in the default exported format and the conversion programs are being developed to convert the base records into the standard ISO 2709 format before they are finally being merged in the Union Catalogues. I would like to mention that the information is also collected from the prominent libraries of the country who may be non-members since they can always be approached for getting the desired references. There is an online facility for uploading the machine readable records to DELNET by the member-libraries. The bibliographical databases do not strictly adheres to the international bibliographic formats and the library professionals are not much familiar with MARC 21 cataloguing.

MEMORY AND FILE MANAGEMENT

MEMORY

Memory is the electronic holding place for instructions and data that the computer's microprocessor can reach quickly. When the computer is in normal operation, its memory usually contains the main parts of the operating system and some or all of the application programmes and related data that are being used.

Memory is often used as a shorter synonym for Random Access Memory (RAM). This kind of memory is located on one or more microchips that are physically close to the microprocessor in the computer. Most desktop and notebook computers sold today include at least 16 megabytes of RAM, and are upgradeable to include more.

The more RAM you have, the less frequently the computer has to access instructions and data from the more slowly accessed hard disk form of storage. Memory is sometimes distinguished from storage, or the physical medium that holds the much larger amounts of data that won't fit into RAM and may not be immediately needed there. Storage devices include hard disks, floppy disks, CD-ROM, and tape backup systems. The terms auxiliary storage, auxiliary memory, and secondary memory have also been used for this kind of data repository. Additional kinds of integrated and quickly accessible memory are Read-Only Memory (ROM), programmable ROM (PROMO), erasable programmable ROM (EPROM).

These are used to keep special programmes and data, such as the basic input/output system, that need to be in the computer all the time. The memory is a resource that needs to be managed carefully.

Most computers have a memory hierarchy, with a small amount of very fast, expensive, volatile cache memory, some number of megabytes of medium-speed, medium-price, volatile main memory (RAM), and hundreds of thousands of megabytes of slow, cheap, non-volatile disk storage. It is the job of the operating system to coordinate how these memories are used. The part of the operating system that manages the memory hierarchy is the memory manager. It keeps track of parts of memory that are in use and those that are not in use, to allocate memory to processes when they need it and de-allocate it when they are done, and to manage swapping between main memory and disk when main memory is too small to hold all the processes.

Systems for managing memory can be divided into two categories: the system of moving processes back and forth between main memory and disk during execution and the process that does not do so.

Mono Programming without Swapping or Paging

The most simple memory management scheme is to run one programme at a time, sharing the memory between that programme and the operating system. There are three variations of this type. The operating system may be at the bottom of the memory in TAM (Random Access Memory) or it may be in ROM (Read-Only Memory) at the top of the memory or the device drivers may be at the top of the memory in a ROM and the rest of the system in RAM down below. With the system organised in this way, only one process at a time can be running.

As soon as the user types a command, the operating system copies the request programme from a disk to memory and executes it. When the process finishes, the operating system displays a prompt character and waits for a new command. When it receives the command, it loads a new programme into memory overwriting the first one.

Mono Programming with Fixed Partitions

It is often desirable to allow multiple processes to run at the same time, even on simple operating systems in which multiprogramming is sometimes used. On time-sharing systems, having multiple processes in memory at once means that when one process is blocked waiting for the I/O to finish, another one can use the CPU. This way, multiprogramming increases the CPU utilisation. It is however preferable to be able to run two or more programmes at once even on personal computers.

Swapping

The process of organising memory into fixed partitions on batch system is simple compared to time sharing systems or graphically oriented personal computers. On batch systems, each job is loaded into a partition when it gets to the head of the queue. It stays in memory until it has finished.

As long as enough jobs can be kept in memory to keep the CPU busy all the time, there is no reason to use anything more complicated.

On time-sharing machines, sometimes there is not enough main memory to hold all the currently active processes, therefore excess processes must be kept on disk and brought in to run dynamicallySwapping as an approach to memory management consists of bringing each process in its entirety, running it for a while, then putting it back on the disk.

THE SCENARIO

The problem we are trying to overcome is simply this: You want to develop some kind of file or text editor, and you want your programme to be able to load, edit and save files of any size. In fact, you want your programme to load and edit the largest sized file possible. Under 32bit Windows this is a 4GB file.

MEMORY MANAGEMENT

Let's forget about actually editing a large file for the moment, and concentrate just on loading a file into your application. So, your have a 4GB file saved on your hard disk, and you want to load this file so you can preview any portion of it. Let's assume that our first application will be a simple hex file viewer, with no editing capabilities. The first decision to take is what memory facilities as suggested, use to gain access to the file's contents.

To make this decision, we need to know what memory facilities are available to our programme, and base our decision on that. Because our file viewer will be a 32bit Windows programme capable of running under Windows 9x and NT/2000, we have the following facilities at our disposal.

VIRTUAL MEMORY

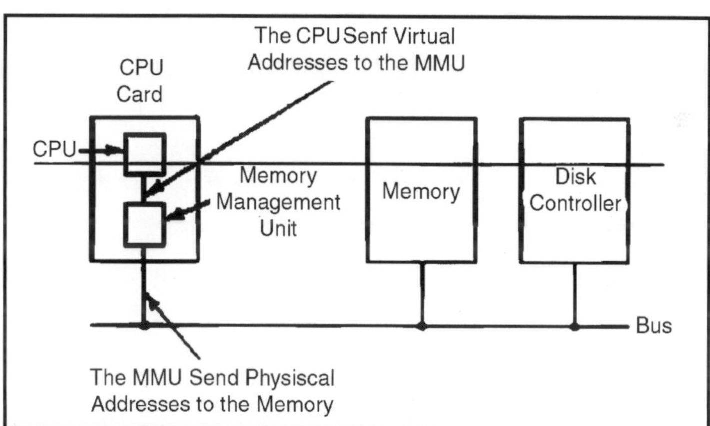

Another strategy for managing memory is the virtual memory, which allows programmes to run even when they are only partially in main memory. The basic idea behind this strategy is that the combine size of the programme, data, and stack may exceed the amount of physical memory available for it.

The operating system keeps those parts of the programme currently in use in main memory, and the rest on the disk. Virtual memory can also work in a multiprogramming system, with bits and pieces pf many programmes in memory at once. While a programme is waiting for a part of itself to be brought in, it is waiting for I/O and cannot run, so the CPU can be given to another process, the same way as for any other multiprogramming system. Most virtual memory systems use a technique called paging.Every 32bit process in Windows has a 4GB virtual address space, regardless of the amount of physical RAM you have installed. Of this total virtual space, only 2GB is available for an application's private use. Actually, the available space slightly less than this - 128KB less in WinNT and 4MB less in Win9x). There are a variety of methods to allocate memory from this 2GB region of space. All depend on how much memory needs to be allocated, and what its intended use is.

Malloc and New

The simplest is to use the standard C or C++ memory allocation routines. Both of these methods use the memory allocation facilities provided by the operating system. In Visual C++ 6.0, malloc and new use VirtualAlloc internally. Anyway, malloc and new[] are only really meant for allocating lots of small objects, not one gigantic memory region.

Heap Alloc

The second method to allocate memory in Windows is to use the Heap function–HeapAlloc. These functions are also meant for allocating many small objects though—just like malloc and new—and are also implemented by calls to VirtualAlloc.

VirtualAlloc

The third way to allocate memory in Windows is to use VirtualAlloc directly. This method is much more flexible because it allows you to specify where you want the memory to be in your address space, and allows you to reserve a region of memory without actually allocating any space from it.

Memory-Mapped-Files

The forth way to allocate memory is by using Memory Mapped Files. Rather than allocating memory, a memory-mapped file is a reserved region of the 2GB address space, which has mapped into it a region a file stored on disk. The great thing about memory-mapped-files is that they free the programmer from having to do any direct file reading or writing. Simply reading and writing to the memory-mapped view causes the file's contents to be accessed. The operating system provides clever page caching to make memory-mapped files a very quick way to read/write to a file.

MANAGEMENT INFORMATION SYSTEM VS. DECISION SUPPORT SYSTEM

Researcher identified four major problem areas of management information systems.

They are:

1. Output is undiscriminating.
2. The information is not analysed for a purpose.
3. The system is not user-friendly.
4. The information which is given by MIS may not be acceptable.

Decision support systems can be seen as an extension of the idea of management information systems to provide a wide range of information in a more flexible and interactive way. They are designed to support decision making needs of management rather than act a useful by-product of transaction processing systems.

The special feature of a decision support system is that it solves a major problem of management information systems, *i.e.*, the poor communication between the system and the users, library managers. Decision support systems have interface outputs which are more live than those of management information systems.

The main interfaces in decision support systems are:

- Regular reports which provide information on parts of the system, which are predetermined by the system's users.
- Event-centred reports in which a report is generated only when a predetermined event has occurred. This will usually be the result of an exceptional condition, which is signalled by the system.
- *Ad hoc* reports which are generated in response to a stimulus by the system user to report on a condition which is not normally monitored.
- A query language which enables the user to interface directly with the system and to test changes in conditions experimentally. This is usually performed with 'goal-seeking' and 'what if techniques.

Beside the interface output, a decision support system also provides the report formats which may be required by the system's user, ranging from simple one-off designs to sophisticated presentations for senior managers. They are:

- *Standard reports* containing details prompted by the system user but in a format determined by standard software.
- *Tailored reports* containing information determined by the user and in a format designed by the user.
- *Tabulations* enabling the user to examine a range of statistical data rapidly, in either a standard or tailored format.
- *Spreadsheet format* allowing the user to transfer data from the system into a separate format which can be manipulated in a statistical layout.
- *Graphic presentations* providing a method of transmitting a trend analysis rapidly, and in a user-friendly manner.

Like management information systems, the data input into decision support systems can be external or internal data concerning the library. The three levels of influence on decision making can be isolated:

- Information from the library's operations.

- Information from the parent organisation.
- Information at the national and regional level.

The differences between a management information system and a decision support system lie not only their features, but also in their users. Management information systems tend to be used by lower and middle management because of their ability to assist in making structured decisions. In contrast, decision support systems tend to be more useful to top management because they can help with decisions on unstructured issues. Where they exist, decision support systems appear to be mainly used at the strategic management level.

MANAGEMENT INFORMATION SYSTEMS AND THE STAFF STRUCTURE

Seven of the eight libraries claimed that they already had a 'flat' management structure, and are trying to avoid a more hierarchical staff structure. However, the current structure was said to be uninfluenced by the existence of a management information system. Rather, it was due to the need to establish a structure which was customer oriented, which provided a clear definition of the responsibilities of staff, and which facilitated the flow of instructions or information. One university librarian also stated that the hierarchy that had been retained was intended to facilitate staff promotion.

OPINIONS ON DECISION SUPPORT SYSTEMS

Libraries which had formal management information systems found that the management information produced by their system needed to be carefully interpreted; moreover, the management information systems were not pro-active. Therefore, their aim was the introduction of decision support systems in the near future.

Those libraries which had only informal management information systems saw that they had the choice of establishing either a formal management information system or a decision support system. They indicated that they were more likely to favour decision support systems.

All of the librarians interviewed were aware of the nature and potential of decision support systems, and saw them as particularly helpful in utilising performance indicators and developing quality assurance processes in the library. One library was already experimenting with a decision support system and performance indicators, and three were aiming to have one.

One librarian, however, had no intention to have a decision support system, as he felt that it could assume too much control, as well as being very difficult to establish. However, all were agreed that decision support systems are more reliable than management information systems.

Nevertheless, in terms of infrastructure for decision support systems, little progress was evident. Only one library had a microcomputer based network, and one other was preparing to have one.

INFORMATION SYSTEMS AND EFFECTS ON DECISION-MAKING

All of the libraries visited already employed automated systems. However, formal and relatively fully automated management information systems existed in only two of the eight libraries visited. They had been established because of the existence of management information systems in the institutions as a whole. In the other libraries, the use of cost centres for resources allocation caused the libraries to have some formal management information. Libraries generally are not fully utilising the capability of their automated systems since some external information remains in printed form, and manual data processing is still a significant element in their analysis of the data available.

Those librarians who had 'informal' or 'partial' management information systems had concluded that a management information system would be not helpful for decision making in budgeting and resource allocation, but they still faced a requirement to produce reports for their institutions, particularly for their finance departments, which incorporate management data.

They also produce summary information for various purposes, profiling their parent institution, finance, staff, users, facilities and equipment, programmes and functions. Those libraries which had management information systems possessed information which was deeper in substance and more readily available, so it was easier for them to make appropriate decisions.

LIBRARY MANAGEMENT AND LEADERSHIP

Leadership and management are two terms that are often used interchangeably. In fact, they describe entirely different concepts, as leadership is more than a component of the functions of management. Management is the process of administering and coordinating resources to ensure than an organisation accomplishes its mission and goals. *Library and information science* (*LIS*) has a managerial focus; librarians manage the infrastructure of a library: its collections, staff, technology, and facilities. For this reason, the interconnection between management and leadership is the domain of LIS theory and practice.

The purpose of leadership is to challenge the status quo as libraries undergo a transition in organisational culture, the services they offer, and workforce restructuring as they try to better fulfill the organisational and broader institutional mission.

Management, on the other hand, prepares the infrastructure for that transition. As early as 1950s, the term *managerial leadership* was coined, but its definition was imprecise. "No definition of the phrase 'managerial leadership' has gained general acceptance. In fact, it is often referred to but left undefined" or merely equated to particular leadership theories and styles. The term recognizes that leadership is not exclusively a top-down process between the *boss* as a leader and subordinates.

This paper, which aligns with the programme in managerial leadership in the information professions at Simmons College, views managerial leadership as encompassing an examination of leaders, followers, the interaction between the two groups, and, in this context, leadership becomes a process whereby people influence others to develop, accept, and carry out a shared vision that guides future actions of the organisation.

As a result, that process is longitudinal and involves events. Because leadership is not always effective or positive, it should not automatically be assumed that goals and events are always successfully met or that staff members are sufficiently motivated or inspired to challenge themselves and others. The purpose of this paper is to build on the international research agenda that Candy Schwartz and I presented in 2008 and that illustrates that LIS research needs to go beyond a preoccupation with under-standing the style, personality, traits, and other characteristics of the boss and that person's influence on organisational dynamics and performance.

LEADERSHIP

In addition to focusing on a shared vision, leadership is about giving people confidence to meet organisational expectations and to serve as change agents. It also encourages them to seek, be given, and benefit from team coaching and mentoring aimed at enhancing their knowledge, skills, abilities, effectiveness, and commitment to the transformation process. A library's staff might consist of both followers and leaders who are willing to collaborate with other institutional partners.As well, the director, if that person is truly a leader, might be more so within the organisation than in representing the library to other stakeholders. With so many libraries organised into teams or small groups and involved in managing change; with new staff members expected to work together to plan, implement, administer, and evaluate services; and with libraries forging new partnerships at the institutional, local, and other levels, more librarians are becoming increasingly interested in knowing about and applying leadership theories, styles, traits, and roles.

They are also trying to develop their leadership potential. Within this context, there is much interest in transformational leadership and emotional intelligence, which helps leaders move beyond basic 'people skills' to understanding how one's own reactions and feelings impact how one is perceived by others.

Leaders and managers need to understand their own emotions and recognize and understand the feelings of those around them. Leaders are more successful when they pay attention to their social interactions with others in the workplace and the impact they as leaders have on those around them. It is also important for leaders to understand the impact that others' emotions have on them. When leaders are aware of the emotional side of the workplace, they are better able to create a working environment that encourages excellence.

As librarians gain an understanding of such theories, it is important to remember that, as Peter Northouse points out, leadership has 'many different meanings;' this is evident when people "finish the sentence 'Leadership is....'" Their responses might ignore social influence, add new elements, or confuse leadership with someone holding a managerial position. They might also fail to recognize that there are also spiritual, legacy, moral, ethical, charismatic, and other types of leadership. Each of these areas actually produces separate leadership theories that have been long investigated but rarely connected to LIS.

CONTEXT

Even though this paper focuses on topical areas for future research and selected methodologies, it is important to remember that methodologies do not frame a research study. Research, which engages in problem-solving, is shaped by a reflective enquiry.

These components, as well as the study procedures and data quality, comprise a framework in which each component should be bonded to the others through, what David R. Krathwohl calls, a 'chain-of-reasoning.' That 'chain,' he points out, 'is only as strong as its weakest link' and 'all links...should be built to about the same strength.' He further explains that, "as the work load is picked up by the first link and passed to successive links, the work load—and therefore the nature of each link—is determined by the previous links."

Furthermore, "where several links together join those above and below them, there may be trade-offs to compensate for weaknesses. It is beyond the scope of this paper, however, to present and relate the entire chain-of-reasoning. Still, I would be remiss if I did not underscore the importance of the theoretical framework.

Vincent A. Anfara, Jr. and Norma T. Mertz provide an excellent overview of theatrical frameworks and the impact of 'good and useful' theory on the chain-of-reasoning. In the case of managerial leadership, like other areas within LIS, there are numerous theories, some of which fit a given problem statement and set of objectives better than others.

One such theory might be constructive-development theory, which relates directly to leadership and which offers a way to view the complex problems that organisations face from multiple perspectives.

This theory describes "how adults develop more complex and comprehensive ways of making sense of themselves and their experience." Another concept relates to trust, which is an essential component in motivating or inspiring others and which is more than a trait.

RESEARCH DESIGNS

As a prelude to methodologies, research designs for leadership research might call for a longitudinal study and a comparison of several organisations.

Widely used research designs centre on either a case study or the application of grounded theory. A case study is a means "for learning about a complex instance, based on a comprehensive understanding of that instance obtained by extensive description and analysis of that instance taken as a whole and in its context."

Grounded theory, on the other hand, "is a method for discov-ering theories, concepts, hypotheses, and propositions directly from data, rather than from a priori assumptions, other research, or existing theoretical frameworks." Theory emerges from, and is grounded in, the data themselves.

DATA-GATHERING TECHNIQUES

This part focuses on some of the most prevalent methodo-logies used in leadership research, especially within LIS. As such, it builds from Karin Klenke's work on leadership research. It is increasingly common for researchers to apply qualitative methods. The accompanying table offers examples of some methodologies applicable to the study of leadership in LIS that will not be discussed in the body of this paper. The sources in that table came from an extensive review of the vast literature on leadership produced outside LIS.

The largest number of research studies related to leadership involves the distribution of a self-report survey or questionnaire. Such surveys are often in paper-and-pencil format, although more recently Web-based surveys have appeared with increasing frequency. The survey might involve the use of a predeveloped, behaviour-based leadership assessment tool that is distributed to those heading the organisation or to subordinates who are asked to evaluate the director or boss as a leader or their immediate supervisor.

As an alternative, surveys might probe respondent preference for a particular leadership theory or style and ask them to rate themselves or identify the most important attributes for individuals in their position. Complementary to a questionnaire that is mailed or otherwise distributed, investigators might use personal or focus groups interviews. Responses to open-ended questions might be subjected to content analysis, which "is a set of procedures for transforming Non-structured information into a format that allows analysis." On occasion, biographies of people identified as leaders have been developed and their content subjected to analysis for discussions of leadership.

Available historical records, however, might focus more on their accomplishments than the story behind those accom-plishments: how did the individual co-opt and navigate different stakeholders and the staff to bring about that change? If a shared vision emerged, how was it developed? Some other means of data collection include an analysis of citation patterns of a body of works on leadership and a characterization of the most cited works and authors, as well as the age of the cited material. Additional insights might be gained from a consideration of the journal's impact factor and the number of copies of a work that libraries hold.Assuming the availability of a body of independent studies focused on the same aspect of leadership and that describes the research design, the methodologies and data-collection instruments used, information about the population and sample, and so on, meta-analysis might be appropriate. Such analysis refers to a set of statistical procedures used to summarize and integrate those studies. It reveals sources of bias and is helpful for posing research questions for future study.Among other things, it cannot exceed the limits of what the researchers report. Another method, known as the Delphi study or technique, is a procedure relies on the use of sequential questio-nnaires in which experts share their perspectives on issues. The Delphi technique is not necessarily designed to generate consensus, but it does involve a systematic refinement of prior responses. It has been applied to seeing which leadership attributes are most critical for future managerial leaders.

Concept Mapping

Concept mapping is both a process for representing data in the form of pictures or maps and a structured methodology for organising the ideas of a group or organisation. The goal is to bring together groups of multiple "stakeholders ... and help them rapidly form a common framework that can be used for planning, evaluation, or both." The maps represent the groups' thinking about a topic, show how their ideas are related to each other, and, in general, indicate "which ideas are more relevant, important, or appropriate."

Interviews and other techniques might produce datasets that might be examined by the use of concept maps. These maps provide a graphic illustration of patterns among the findings. Jan Schilling, for instance, takes interview data about negative leadership and produced maps that show the antecedents of such leadership, negative leadership behaviours, and the consequences of negative leadership.

Simulation and Scenarios

A simulation study, as G. Yukl explains, involves a realistic task that continues for several periods of time and asks participants to assume the role of top executives in an organisation and to engage in team and organisational learning. Simulation "is also relevant for understanding how collective learning occurs among people whose decisions and actions affect organisational processes and performance." Instead of doing a simulation exercise, researchers might develop scenarios that make projections for the next fifteen years; forecaster Joseph P. Martino indicates that the accuracy in predicting what will likely occur declines dramatically with a longer time frame.Scenarios, as a prime technique of future studies, have long been used by government planners, corporate managers and military analysts as powerful tools to aid in decision making in the face of uncertainty. The idea behind them is to establish thinking about possible futures which can minimi[z]e surprises and broaden the span of managers' thinking about different possibilities.

They recommend that the number of scenarios not exceed four and that any scenario should meet criteria such as:

- *Plausibility* (each is capable of happening),
- *Differentiation* (each differs from the others and together they offer multiple futures),
- *Decision-making utility* (each offers insights into the future that help in planning and decision-making), and
- *Challenging* (each challenges conventional wisdom about the future).

RESEARCH AGENDA

The accompanying figure, which updates the depiction that Schwartz and I created, centres on three broad areas that relate to planning:

- Accomplishments (translating vision into effective organisational performance);
- People (creating an organisational climate that values staff and inspires them); and
- Transformation abilities (focusing on the change process that brings people together to accomplish the organisation's mission and goals—preparing the organisation of the future).

These areas match those that guide the doctoral programme in managerial leadership in the information professions (Simmons), which the Institute of Museum and Library Services has funded since 2005 with two multi-year grants. Those areas, originally modeled by the National Centre for Health care Leadership, cover twenty-five distinct leadership competencies. Under each of the broad areas, numerous topic areas emerge.At the same time, relationships among the areas might be probed. As directors or other members of the senior management team retire or depart, their replacement might be someone who serves on an interim basis. Are such people leaders or caretakers? The answer might take into account the library but also engagement beyond the library, transformation abilities, mentoring, and talent management. Focusing solely on talent management, many businesses engage in succession management or planning, but do libraries?Succession planning and management are not synonymous with mentoring. In some countries, if there is leadership, it might be characterized as autocratic. Such leadership merits analysis. Finally, various aspects of the figure might be probed in the present recession as libraries make significant decisions about collections and staff that will likely have a long-term impact. Turning to other topics, James G. Neal discusses 'feral library professionals,' which refers to the hiring of more people into traditional and nontra-ditional library positions who do not have the credentialed degree from an accredited library school programme.

Comparative case studies might analyse the emergence of leadership in organisations that employ both feral and non-feral professionals and that include staff who represent different generations. How cohesive are staff within and across departments? Do they share a common vision—do they need to share one? Studies might probe LIS educational programmes and see whether they incorporate leadership as a student learning outcome, one that reflects what students have learned throughout their programme of study and demonstrates what they can apply upon graduation.

Some other possible topics include the role of power in effective leadership, the major trends in making leadership effective, the communication networks of leaders, transformational leadership and its relationship, for instance, to

- Emotional intelligence, which deals with one's ability to manage emotions and relationships and to use this ability to advance the organisation's mission and goals. Emotional intelligence presumably requires *sense-giving* or shaping how people understand themselves, their work, and others engaged in that work.
- Resonant leadership, which focuses on self-awareness and self-renewal, and which enables individuals to recognize and cope with work stress.
- Distributed or shared leadership, which views leadership as more than a top-down approach. Leadership moves up the organisation as well and is distributed among a number of people working in teams and groups.
- Servant leadership, which recognizes that leadership is not confined to those in formal managerial positions and who lead as a way to extend service to others. The servant leader focuses on the needs and the development of followers.

Recognizing that libraries serve multicultural communities, employ a diverse staff, and deal with myriad stakeholders, it is critical to assess different leadership theories, recognizing the strengths and weaknesses of each. Many of the prevailing theorists have not considered how multiculturalism influences what they propose. Perhaps the best illustration of this comes from Linda Sue Warner and Keith Grint, who adopt a historical perspective and compare American Indian and western approaches and perspectives on leadership. There are differences between the practice of leadership in a tribal setting and in other organisational settings.

EXAMPLE

Although library directors cannot be equated with the president of the United States and other heads of government, political commentators have identified areas in which the leadership of those aspiring to be president might be probed. Prompted by the lack of penetrating questions raised in presidential debate and the quality of the responses, David Gergen and Andy Zelleke identify a series of important questions that deal with leadership and that require answers of more than a number or brief response. Their categories and questions have been reorganised and combined with the categories that Jack and Suzy Welch would like considered. The revamped questionnaire was pre-tested with one university library director and one library consultant. Based on their comments the questionnaire was revised. As of this time, the author of this paper is conducting a study to fine-tune the instrument and to gauge the responses of some library leaders. Instead of presenting preliminary data, this part probes relevant methodologies that might be used to address the open-ended questions and determine the relative rating of the categories. The methodology part of a hypothetical study might be based on a survey that is most likely administered in the form of an interview, either in-person or by telephone.

Directors might be unwilling to devote the time necessary to complete a paper-and-pencil survey or be unwilling to write detailed responses to each question. It might be difficult to find a time when five to ten directors could meet and participate in a focus group interview. For additional data collection, the inves-tigator might ask for historical documentation or visit the institutional repositories of selected institutions to gather data for event history analysis, assuming such information has been gathered and is publicly available.

Interview results might be analysed in terms of grounded theory and content analysis. The rating of the categories on a seven-point scale might be visualized in terms of concept mapping, and such mapping might also apply to the responses to the various questions within a category, especially if responses can be gathered from the same scale. A follow-up study might concentrate on selected categories and probe responses more deeply.

For instance, under 'Coalition Building/Advocacy,' partici-pants might meet and be asked for an example of when they became a catalyst who brought groups with polarized opinions together so that all voices were at the table. The examples generated might be cast in terms of a concept map, or the investigator could make the topics recurring most frequently and pursue them more with the Delphi technique. A different study might recast question responses to the initial study or one focusing on selected categories as scenarios or as simulation exercises.

It is also possible to take selected responses from the first study and select particular sites for in-depth case study analysis. That instrument, however, is framed in such a way that the research focuses on leadership as events and assorted methodologies are applicable. Leadership, after all, "is a process, a series of activities and exchanges engaged in over time and under varied circumstances." As such, accomplishments might be viewed as events in that leadership is an ongoing, never-ending process. To gain a more complete understanding of the phenomena under investigation, it is common for studies on leadership, like other topical areas, to incorporate more than one method of data collection.

Mixed methods, which are most prevalent with case studies, integrate quantitative and qualitative methods into one study and therefore strengthen the chain-of-reasoning presented in study findings. While it is important to expand the methodo-logical tool-chest that researchers within LIS use, it is also important to shift from studying leaders to investigating leadership events.

Many aspects of leadership presented in the figure have not been addressed, and a need emerges for a fuller body of evidence-based research relevant to change management within libraries and similar complex organisations on a global basis. It is also important that those within LIS contribute to the broader literature on leadership and that their works be recognized by those in other disciplines.

9

Automatic Identification and Data Collection Technology

INTRODUCTION

There are three important identification and data collection technologies that are used in libraries, namely, bar code technology, RFID and Smart card.

BAR CODE TECHNOLOGY

Bar code technology is being used in library and businesses for the past 30 years to minimize data entry errors, speed processes and reduce costs. Most books, journals as well as other consumer products in the market carry black and white thin and thick strips called barcodes. Barcode technology offers a mechanism that can be used for identification, location and tracking of items that are bar coded. Barcode is not a new technology, it was introduced in 1940 although it was first applied commercially in 1960's as a method for tracking rail road cars. Since, then, it has been used extensively in consumer industry, material handling, industries and libraries. A bar code is a machine readable code consisting of a series of bars and spaces printed in defined ratios.

Bar code symbologies are essentially alphabets in which different widths of bars and spaces are combined to form characters and ultimately, forms a message. Because there are many ways to arrange these bars and spaces, numerous symbologies are possible. Common linear symbologies include UPC/EAN, Interleaved 2 of 5 (I of 5), Codabar, Code 39 and Code 128. While each symbology is in some way unique, the composition of a complete message (bar code) is regardless of the symbology used. Barcode by itself, is not a system but is an identification tool that enables accurate reading of data for sophisticated management systems. Use of barcode increasing accuracy in data collection, saves time and brings about the efficiency in library activities. Bar code technology is being used in libraries all over the world especially for circulation of books as well as for several other functions including location control or book tracking, stock verification, receipt of issues of journals, cross checking of documents issued from the library, ,etc.

RADIO FREQUENCY IDENTIFICATION (RFID)

RFID (Radio Frequency Identification) is a term used for a radio-enabled device that communicates with or interrogates a tag or smart label, which is embedded with a single microchip processor and an antenna. The origin of the term lies in the invention of 'tags' that reflects back or re-transmit a radio frequency signal. The two components of RFID are tags and readers. The tags or label is equipped with a single microchip processor, an antenna and an ID code that can be embedded in almost any object. RFID readers are radio-enabled devices that communicate with or interrogate RFID tags or labels wirelessly and obtain the ID code on the tags from a distance of several inches.

The RFID readers can be fixed or made portable just like barcode scanners. RFID can also be referred as a high-tech version of the barcode. In the past few years, the cost of RFID tags have come down drastically. Low cost RFID tags, typically costs less than ₹ 30.00 each for up to 1 metre range making the technology affordable as an alternative to the barcode, magnetic strip or printed label. RFID has advantages that include tolerance of mis-orientation and obscuration, lower cost over life and ability to 'read'. Most importantly, RFID tags are cheap enough to be disposable and thin enough to go even inside the sheets of paper in some cases. An RFID tag is a means of storing and retrieving data through a radio frequency transmission to the chip inside the tag. An RFID tag is simply an integrated circuit (chip), which includes memory for data storage and a substrate backing material with an antenna pattern.

The chip can typically hold up to 1,024 bits (128 bytes) of information. In a typical library implementation, each book is equipped with smart labels and library patrons are given library cards imbedded with smart labels. Tags or smart labels can be programmed to store i) unique accession number of documents; ii) class number of a document; and iii) a unique security code for EAS. While accession number is used for carrying out functions of circulation, stock verification and other library applications, class number can be deployed for sorting documents according to class numbers and segregating then into bins for different shelving areas.

The RFID tags can also be used as antitheft devices in libraries. Such applications of RFID are called Electronic Article Surveillance (EAS). New forms of RFID perform EAS functions as well, obviating the need for a separate device. An interrogator, or reader, is a radio frequency device used to write data to and read data from the chip. Smart tags used in a library are passive, having no internal power source such as a battery. The interrogator provides enough RF energy to power and activate the tag to reflect or to present information stored on them. RFID tags transmit data, antennas receive or transmit the RF signal through the air and readers decode the RF information received from the RFID tag through the antenna. The data is then transmitted to the host application for necessary processing.

SMART CARDS

A smart card, chip card, or integrated circuit card (ICC), is a pocket-sized card with embedded integrated circuits which can process data. Effectively, a smart card can receive input, process it and deliver the processed data as an output. There are two broad categories of smart cards, memory cards contain only Non-volatile memory storage components and specific security logic.

Microprocessor cards contain volatile memory and microprocessor components. The card is made of plastic, generally PVC. The card may embed a hologram to avoid counterfeiting. Smartcards are generally used as security authentication mechanism for single sign-on within large companies and organisations.

A quickly growing application of smart card is as digital identification cards. In this application, the cards are used for authentication of identity. When combined with biometrics, smart cards can provide two- or three-factor authentication. The libraries generally use smart cards to identify and authenticate its patrons.

COMPUTER TECHNIQUES AND PROCEDURES IN LIBRARY SCIENCE

The following studies are concerned with early steps along the course from present digital-computer system to future pro-cognitive systems. Let us consider the studies in the order of their locations along that course. The first ones were intended merely to make it convenient to carry out some of the functions that are required in research on library and pro-cognitive problems or in the efficient use of large collections of documents. The last ones in the sequence were intended to explore functions that we think will actually be involved in future pro-cognitive systems.

AN 'EXECUTIVE' PROGRAMME TO FACILITATE THE USE OF THE PDP-1 COMPUTER

One of the first needs of the study was a computer programme to facilitate the programming and use of the laboratory's digital computer. The computer is a small but excellent machine, Digital Equipment Corporation PDP-I, specialised to facilitate interaction with users who work 'on line.' The PDP-1 has an oscilloscope display with light pen, several electric typewriters, a set of programmable relays, an analogue-to-digital converter, and an assortment of switches and buttons. Its primary memory is small but it is capable of transferring information rapidly between the primary memory and a secondary drum memory that holds about 90,000 eighteen-bit words. Associated with the computer are two magnetic-tape units. With the computer, it is possible to implement, in a preliminary and schematic way, several of the functions that were described in Part I as functions desirable in a pro-cognitive system. One encounters two main difficulties in trying to do, with the PDP-1 computer, research oriented towards a future period in which information-processing machines will have more advanced capabilities.

First, although the machine is reasonably fast, and although its secondary and tertiary memories make it possible to work with significantly large bodies of information, the machine is not capable of performing deep and complicated operations on really large bodies of text with the speed that would be desired in an operational system. The result is that it may take 30 seconds or a minute to get something that one would like to have almost instantly, that the display flickers on the oscilloscope screen, and so forth. Second, there is not available, at present, on any machine, either a programming language or a man-machine interaction language that makes it easy to do, or possible to do rapidly, many of the things envisioned in the discussion of pro-cognitive systems in Part I of this report. Our approach, during the study, was simply to put up with, and make allowances for, the shortcomings of the hardware system. It was easy to do that in informal experiments conducted by members of the research group; it was not realistic, however, to hope that all the observers of demonstrations would make the necessary allowances, and the shortcomings of the equipment effectively precluded formal experimentation.

Nevertheless, the equipment situation was at least tolerable, in terms of absolute assessment, and it seemed superb when we compared our man-computer interaction situation with any but two or three of all the others with which we were acquainted. The unavailability of highly developed languages and, of course, the interpreter and compiler programmes that would be required to make them useful - was, however, a seriously inhibiting factor. During the period of our study, two good programming-language systems came into being: DECAL, which is a quite elegant and powerful language and compiler of the ALGOL type, suitable for a small computer, and MACRO, which is an ingenious language and assembler system that incorporates several of the features that DECAL lacks and lacks several of the features that DECAL incorporates.

However, neither DECAL nor MACRO was designed for on-line programming, and neither was designed particularly to handle the problems that seem likely to present themselves to users of pro-cognitive systems. Those considerations led to the effort, which was never quite completed, to develop a composite programme oriented and user-oriented system to facilitate our research in man-machine interaction. The system is called 'Exec,' which stands, of course, for 'executive program'– and thus expresses something about the mode of operation: statements of the input language, coming into the computer, are examined by the executive programme, and, depending upon whether or not they fall into the class requiring interpretation, are either interpreted and executed with the aid of a set of subroutines associated with the executive programme or simply executed as machine instructions. Exec was written originally in the symbolic language called 'FRAP' and had, as its main function, simplification of the preparation of programmes and subroutines to be translated and assembled by FRAP. When DECAL became available, Exec was rewritten in DECAL, and slight modifications were made to facilitate the use of Exec in the preparation of programmes and subroutines to be translated and compiled by DECAL. The original intention - to develop Exec to the point at which it could operate as an on-line language as well as an adjunct to a programming language—was not accomplished.

One of the main themes in the work on Exec was to simplify and regularise the 'calling' and 'returning' of subroutines. In most computer-programming systems, and especially in the computer-programming systems that will be required in the implementation of plans of the kind, a computer programme is a complex arrangement of parts. The highest echelon of the structure does little more than represent the chapter headings of the general plan.

The actual work—the detailed processing of data - is handled by subprograms or 'subroutines' that break the task down into successively simpler sub packages at successively lower levels of detail until, finally, there is nothing left for the lowest-echelon subprograms to do but to perform simple, explicitly defined operations upon the few codes or numbers that are supplied to them. In this process of successive delegation of responsibility, the transactions that appear repeatedly are the 'calling' of a lower-echelon subroutine by a higher-echelon subroutine and the 'returning' of control from the lower-echelon subroutine to the higher-echelon subroutine.

Calling usually includes transmission of instructions, and also the designation of the arguments upon which the lower-echelon subroutine must operate, from the calling subroutine to the called subroutine. The transmission of information down the line we shall call 'briefing'. Transmission of results up the line we shall call 'debriefing.' In the conventional way of handling calling and returning, a subroutine eventually returns control to the subroutine that called it, but it may first call one or more lower-echelon subroutines. Fortunately or unfortunately, depending upon one's point of view, there are many different ways in which subroutines can be called and briefed and in which they can return control and do their debriefing. As indicated, one of the main purposes of Exec is to simplify and regularise this whole process.

In order to simplify the process of calling and returning, Exec is interposed between the calling subroutine and the called subroutine at the time of calling and between the called subroutine and the calling subroutine at the time of returning. With each subroutine is associated a compact code, that provides Exec with a description of the needs.of the subroutine. Exec can therefore handle in a systematic, centralised manner several of the functions that would otherwise have to be handled by each subroutine. In taking a burden off the routines, Exec takes a burden off the programmers who prepare them. The arrangements in Exec for calling and returning are set up in such a way that the chain of subroutine calls can be recursive. That is to say, it is possible for subroutine A to call subroutine A, or for subroutine A to call a subroutine B which, directly or through one of its minions, called subroutine A. To permit recursive operation, one must handle 'temporary storage' - storage of the scratch-pad jottings made by each subroutine during its operation - in such a way that results written by B, for example, do not destroy results that A calculated before calling B and will need to use after B returns control.

The functions just described have been implemented in a few programming systems - notably in the systems called IPL and LISP. In IPL and LISP, however, one either works wholly within the system or does not use the system at all. Exec extends the basic programming language and provides the new capabilities and conveniences within the structure of DECAL. In implementing the handling of subroutines, we made use of the technique of the 'pushdown list'. A pushdown list is an arrangement for storing information that resembles the spring-supported tray on which plates are stored in restaurants. If one puts a plate onto the top of the stack, it pushes all the others down, and if one then takes the plate off the top, the others pop up again. Exec, itself, employs one pushdown list.

Another pushdown list is available to the programmer or user through simple commands. He has only to give the name of the entity to be stored into the pushdown list or returned from it and to say whether he wants to push it down or pop it up. In the process of handling a call to a subroutine or a return from a subroutine, Exec examines the subroutine's heading code – determines whether or not, and how, to fulfill each of a number of functions, and then carries out those required. These functions include protecting contents of certain special registers of the processor against destruction during the running of the subroutine, finding the arguments needed by the subroutine and displaying them for its use, accepting the results obtained by the subroutine and communicating them to the calling routine, and protecting the contents of various temporary storage registers and 'flag' registers against modification by the called subroutine.

Exec protects information by putting it into the pushdown list. A second general purpose of Exec is to provide the advantages of generality and the advantages of specificity both at the same time and within the same system. If a computer programme is written in such a way as to make it useful in a particular situation. On the other hand, if the programme is written so that for example, it alphabetises or orders any kind of strings of alphanumeric text in any file or table, then he has to communicate to it, or have the routine that calls it communicate to it, that it should operate on words and that it should alphabetise according to a specified alphabet. In Exec, an effort is made to accommodate very general subroutines and to make it maximally convenient to communicate to them the information required to prepare them for specific applications. This is done by setting up and maintaining a description of the prevailing context of operation. In the terms of the example, his description may contain a specification that the currently prevailing string class is the class of 'words.' It contains the specification that the *x,* in any subroutine prepared to operate upon 'Table *x,* ' should be interpreted as 3. The subroutine, therefore, automatically performs on the operation intended by the programmer, despite the fact that the programmer was thinking in terms of abstractions and not in terms of the particular present task.

With arrangements of the kind just suggested, Exec makes it possible to use a subroutine that contains the expression, 'next string,' for example, to operate on the next character, or the next word, or the next sentence, or the next paragraph, or the next section, or the next chapter, and so forth. Exec keeps track of three 'string classes' simultaneously, class *u,* class *v,* and class *w.* At any time, the programmer can set anyone of the string classes to anyone of seven levels. He can write, for example, '*SSCU* word,' meaning to *set* the string class *u* to have the value, *word.* From that time on, until the instruction is superseded, all the subroutines that deal with the string class hierarchy *u* will consider the *u* strings to be words.

The procedure for designating tables is similar to that for designating strings. If the programmer would like to have programmes written in terms of Tables *x, y,* and *z* operate on the contents of Table zones 2, 5, and 7, he writes '*ntox* 2, *ntoy* 5, *ntoz* 7.' * When Exec sees those instructions, it does more than merely substitute 2 for *x,* 5 for *y,* and 7 for *z.* It finds the descriptions, in its file of table descriptions, that characterise the three numbered tables, and it substitutes these descriptions for the pre-previously prevailing descriptions of Tables *x, y,* and *z,* respectively. When a subroutine operates on the contents of the table, it examines the table's description and controls its processing accordingly. This makes it possible to accommodate diverse formats and conventions. Inasmuch as the adjustments are made 'interpretively' during the running of the programme, the user can change his mind and reprocess something in a slightly different way without having to go through extensive revision and recompilation of his programmes. This is an advantage that the present technique has over the technique, based on the 'communication pool,' that has been developed in connection with the programming of very large computer systems—systems programmed by teams so large as to discourage the effort to enforce the use of a single, standard set of conventions and formats.

The part of Exec that we have been describing is approximately an interpretive communication pool. The third set of functions with which Exec is concerned has to do with the display of alphanumeric information on typewriters and on the oscilloscope screen. Although these are very simple functions, they involve enough detailed programming to be a nuisance unless they are handled in a systematic way. Exec makes it convenient to separate specification of the information to be displayed from specification of the equipment through which it is to be displayed. It uses standard programmes to handle strings that are long enough to be considered messages or texts, but it provides special arrangements to facilitate preparation of labels, headings, and the like. For example, the programmer can call for the typing of any particular character *x* on whatever typewriter is currently specified to be typewriter *b* simply by writing *'type x.'* If the programmer wants the character to appear upon the screen of oscilloscope *a*, he writes *'scpa x.'* With the aid of Exec, the programmer can define in equally short instructions the size of the print, the vertical position at which the text should begin, and other parameters of the visual display.

Exec's arrangements for displaying capital and lower-case letters on the oscilloscope are primitive, but it is a step in the right direction to have both capital and lower-case letters. At present, a 'lower-case' letter is simply a small capital letter. We settled for that stopgap solution only in the interest of economy. The fourth and final set of functions handled by Exec has to do with display, by the computer, of what the computer is doing. One technique developed for this purpose, a technique called 'Introspection,' because it was developed as a separate project. The arrangements described here are integral to Exec. One of the main causes of difficulty in man-computer interaction is that the computer does not give the man any good clues about what it is doing until it completes a segment of processing and spews forth the results.

When the computer is running, its lights flash so fast that they are scarcely interpretable. It seems important to provide a way of having the computer give a running account of its processing. A part of Exec called the 'Reporting Subsection 'an optional part - is brought into play each time a subroutine is called and each time a subroutine returns control to its caller. When the reporting subsection is brought into action, it examines the list of things that it should do. This list can be changed while Exec and other programmes are running. Ordinarily, the first thing on the list is to give the address, and, if it is available in the directory, also the name, of the subroutine that is being called or that is returning control to its caller. Since the subroutines operate very rapidly, the names and addresses would appear to be presented simultaneously, one on top of another, if they were shown in a fixed location on the screen.

Therefore they are displayed in a format corresponding to that of a conventional outline. If a chain of subroutines is called, each one operating at a level just lower than its caller, the names and addresses appear on successive lines of the display with increasing indentation. Then, as the subroutines return control, each to its caller, the names and addresses are displayed again in such a way as to redisplay the outline pattern from bottom to top. To the display just described can be added, at the option of the operator, a display of the contents of the active registers of the computer. In addition, the operator may see the contents of whatever parts of the computer's memory he wants to examine. He designates the various parts of memory to Exec by typing on the typewriter while the programme is running. He can change his prescription at will. The current version of Exec allows him to specify nine different sectors of memory, either symbolically or in terms of absolute addresses. When he indicates that he wants to see 'the subroutine,' Exec interprets 'the subroutine' to mean the particular subroutine that is being called, or that is returning control to its caller. That will, of course, be one subroutine at one moment and another at another moment. When the operator wishes to examine a table or a programme in detail, he touches the space bar of the typewriter. That causes the system to pause in its progression through the sequence of things to be displayed, and to hold the current display until the operator releases it by touching the tab key. The Reporting Subsection provides a few additional conveniences - minor ones introduced from time to time on an *ad hoc* basis - but the foregoing will suffice to give an idea of the existing arrangement. Let us mention a few of the steps not yet accomplished, however. It seems worth while to connect to the Reporting Subsection the 'Introspection' programmes that will be described later.

It is necessary to complete the arrangements that associate the tables that reside in the primary memory to corresponding structures in secondary and tertiary memory and, in the manner of the Atlas computer system, to arrange it so that information structures are automatically shifted up through the memory hierarchy whenever they are addressed. It is necessary, also, to expand the mechanism that associates symbols with machine addresses. That mechanism is only a simple table-searching system, but it is inherently capable of effecting the translation required to make conveniently readable the reports of 'what is currently going on in the computer.' We found it useful to distinguish, in Exec, between 'intrinsic' and 'extrinsic' subroutines. Exec is highly 'subroutinised' and has the partly hierarchical, partly recursive, structure that we have described as essential for pro-cognitive systems. Each sub-function of Exec that appears to have any likelihood of proving useful in future applications is separated out and set into the form of a subroutine. In the process of writing subroutines to handle substantive problems - subroutines that made use of Exec but were not at first intended to be part of the Exec system - we encountered repeatedly several sets or clusters of functions. By associating with Exec the subroutines prepared to handle those functions, we were able to build up a system of considerable convenience and power. The part of the system not intrinsic to Exec was too extensive to be held in primary memory at all times. However, it was clearly desirable to bring parts of it into primary memory - coherent clusters of it corresponding to major functions - whenever required in the execution of a programme. The easiest way to accomplish dynamic storage and transfer of subroutines, and to handle the associated bookkeeping, was to take care of it automatically through Exec's ability to examine calling sequences and subroutine headings. We did not make much progress towards that end during the course of the study.

However, we did work with the problem enough to see the great convenience and power that reside in a coherent structure of computer subroutines and a largely automatic arrangement for calling them and transferring information among them. Evidently, the more sophisticated the arrangements, the larger the fraction of the subroutines that will be intrinsic to the arrangements. We visualise a system in a continual process of development, with a set of intrinsic subroutines, a set of extrinsic subroutines, and a continual flow from the extrinsic set to the intrinsic set as more and more functions are brought within the scope and capability of the system.

RECRUITING ON THE INTERNET

Using the Internet is faster and cheaper than many traditional methods of recruiting. Jobs can be posted on Internet sites for a modest amount, remain there for periods of thirty or sixty days or more - at no additional cost - and are available twenty-four hours a day. Candidates can view detailed information about the job and the organisation and then respond electronically. Most homes and workplaces are now using computerised equipment for communication; the Internet is rapidly becoming the method of choice for accessing and sharing information. First-time job seekers are now more likely to search web sites for job postings than to peruse newspapers, magazines and journals. The prevalence of eadvertising has made it easier.

The Internet speeds up the hiring process in three basis stages:

- Faster posting of jobs.
  - The submission of information to the media house and its appearance in print disappears. On the internet, the advertisement appears immediately and can be kept alive for as long as the recruiter requires it.
- Faster applicant response.
  - Jobs posted on the Internet and requiring responses via the same medium receive responses on the same day.
- Faster processing of résumés.
  - An applicant sending a résumé electronically can immediately have the application processed, receive an acknowledgement, be screened electronically, and have details of the application and résumé despatched to several managers at the same time.

On-line recruiting also provides access to passive job seekers, that is, individuals who already have a job but would apply for what appears a better one that is advertised on the Internet. These job seekers may be of a better quality Since, they are not desperate for a job change as are the active job seekers who may be frustrated, disgruntled workers looking for a new position. Companies that are likely to advertise on-line usually have a Web site that allows potential candidates to learn about the company before deciding whether to apply, thus lowering the incidence time-wasting through the submission of unsuitable applications.

The Web site can be used as a tool to encourage potential job seekers to build an interest in joining the organisation. Job web sites offer unlimited space which can be used, by management, to sell the organisation. The site can then be used, not only to post vacancies, but also to publicise the organisation. That will allow candidates to become more familiar with the company, know what skills the company is looking for and get to know about its culture. Most importantly, the system will provide a proper path to securing quick responses to job openings. On-line recruiting facilitates the decentralisation of the hiring function by making it possible for other groups in the organisation to take responsibility for part of the function.

- Some applicants still place great value on face-to-face interactions in the hiring process. Such applicants are likely to ignore jobs posted, impersonally, on-line.
- Companies are overwhelmed by the volume of résumés posted on the Internet. This can, in fact, lengthen the short-listing process. If the screening process is not well done, the quantity of applications/ résumés logged-on may be more of a hindrance to the process that an aid to selection.

Job seekers who demand confidentiality in the recruitment process may be reluctant to use the Internet as a job search mechanism.

For effectiveness in the use of the strategy of e-Recruiting, companies are advised to:

- Use specialised Job Sites that cater to specific industries; interested in joining the company;
- Take advantage of the fact that Internet job advertisements have no space limitations so recruiters can use longer job descriptions to fully describe the company, job requirements and working conditions offered;
- Use valid Search Engines that will sort candidates effectively, but will not discriminate against any persons or groups;
- Create attention-grabbing newspaper advertisements that prompt people to visit the company's Web site. They will then see all vacancies that are advertised;
- Encourage employees to e-mail job advertisements to friends;
- Design and implement a successful e-Recruitment strategy.

COLLEGE RECRUITMENT

College recruiting – sending an employer's representatives to college campuses to prescreen applicants and create an applicant pool from that college's graduating class – is an important source of management trainees, promotable candidates, and professional and technical employees. To get the best out of this hiring strategy, the organisation and its career opportunities must be made to stand out.

Human resource professionals are aware that few college students and potential graduates know where their careers will take them over the next fifteen to twenty years. Therefore many of the an opportunity for recruiters to select the potential employees with the personal, technical and professional competencies they require in their organisation. The personal competencies identified may include, *inter alia*, a positive work ethic, strong interpersonal skills, leadership capacity and an ability to function well in a work team. The opportunity to discuss a student's current strengths and potential future value to an organisation cannot be replicated in any other setting. Two major advantages of this strategy are the cost (which is higher than word-of-mouth recruiting but lower than advertising in the media or using an employment agency), and the convenience (Since, many candidates can be interviewed in a short time in the same location with space and administrative support provided by the college itself).

Unfortunately, suitable candidates become available only at certain times of the year, which may not always suit the needs of the hiring organisation. Another major disadvantage of college recruiting is the lack of experience and the inflated expectations of new graduates and the cost of hiring graduates for entry-level positions that may not require a college degree. To make college recruiting effective, the recruiting organisation must first determine how many and which schools should be targeted. It may prove cost-effective to do intensive recruiting in a few, carefully-selected institutions, establishing a presence and building the organisation's reputation among students and faculty.

Timely and frequent dissemination of literature, the offer of internships and the award of prises for academic and/or social prowess help to advertise the organisation as a preferred place of employment. Subsequent invitations to the organisation's offices, made to students identified as potential employees, may serve to solidify the firm's image. Public Service organisations are usually unable to compete financially with their Private Sector counterparts and are therefore less likely to pay competitive salaries.

However, most public service agencies provide their employees with a wealth and range of experiences that are available nowhere else. It is for that reason that many college graduates use the Public Service as an employer of first resort to gain the experiences that will make them marketable in the short term. The strategies may not work as smoothly for public service recruiters, Since, the laws that govern their organisations' recruitment practices may be more stringent than those that apply in private sector companies. There may also be questions about the legality of the on-line application form. If this strategy were to be employed, public service recruiters must first decide on the criteria that should guide the process. The Public Service is seldom immediately seen as an attractive employer, mainly because salaries are uncompetitive.

Except for those students who have a commitment to public service, the top ten percent of college graduates will select the Private Sector as the employer of choice, partly because of the prestige value but primarily because of the remuneration package and because the recruiters may have been more successful in marketing their company. Therefore, it is understood that many of the graduates who enter the Public Service will stay for a short time and either return to school or proceed to another sector once they have acquired the requisite skills and experience that make them marketable.

Recruitment and retention strategies in the Public Service must, therefore, reflect this reality and efforts made to get the most out of college graduates before they move on; conversely, the organisation may need to plan to recruit those students whose academic records suggest that they will remain in an organisation that pays less.

Retention strategies will focus on ensuring opportunities for intense training and development for skill enhancement and personal satisfaction. College recruitment also offers opportunities for internships. These programmes may provide the organisations with quality employees at low cost per hire. Some interns are hired at low cost (perhaps minimum wage) and are offered work experience.

Interns are able to have business skills, check out potential employers, and learn more about employers' likes and dislikes before making final career choices. Some of the better interns are recruited after graduation. College recruitment is relatively expensive and time consuming for the recruiting company. The process involves screening the candidate, that is, determining whether he/she is worthy of further consideration and marketing the company as a preferred place of employment. An alternate strategy for college recruitment is the career planning workshop.

These activities are usually (but not exclusively) associated with adolescent school leavers. They do not immediately produce ready candidates for the job market but provide the opportunity for an organisation to present itself as an employer worthy of consideration. Co-ordinators of career planning workshops co-opt professionals and organisations to present career options to potential school leavers in a controlled setting so as to lay out the range of possibilities to young job seekers.

Career planning workshops are used mainly as information-giving tools which the school leaver can use to make informed career choices. Some organisations use the workshops as a base for internships.

Job Fairs

The concept of a job fair is to bring those interested in finding a job into those companies who are searching for applicants. Job fairs are open fora at which employers can exhibit the best their companies have to offer so that job seekers can make informed choices. They are considered one of the most effective ways for job seekers to land jobs. At the job fair, employers have a large pool of candidates on which to draw, while job seekers have the opportunity to shop around for dozens – sometimes hundreds – of employers, all in one place.

Notwithstanding the fact that the atmosphere at the fair is more relaxed than at an interview, employers are still on the look out for qualified, potential employees who have interest, dedication and initiative.

Maintaining Fairness/Equity in the Recruitment Process

It is often difficult to ensure and maintain fairness/equity in the recruitment process although, in every jurisdiction, there are laws that protect individuals and vulnerable groups from the negative impact of discriminatory practices. Where necessary, systems, detailed procedures and processes exist or must be established to minimise discrimination.

Each country designates/identifies a group or groups for special notice; women, visible minorities and the disabled are usual targets. The Government of Canada, in articulating its "Employment Equity Act and Regulations", identified four designated groups as employment equity targets: women, Aboriginal people, members of visible minority groups, persons with disabilities.

In the legislation, managers' responsibilities for employment equity are stated as:

- Ensuring effective overall performance and continuous progress of the employment equity goals within the operation;
- Achieving, fostering and maintaining a representative workforce;
- Showing leadership in employment equity and demonstrating commitment to it by ensuring that discrimination and stereotyping are not tolerated; and
- Informing and educating employees in the organisation about employment equity and diversity.

The Australian Public Service Commission, in ensuring that there were no infringements against individuals rights, issued general guidelines on workplace diversity, some of which related to recruitment:

- Integrate workplace diversity with the agency's goals and business.
- Reflect agency workplace diversity objectives in workplace agreements and certified agreements.
- Integrate workplace diversity principles into human resources policies and practices.
- Include implementation of workplace diversity objectives in the corporate plan, business plan and client service charters.
- Ensure information about employment opportunities is available in accessible formats.
- Review recruitment and selection processes to ensure that current and potential employees are not discriminated against.

Gather information on demographics. It is the goal of every jurisdiction to minimise or eliminate any instance of obvious discrimination against individuals or groups. In discussing policies on employment equity, scholor explains: "Employment equity policies and Programmes are about fairness in the workplace, not about reverse discrimination. Fairness is achieved when no one is denied employment opportunity and no one benefits for reasons unrelated to ability. Employment equity Programmes attempt to change the composition of the Workforce so that employees better reflect the community. The facts (both historical and current) show that members of the four designated groups face discrimination, enjoy less access to educational Programmes and training, and are often denied employment and promotions even when they have the necessary skills and experience."

The University's policies give special attention, *inter alia*, to the existence of systemic barriers and instances of intentional discrimination in the process of recruitment. Service Commissions were enshrined in the Independence Constitutions of the territories of the Commonwealth Caribbean and given *inter alia*, the power to recruit/appoint persons into the Public Service and, in so doing, reduce the influence of politicians on the staffing process.

In order to discharge their authority for making appointments, the Commissions have influenced the development of legislation and regulations that circumscribe the practice of recruitment, primarily to ensure that no discrimination attends the exercise.

To this end, entry into the Public Service follows the procedures of:

- Application on prescribed forms;
- Selection on the basis of seniority of application; application of age limits for entry into certain defined grades/classes; the use of written examinations and/or competitive interviews as the basis for permanent appointment to certain grades/classes.

The rules established by the Commissions enforce compliance in an attempt to minimise or eliminate the possibility of bias in staffing on the basis of race/ethnicity, creed, age, social status or physical disability.

INFORMATION SOURCES IN THE LIBRARY/INTERNET

The Internet has become a big library for all kinds of information. Some information sources are available online free of charge while others are fee-based. Examples include online books, databases, journals and reference resources. Some of these are free on the Internet while others are based on subscription or purchase. MEDLINE/PubMed is a good example of a free online database while EMBASE is based on subscription.

The various categories of information sources that could be accessed through the Web:

- Reference;
- Monographs;
- Periodicals;
- Indexes and abstracts;
- Drug information; and
- Databases.

REFERENCE SOURCES

These are authoritative works that provide specific answers or information. As you go through school, you will need to use reference sources to find information about topics, locate facts, and answer questions. There are many types of reference sources, including atlases, dictionaries, Encyclopaedias, thesauri, directories, almanacs, manuals, biographies, and handbooks, among others. Each type is available either in print, on CD-ROMs and the Internet. Reference information sources can be general or subject specific. For example, The Encyclopaedia *Britannica* is general while *The Encyclopaedia of Stem-Cell* Research, *The Encyclopaedia of Pain*, and *The Gale Encyclopaedia of Medicine* are subject Encyclopaedias. Other reference sources such as dictionaries, atlases, directories also have both general and subject categories.

Fig. A Set of Encyclopaedia Britannicagale Encyclopaedia of Medicine.

MONOGRAPHS

A monograph is a scholarly piece of writing in form of an essay or book on a specific, often limited subject. It is a book that stands on its own rather than being part of a series. National Research Council (NRC), a monograph is a specialized scientific book.

Monographs are written by specialists for the benefit of other specialists and demand the highest standards of scholarship. Most monographic manuscripts are critically reviewed and edited resulting in books that are expected to have a reasonably long shelf life. Monographs serve as an important means for conveying basic background information, such as a narrative description of a disease, path-physiology, diagnostic techniques and common therapeutic regimes etc. This trend remains true today, whether the monograph is in the print or electronic format.

Monographs can be located using bibliographies that list references of books with detailed bibliographic information (author, title, year of publication, publisher and date of publication). Bibliographies serve as tools for verification, location and selection of monographs. Today, many print sources for monographs are now in electronic formats. To locate monographs in a library collection requires using the library catalog and most libraries now have Online Public Access Catalog (OPAC). A good example is the National Library of Medicine LOCATOR plus.

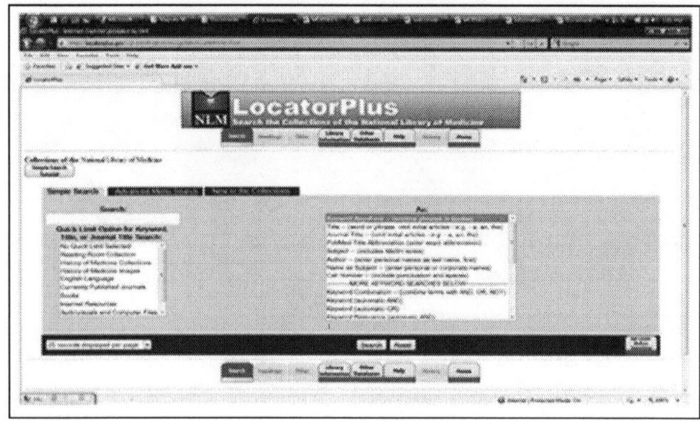

PERIODICALS

Periodicals are publications such as journals, newspapers, or magazines published on a regular basis-daily, weekly, bi-weekly, monthly, bimonthly, quarterly, yearly, etc. The information in periodicals covers a wide variety of topics and is very uptodate. Periodicals are available in both print and electronic formats. Common examples of periodicals include popular magazines (or general interest magazines), professional and trade magazines, scholarly journals, newsletters, and newspapers. The two basic types of periodicals are: popular (or general interest magazines), and scholarly.

POPULAR

Popular magazines are periodicals of non-specialist nature. The published articles are usually written by staff writers, and chosen by the editor of the publication. Magazine articles are usually shorter, written in non-technical language, and designed for the general population. Articles in popular magazines are reviewed by one or two members of staff of the organization where they are published. Popular magazines have a glossy appearance, contains many photographs and advertisements.

Examples of popular magazines are:

- O, The Oprah Magazine.
- Readers Digest.
- People.
- Time Magazine.

TRADE MAGAZINES

These are magazines that present information about a profession or a particular trade. They are written for members of a specific business, industry or organization. Trade magazines cover industry trends, new products or techniques, and organizational news written by staff or contributing authors. Good examples of trade magazines are: *The Economist, APA Monitor* and *Computer World.*

SCHOLARLY JOURNALS

Journals are written by experts or specialists in a particular field/discipline and geared towards other scholars. The purpose of scholarly publications is to report research or advance knowledge. The articles are usually longer and may contain charts, graphs, statistics, etc., as well as extensive bibliographies. The articles usually involve extensive research and in-depth studies. The writing style is more complex and the language may be technical.

Examples of this type of periodical are academic journals and professional journals. Academic journals are written by members of an academic community and are reviewed by their peers while professional journals are written by member of a professional body including librarians, lawyers, doctors and nurses.

Examples of academic journals are:

- *British Medical Journal.*
- *New England Journal of Medicine.*
- *African Journal of Medicine and Medical Sciences.*
- *East African Medical Journal.*
- *African Health Sciences.*

Examples of professional/academic journals include:

- *Journal of the American Medical Association.*
- *Journal of the Medical Library Association.*
- *African Journal of Library, Archival and Information Science.*

Access to journals either in print or electronic formats is based on subscription, however; fulltext articles of some electronic journals can be accessed free on the Internet. Also, more than 7000 electronic journals are available to students, researchers, scientists, Health care workers, and policy makers in Africa through the Health Internetwork Access to Research Initiative (HINARI). Using this resource requires institutional registration and login with the User Identification and Password.

NEWSPAPERS

Newspaper articles are short and written in non-technical language. They provide first-hand account of an event and so are primary sources. Newspapers come in different forms and are designed for the general public and are business in nature. Newspaper articles are usually short and written in an easy to understand language by staff reporters and reviewed by staff within the organization. Newspapers are also good sources for secondary information. However, not all information in newspapers is reliable. Newspapers are published daily, weekly or monthly. Example of newspapers include: *The New York Times, The Guardian*, and *Nigerian Tribune* etc.

INDEXES AND ABSTRACTS

Abstracts and indexes provide citations to papers dealing with specific topics in a field of knowledge. Indexes provide the essential bibliographic information needed to identify an article or other publications and usually include information about the author of the work, the source journal or other publication, volume, issue, and pagination. Abstracting tools include the same key elements but also a summary of the work usually written by the author or sometimes generated by the reviewer where an author did not submit one.

Most indexing and abstracting services allow access to their content through subject and author indexes. However, each tool differs on how data is presented and the nature by which access is organized.

Examples of abstracts and indexes include:

- *Index Medicus.*
- *International Pharmaceutical Abstracts.*
- *Index to Dental Literature.*
- *Science Citation Index.*
- *Current Contents: Clinical Practice.*
- *Psychological Abstracts.*
- *Cumulative Index to Nursing and Allied Health Literature* (*CINAHL*).

Most of the popular databases searched by librarians and library users originated from printbased abstracting and indexing services. For example, the Index Medicus resulted in MEDLINE now accessible online through PubMed.

DRUG INFORMATION SOURCES

Butros and McGuinness, drug information sources cover the fields of pharmacology, pharmacy and toxicology. There are as many drug information sources as there are various specialties.

DATABASES

These are systematically organized collections of infor-mation covering different subject matters or specializing in one given subject or topic. They may be arranged in a table of contents, alphabetically, in numerical order, in an index or in subject categories. A database is made up of records. Each item in the database has one record. Records consist of smaller units of information called fields.

Common bibliographic database fields are: author, publi- cation title, article title, subject or keywords, publication date, volume, issue and page number. For example, in the MEDLINE/PubMed database, each journal citation has one record.

The record consists of the following fields: author, article title, journal title, date of publication, volume, issue, page number, PubMed ID, and abstract.

A digital database (8.3) is a computer programme that organizes, describes, and indexes information. It permits the user to search for specific types of information, depending upon the selected search parameters.

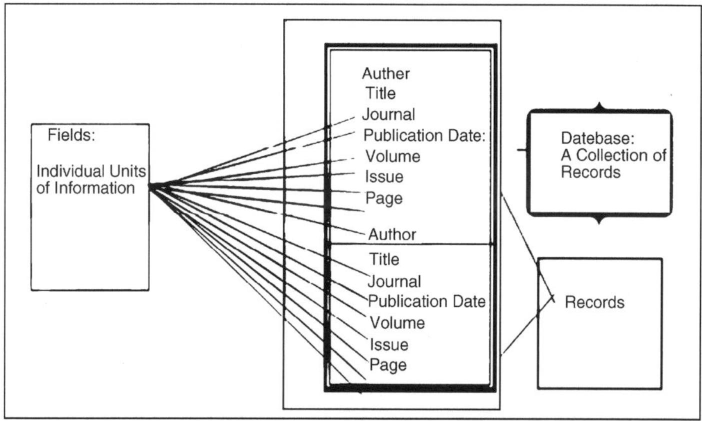

Fig. Components of a Biblographic Database

INVISIBLE OR DEEP WEB

The "invisible Web" is what you cannot find using search engines and what you see in almost all subject directories. They are gold mines of information you need to search directly. These includes all of the licensed article, magazine, reference, news archives, and other research resources that libraries and some industries buy for those authorized to use them. There is lots of helpful information locked away in databases that can never be indexed by search engines. The services that let you search this "invisible Web" or "deep Web include: Invisi-bleweb.com, Lycos Invisible Catalog, Direct search and WebData.

Examples of searchable databases containing invisible web pages valuable in academic research are:

- Ipl2.
- Infomine.
- Online Bibliographic Databases:
  - African Index Medicus (AIM);
  - MEDLINE/PubMed;
  - Cumulative Index to Nursing and Allied Health Literature (CINAHL);
  - Web of Knowledge;
  - Scopus; and
  - EMBASE.

African Index Medicus (AIM)

African Index Medicus (AIM) is a collaborative effort between the World Health Organization (WHO) and the Association for Health Information and Libraries in Africa (AHILA). AIM gives access to information published or related to Africa and also encourages local publishing. A total of 140 journals published in Africa are indexed in AIM as of October 1, 2010. This database provides access to mainly abstracts and a few full-text articles published in African journals.

MEDLINE/PubMed

MEDLINE is the premier bibliographic database of the National Library of Medicine, Bethesda, Maryland, USA. It covers the field of medicine, nursing dentistry, veterinary medicine, the Health care systems, the preclinical sciences and other areas related to the life sciences and is updated daily. MEDLINE records contain bibliographic citations from over 5,000 print and electronic biomedical journals published across the globe. It has over 12 million citations of which approximately 76per cent include abstracts.

Cumulative Index to Nursing and Allied Health Literature (CINAHL)

Cumulative Index to Nursing and Allied Health Literature (CINAHL) CINAHL gives access to citations and abstracts for nursing and allied health information. It includes citations from over 2000 journals and abstracts are available for over 1200 titles with full text of over 7,000 records available in the database. This database also provides some coverage of biomedicine, alternative/ complementary medicine and consumer health information. CINAHL is based on subscription. However, it could be accessed free of charge through HINARI by institutions in Africa.

Web of Science

Web or science Provides access to the Science Citation Index Expanded and Social Science Citation Index. It covers science and provides technical journals in biochemistry, biology, genetics, biomedicine, genetics, microbiology, nuclear science with abstracts. It covers more than 8,000 journals. It offers current and retrospective bibliographic information, author abstracts and cited references and allows users to conduct broad-based comprehensive searches that uncover all the relevant information they need. It provides cited reference searching, the unique ISI search and retrieval feature that lets users track the literature forward, backward and through the database. It is updated weekly. Web of Knowledge (PubMed) is accessible free of charge via HINARI.

Scopus

Scopus is an interdisciplinary bibliographic database that indexes the content of more than 15,000 peer-reviewed journals from more than 4000 international publishers. It covers subjects such as the physical sciences, engineering, earth and environmental sciences, life and health sciences, social sciences, psychology, business, and management. Scopus content includes MEDLINE and EMBASE citations. Also, Scopus covers 1,000 Open Access Journals, 500 Conference Proceedings, Over 600 Trade Publications and over 125 Book titles. In addition, Scopus covers 386 million quality Web sources including 21 million patents.

Embase

Provides content to biomedical (clinical and experimental) information with extensive coverage of drug research, pharmacology, pharmacy, and toxicology, public health and mental health topics with abstracts back to 1974 and it is updated daily with pharmacological information. The database indexes more than 7000 journals, has over 18 million records. It has more than the 11 million EMBASE records from 1974 to date and seven million for unique MEDLINE records from 1966 to the present.

EVIDENCE-BASED MEDICINE (EBM) RESOURCES/DATABASES

Evidence-Based Medicine is about using information from the medical literature in making informed decision about patient care.

Many EBM databases are now accessible online including, among others:

- Clinical Queries.
- Cochrane Library.
- Clinical Evidence.
- DynaMed.
- Best Evidence.

In this module, Clinical Queries and the Cochrane Library will be discussed

Clinical Queries

This is accessible through PubMed and covers three main areas namely:

- *Clinical Study Category Query*: This filters citations to a specific clinical study category and scope.
- *Systematic Reviews:* These filter citations for systematic reviews, meta-analyses, reviews of clinical trials, evidence-based medicine, consensus development conferences, and guidelines..
- *Medical Genetics:* Filter citations to topics in medical genetics.

The Cochrane Library

The Cochrane Library is a collection of databases, published on CD-ROM and the Internet and updated quarterly, containing the Cochrane Database of Systematic Reviews, the Cochrane Central Register of Controlled Trials, the Database of Abstracts of Reviews of Effects, the Cochrane Methodology Register, the HTA Database, NHSEED, and information about The Cochrane Collaboration. The Cochrane Library has about 4,000 reviews meant for use by health care workers to enable them to make informed decisions with respect to patient care. Reviews are unique because they are both produced by, and are relevant to everyone interested in the effects of health care. Based on the best available evidence, Health care providers can decide if they should fund production of a particular drug. Practitioners can find out if an intervention is effective in a specific clinical context.

Patients and other Health care consumers can assess the potential risks and benefits of their treatment:

- Systematic reviews seek to collate all evidence that fits pre-specified eligibility criteria in order to address a specific research question.

- They aim to minimize bias by using explicit, syste-matic methods.
- The Cochrane Collaboration prepares, maintains and promotes systematic reviews to inform Health care decisions (Cochrane reviews).
- Cochrane reviews are published in the *Cochrane Database of Systematic Reviews* in *The Cochrane Library.*

DIGITAL LIBRARIES ON THE INTERNET

The Internet and the Web have been growing in leaps and bounds over the past few years, accelerating the problem of information explosion, a well-known phenomena to all of us. According to Nature, the publicly indexable Web contains an estimated 800 million pages as of February 1999, encompassing about 15 terabytes of information or about 6 terabytes of text after removing HTML tags, comments, and extra white-space. Indeed, the growing amount of Search Engines (SEs) that have popped up everywhere, reaching more than 2400 different SEs, enable us to access the cyberspace, but they also flood us with vast amounts of irrelevant information. Search engine coverage, relative to the estimated size of the publicly indexable Web, has recently decreased substantially, with no engine indexing more than about 16 per cent of the estimated size of the publicly indexable Web. It is interesting to note that 83 per cent of the Web sites contain commercial content and only 6 per cent contain scientific or educational content.

The object is structured as follows. This part presents the resource repository hierarchy, defines the notion of the library and the development from paper to digital libraries. The next part classifies digital libraries, compares between the different types and introduces the logical harvesting model. The part following provides additional aspects regarding digital libraries. A concluding discussion ends the object.

RESOURCE REPOSITORIES HIERARCHY

Both Search Engines (SEs) and Digital Libraries (DLs) are Internet Resource Discovery (IRD) Tools. We introduce a resource repositories hierarchy with two major paradigms: search engines and digital libraries, where each branches to categories. SEs can be classified into three categories: Basic-SE, Directory, and Meta-SE.

All the categories support search user interfaces, but with significant differences in their construction method:

- Basic-SE/Index - a tool that uses an automatic robot/crawler to gather metadata on items.
- Directory/Catalog/Guide - a tool that uses human judgement to collect and catalog items.
- Meta-SE - a tool that holds no database of its own, but rather queries Basic-SEs upon a user request.

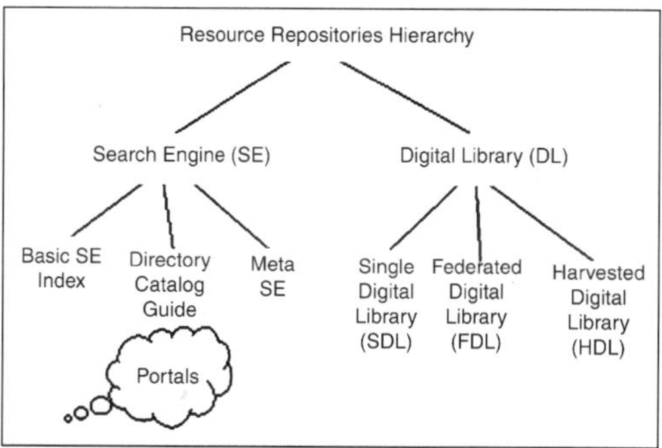

Fig. Resource Repositories Hierarchy.

LIBRARY

Before we delve into digital libraries, we define the notion of a library in general and of a digital library specifically.

Collection of Data Objects

A library holds a collection of data objects, also called holdings, items, resources, or just material.

The items can be:

- Books and journals.
- Documents (*e.g.,* HTML pages)
- Multimedia objects (such as pictures or images, tapes or video files, etc.).
- The library objects can be available locally in the library, or indirectly, by using a network to access them.

Collection of Metadata Structures

A library contains a collection of metadata structures, such as catalogs, guides, dictionaries, thesauri, indices, summaries, annotations, glossaries, etc.

Collection of Services

A library provides a collection of services, such as:

- Various access methods (search, browse, etc.) for different users.
- Management of the library (purchase, shelf arranging, computerisation, communication).
- Search (query formulation), browse, and consultation.
- Logging/statistics and Performance Measurement Evaluation (PME).
- Selective Dissemination of Information (SDI) or as it is called Push mode on the Internet.

Domain Focus

A library has a domain focus and its collection has a purpose. For example:

art, science, or literature. Also, it is usually created to serve a community of users, and therefore is finely grained. For example: academic, public, special, school, national, or state library.

Quality Control

A library uses quality control in the sense that all its material is verified and consistent with the profile, or stereotype, of the library. The material is filtered before it is included in the library, and also its metadata is usually enriched (*e.g.,* annotated), etc.

Preservation

Libraries and archives have served as the central institutional focus for preservation, and both types of institutions include preservation as one of their core functions. The purpose of preservation is to ensure protection of information of enduring value for access by present and future generations. Preservation includes regular allocation of resources for persistence, preventive measures to arrest deterioration of materials, and remedial measures to restore the usability of selected materia ls.

FROM PAPER TO DIGITAL LIBRARIES

In any case, the Web and the SEs do not substitute the classical, loved libraries. Looking backwards, libraries can be classified into three types:

- *Paper/Analog Library (PL)* - the classical paper library with its card catalog;
- *Automated/Hybrid Library (AL)* - a paper library with a computerised catalog; and
- *Digital Library (DL)* - a computerised library in which most of the information is digital.

No one questions or disputes the long and lasting contribution of existing classical libraries. The concept of the paper library and the various services it provides are well established. The idea is that DLs should provide all these and more. We use the term 'integrated services' in DLs to allude to that. These integrated services will add services that are made possible by use of the digital medium such as: varied search techniques resulting in focused results, faster provision of relevant resources, and access also to multimedia resources. The problems of our regular libraries are well known and need not be detailed here. On the other hand, it is less clear to us what a digital library is and how it works-this is the subject of this paper.

CLASSIFYING THE DIGITAL LIBRARIES

We classify the digital libraries into three categories:

- Stand-alone Digital Library (SDL),
- Federated Digital Library (FDL), and
- Harvested Digital Library (HDL).

We now detail:

- *Stand-alone Digital Library (SDL)*: This is the regular classical library implemented in a fully computerised fashion. SDL is simply a library in which the holdings are digital. The SDL is selfcontained–the material is localised and centralised. In fact, it is a computerised instance of the classical library with the benefits of computerisation. Examples of SDLs are the Library of Congress (LC) and its National Digital Library (NDL), and the Israeli K12 Portal Snunit.
- *Federated Digital Library (FDL)*: This is a federation of several independent SDLs in the network, organised around a common theme, and coupled together on the network. A FDL composes several autonomous SDLs that form a networked library with a transparent user interface. The different SDLs are heterogeneous and are connected via communication networks. The major challenge in the construction and maintenance of a FDL is interoperability. Examples of FDLs are the Networked Computer Science Technical Reference Library (NCSTRL) and Networked Digital Library of Theses and Dissertations (NDLTD).
- *Harvested Digital Library (HDL)*: This is a virtual library providing summarised access to related material scattered over the network. A HDL holds only metadata with pointers to the holdings that are "one click away" in Cyberspace. The material held in the libraries is harvested (converted into summaries) according to the definition of an Information Specialist (IS). However, a HDL has regular DL characteristics, it is finely grained and subject focused. It has rich library services, and has high quality control preserved by the IS, who is also responsible for annotating the objects in the library. Examples of HDLs are the Internet Public Library (IPL) and the WWW Virtual Library.

COMPARISON

To emphasise the different aspects of this DL categorisation, let us get into the various DL types. In SDL and FDL, the items are electronically purchased or fully digitised/scanned. These items are stored in the local repository (in SDL), or in separate SDL repositories accessed using a network protocol (in FDL). Each SDL (and all together in a FDL) holds a huge repository containing both the items and some metadata structures to enable efficient retrieval. This material is updated every now and then, in a process similar to the one in classical library. It is important to note that composing a FDL out of SDLs requires interoperability capabilities, and the use of a common protocol. In contrast to the SDL and FDL, the HDL's items are gathered from the network. These items are scattered on many servers, and accessed via direct retrieval using standard protocols such as HTTP, FTP, etc. The HDL holds only metadata on the items, and therefore its repository is small and compact.

Because the items that belong to the HDL can be updated any time by their authors, their summaries have to be dynamically refreshed in the HDL using computerised procedures that are triggered automatically or initiated explicitly by the IS. An interesting point is that the profile of a HDL can be changed by the IS to enhance the library contents.

HARVESTING MODEL FOR HDLs

As suggested, now describe our developed logical model for constructing HDLs. The model includes processes, data repositories (represented by rectangles) and auxiliary repositories (represented by parallelograms). The initiating IS invokes the Harvester with the DL harvesting request. The Harvester generates the initial DL profile and passes this as the harvesting query to the Locator component. The Locator uses various network search techniques to enrich the initial collection of URLs to be harvested. The next component to be invoked is the Gatherer. It uses each top-level URL, in a recursive manner, to gather all referenced resources from the network providers, and passes them to the Filtering component. The Filtering component is responsible for blocking the Non-relevant documents from reaching the focused DL. It uses various levels of filtering that all remaining documents have to pass to be considered relevant. A first level, for example, can use 'regular expressions' to match query keywords with the URL string tokens. A second level can use statistical techniques on the document itself, based on keyword counts and frequencies. A third level might use a Categoriser to classify the document and check if it belongs to the gathered DL categories. More levels or any geared combination of levels can ensure a cleaner DL devoid of 'noises'.

All relevant documents are passed now to the Summariser. It extracts a summary of the document, and passes a stream of summaries to the Broker. The Broker indexes the summaries and organises the DL. The IS builds for the DL a relevant topics-tree, possibly using advanced IR tools for categorisation and clustering. The Retriever provides the DL user with a user-friendly interface.

IMPLEMENTATION OF HARVEST/KATSIR SYSTEM

To demonstrate HDLs, we focus on the Katsir HDL based on the Harvest system, an initial/partial implementation of the harvesting model for HDL. Katsir is currently being developed in Bar-Ilan University (BIU) as cooperation between the Mathematics and Computer Science department and the Department of Information Studies. The Harvest system, developed mainly at University of Colorado, USA, is an integrated set of tools to gather, extract, organise, search, cache, and replicate relevant information across the Internet. With modest effort users can tailor Harvest to digest information in many different formats, and offer custom search services on the Internet. Moreover, Harvest makes very efficient use of network traffic, remote servers, and disk space. The Katsir system is based on the Harvest system. Katsir can be directed to build a focused DL, based on both local and networked harvested materials.

Katsir's enhancements over the original Harvest system are:

- *Hebrew support*: Full Hebrew support for both resources and interfaces was added to Harvest.
- *Improved user interface*: While Harvest's user interface supports keywords query, Katsir enable to user to retrieve information by keywords or conduct a guided tour by following a topics-tree that enables hypertext access to relevant materials.
- *Improved Graphical User Interface for the IS*: While the IS interface to Harvest is through Unix, using file editors to define harvesting options, Katsir implemented a GUI interface to define DL profile. The interface includes URLs for initialisation, harvesting options, ports selection, etc. It also employs the standard browsers Bookmarks/Favorites utilities to define the initial DL Harvesting URLs.

The initial Katsir system was developed and implemented in an educational environment as a response to the unique requirements of the Israeli educational system. This project was part of a drive to enhance and assimilate information and telecommunication technologies in Israel, based on the public Internet. Both researchers and students of the departments of Information Studies and of Mathematics and Computer Science at BIU were involved in the development of Katsir.

Their cooperation in the framework of the demonstrative Gilo High-School project was complementary in knowledge and experience, and fruitful in its results. Moreover, the project itself was planned and executed with full cooperation of the Gilo user community. This begun in requirements analysis, in deciding the topics to be harves ted, in training the users in accessing the system, in conducting the control and evaluation process, and in reviewing and implementing the conclusions reached as part of the working methods of Katsir.

INTERNET AND ITS USE IN ACADEMIC LIBRARIES

Many of us by now are familiar with Internet especially those working in the academic libraries. This is because the academic libraries have been the pioneer in the field of automation and Internet. Internet has become essential for today's education and research in the academic institutions. Library being a hub of research and academic activities are therefore being provided with Internet connections. The Internet is a unique information resource, bringing a wide range of material from around the world to a local machine.

One of the earliest usages of the Internet was to access the OPAC ,*i.e.*, the Online Public Access Catalogues of different libraries or within a campus. The union catalogues which lists the holdings of several libraries was another important tool accessible through net. Another area of growing importance for academic libraries is that of electronic journals. Big publishing houses like

Elsevier, Springer, ACM etc. are providing packages of their journals to libraries in electronic form via Internet. So at nominal subscription the libraries can access to these costly journals, which are becoming increasingly popular with the users.

Thus grew consortia based subscription in India. INDEST, INFONET and CSIR Consortium are the examples of library consortia for sharing journals and bibliographic information. These consortia based journal subscription are available through the Internet. The Indian National Digital Library in Engineering Science and Technology, *i.e.,* INDEST was set up by the Ministry of Human resource Development (MHRD) for subscription to electronic resources for 38 institutions including IISc, IITs, NITs, IIMs, etc. Over 6000 e-journals are accessible through this consortium, which has its headquarters in IIT Delhi. Infonet Contortia is set up by UGC and operated through its INFLIBNET Centre, Ahmedabad. Over 100 Universities are its members. It covers disciplines like Arts, Sciences, Mathematics and statistics etc. About 4000 full text electronic journals from 25 publishers are currently accessible. CSIR e-journal Consortia provides access to 3300+ e-journals from 11 publishers to all CSIR SandT staff of different CSIR institutions located around India.

These consortia not only provide full text access but they also give access to bibliographic databases like COMPENDEX, INSPEC SciFinder Scholar, and Web of Science etc. Many open access materials important for education and research are available on the Internet. They are very useful in the context that they are not fee based and also don't have restricted access and are thus becoming very popular with students and researchers. Communicating with users is very important in academic libraries.

Widespread access to the Internet has also created new means of communicating with users. In some cases, Internet technologies (*e.g.* e-mail and publishing on Web pages) are used to reproduce an existing service in another medium, such as online "suggestion boxes". However, there is "added value" to such a service as users can mail in their suggestions from terminals on or off campus at a time convenient to them. E-mail enquiry or reference services also represent an extension of mainstream library activity - although some academic librarians initially had concerns about being able to meet the demand of such a service. Reference and enquiry services in academic libraries in the main seek to teach their users how to search for information themselves, rather than answering the enquiries themselves, as is more likely to be the case in a special library.

A significant number of British academic libraries have adopted electronic mail enquiry or information services - at the University of Hull the "e-mail help line" is treated as an extension of the Enquiry Desk service. Anecdotal evidence suggests that electronic enquiry services are not overwhelmed, and most users do stay within the parameters of the service. The most successful e-mail enquiry services have developed their procedures and boundaries prior to the service going live. As many enquiries fall into the category of Frequently Asked Questions, these can thus be answered by existing position statements. Electronic mail also has great potential to cut down on the mountain of paperwork involved in sending out recall notices, notifying readers that items can be collected etc.

Some library systems allow students to renew loans (provided no other reader is waiting for the book) directly via the OPAC or to request a renewal via e-mail. Similarly, weblogs or simply blogs are now becoming very popular on the Internet as a communication medium. A library weblog can be used to:

- Providing news information for users
- Providing links to recommend internet sources
- Book reviews, information about new books
- Providing entertainment or amusement for users
- Providing news or information for librarians
- Book discussions
- Provide news or information for the trustees
- Provide research tips
- Communication among the librarians (in a library system).

The library can make good use of the electronic mail system of Internet ,*i.e.,* E-mail to communicate reservation alert, current awareness services like SDI, new arrivals of books and journals, receiving interlibrary loan request and sending overdue notices to the users.

In addition to these specialist services academic librarians also make use of the Internet information that is available to all users. Much bibliographical and price information can be found from online bookstores and Web sites for professional organizations and publishers. A wide range of factual information from government and NGO sources is available too.

Although librarians have more skepticism about the well-publicized Web search tools than most users, such services can be valuable, particularly for easily defined topics (such as names or abbreviations) and the sheer range of material indexed, subjects covered and the speed with which they search can make them useful when a clear starting point is not obvious. They may not always retrieve a full answer, but may give helpful clues.

Internet resources are just another information medium academic librarians are extending their skills to encompass it. So they may offer a current awareness service to teaching and research staff to inform them of new Web sites and discussion lists; they will apply established criteria to assessing the content of information sources or the effectiveness of secondary services like search tools.

The hypertext nature of the Web makes it easy to make additional explanation or instruction for a resource as an optional choice. This concept of instruction at the point and time of use is harder to achieve in the physical library.

ACUTE NEED OF INTERNET SPECIALISTS

In the Internet age there is acute need of Internet specialists. These specialists will be armed with the necessary skills and training to help the users to locate their information pin pointedly and efficiently on the net. Libraries specially the academic libraries would have a great demand for these specialists.

Internet connectivity in the academic libraries is growing day by day. So, the present administration of the academic institutions should take necessary steps to equip the library staff with the required skills and training on Internet. Training can help to understand many essential aspects of the Internet such as follows:

- Are we using the right type of Internet connection for our needs? Are we getting a good deal?
- How quickly can we find what we looking for on the Internet? We should be able to find useful information about virtually any topic in less than a minute. If you're taking longer, you're doing something wrong.
- How do we know if we are safe? Most people who contract viruses or other nastiest thought they were protected.
- Are we using e-mail correctly? Or are we really annoying we our colleagues and they are too polite to tell us? We might be unpleasantly surprised to learn the truth.
- How do we avoid those terrible pop-up windows?
- How do we know if information is real or a hoax?
- How can we make surfing faster?
- How can we get the maximum satisfaction without spending more time on net?

As noted by Paula L. Matthews while employing Internet in academic libraries one of the important issues for the administrator is the implementation library staff training. "A lack of training can result in:

- Poor staff performance;
- Lack of motivation;
- High staff turnover;
- Resistance to change;
- Costly errors or accidents;
- Unfulfilled objectives;
- Undesirable low standards of service.

Academic librarians may well draw on training materials available on the Internet for the higher education community. Recently the issue of whether librarians should learn HTML (Hyper-Text Markup Language) was debated on a North American discussion list. The conclusion was that knowledge of basic HTML was necessary in order to prepare presentations and information guides, which are an integral part of the librarian's professional role. As an increasing number of academic libraries experience some measure of "convergence" with other academic support services, library staff has many opportunities to augment their IT skills and collaborate with colleagues in other services. The combination of technical knowledge and the ability to evaluate information sources is a powerful argument for the continued need for LIS professionals in higher education.

The users of the Academic libraries including some faculty member do not have net skills. In such cases the academic library staff has to come forward to help them. For readiness the staff should have some kind of net skills. The transition of traditional library resources to technology based library resources has put a lot of pressure on the academic library staff. Unless the staff is kept up to date on Internet skills he will face more pressure to work in such conditions. So training of staff has become a necessity in today's context

INTERNET TECHNOLOGY AND ITS SERVICES

The Internet has revolutionised our society, our economy and our technological systems. Over the past century, important technological developments have created a global environment that is drawing people of the world closer and closer together. About fifteen years ago, most of the world knew little or nothing about the Internet. The Internet was then a private network accessible only to computer scientists and researchers who used it to interact with colleagues in their respective disciplines.

It is estimated that about 60 million host computers on the Internet today serve about 200 million users in over 200 countries and territories. Also, the total numbers of host computers and users have been growing at about 33 per cent every six months Since, 1988 – or roughly 80 per cent per year. The Internet has revolutionised the computer and communications world like nothing before. The invention of the telegraph, telephone, radio, and computer set the stage for this unprecedented integration of capabilities.

The Internet is at once a world-wide broadcasting capability, a mechanism for information dissemination, and a medium for collaboration and interaction between individuals and their computers without barriers of geographic location. The Internet represents one of the most successful examples of the benefits of sustained investment and commitment to research and development of information infrastructure. Beginning with the early research in packet switching, the government, industry and academia have been partners in evolving and deploying this exciting new technology. Today, terms like 'Yahoo' and 'Google' are common part of our vocabulary. Internet-based communication services, content creation and delivery tools applicable in libraries.

INTERNET-BASED COMMUNICATION SERVICES

Libraries use Internet-based communication system while attending their day-to-day routine works. An Internet-based communication system allows communication between computer users hooked into a network.

Internet-based communication system is used for communication between person-to-person, person-to-group and group-to-group. A document or message sent through electronic system may contain text, graphics, image, speech as well as other types of information.

Electronic Mail (E-mail)

Electronic Mail, or e-mail, is a fast, easy and inexpensive way to communicate with other Internet users around the world. It is the most popular and widely used services of the Internet. E-mail is the term given to an electronic message, usually a form of simple text message that a user types at a computer system and is transmitted over some form of computer network to another user, who can read it. E-mail offers speedy and economical transfer of messages anywhere in the world. Sending e-mail messages are virtually free even to long-distance destinations. Most integrated library system support e-mail-based communication to library users (for circulation and acquisitionrelated activities) and to the vendors/ publishers (for placing orders, reminders, cancellation, etc).

Listserv

Listservs are electronic groups that typically centre around broad topics such as Digital Libraries or Reference Service, ,etc. Listservers of IFLA with the name IFLA-l, Digilib-l LIBJOBS-l are good example of this. Every e-mail message sent to the listserv is distributed to all members of that listserv, which is potentially hundreds or thousands of people. It does not cost anything to subscribe to a listserv, but simply requires that the user sends an e-mail message to the appropriate address with the message: subscribe (listserv) Firstname Lastname. Each Listserver has one address where a user sends requests to subscribe, un-subscribe, search the archives, etc., and another address to send actual questions or responses to the readers of the list. Apart from organising discussions, job announcements and conference announcements are popular usage of Listservs.

Chat or Instant Messengers

Chat refers to any live discussions conducted using the Internet, usually between more than two persons using their keyboard to communicate. Chat Programmes allow users on the Internet to communicate with each other by typing in real time.

It is a feature offered by many online services or Web sites that allows users to 'chat' by typing messages which are displayed almost instantly on the screens of other users who are using the chat room at a given time. After entering a chat room, any user can type a message that will appear on the monitors of all the other users. Chatting is one of the most popular uses of the Internet. Generally the users remain anonymous by using nicknames or pseudonyms to identify themselves online. A variation of chat is the phenomenon of the instant messenger. Instant messaging can be used to communicate privately with friends, relatives or co-workers.

To send and receive instant messages, a user needs a connection to the Internet and instant messaging software such as Gmail Messenger, Yahoo Messenger and MSN Messenger. The instant messaging software enables a user to set up a list of contacts who also use the same Programme. Once this list is set up, one can see each contact as they come online. A chat session can be started with them quickly and easily. Most conversations are typed text messages that are sent back and forth, though more advanced users can exchange voice, video, files and more.

Conferencing

One of the most exciting features of Internet is to communicate, talk, and see groups of people in different locations around the world, without the expense of travel. Conferencing can take many forms, such as web chat, audio conferencing, video conferencing, multimedia conferencing, screen-sharing, etc.

The conferencing Programmes, such as the popular CU-SeeMe, allow workgroups to use the Internet to see each others' faces in small windows on the computer screen and to hear their voices through computer speakers. One can use desktop video and audio simultaneously or audio can be used alone, or just use the screen-sharing capability without either audio or video.

Audio Conferencing or Internet Telephony

Internet telephony also called IP telephony is a combination of hardware and software that allows the Internet to be used as a telephone carrier. Internet telephony is the conversion of analogue speech signals used on current telephone systems into digital data, allowing calls to be sent over the Internet, bypassing long distance charges.

While the Internet was first devised as a way of transmitting data, it is now being used to make voice calls. Internet telephony is projected to explode as the costs plummet. After the costs of initial set-up and access to an Internet Service Provider, long-distance voice calls can be made via the Internet free of charge, but current quality of voice transmission over the Internet is not always as good as direct telephone service. There are also PSTN/ Internet gateways that allow regular telephone callers to make Phoneto- Internet-to-Phone connections. There are PC-to-Phone connections and Phone-to- PC connections.

Video Conferencing

Video conferencing is one of the most exciting areas of development in telecommunications, with applications ranging from business to government to education to home and family. Video conferencing involves sending video signals as well as audio and computer data signals. Conferencing can be done one-to-one, one-to-many (called multicast), and many-to-many (called multipoint). While video conferencing, one can talk as well as see the people sitting miles away as if all are discussing in one room facing each other.

One of the most popular applications is transmission on news from various locations by the TV news channels. It also has enormous potential for enhancing communications for small and mid-sized companies, as well as distance learning. However, video conferencing requires sufficient bandwidth to transfer video files of acceptable quality. Desktop conferencing, therefore, is not yet widely implemented for business and educational use. As bandwidth increases, desktop video conferencing is expected to blossom. The PictureTel and Vtel are two of the largest companies that sell video conferencing equipment.

NetMeeting

Microsoft NetMeeting facilitates a new way of talking, meeting, working and sharing over the Internet. It uses Internet phone voice communications and conferencing standards to provide multi-user applications and data sharing over Intranets or the Internet.

Two or more users can work together and collaborate in reach time using application sharing, whiteboard, and chat functionality. NetMeeting can be used for common collaborative activities such as virtual meetings. It can also be used for customer service applications, telecommuting, distance learning, and technical support. The product is based on ITU (International Telecommunication Union) standards, so it is compatible with other products based on the same standards.

NetMeeting supports text chat, video shared whiteboard, transferring of files, directory of connected users. Files, such as documents or pictures, can be exchanged. One of the problems with net meeting is the break-up in audio that sometimes becomes inaudible when using it on the Internet, though it works fine over a high-speed company network.

News Groups

Another Internet service similar to listservs is a newsgroup. News Groups are like an International bulletin board. Each group is a forum for a different subject, where a subscriber can post his/her questions or answers.

There are thousands of groups covering just about every area of interest. The difference between listserv and news group is that when a user joins a group, the mail is no longer automatically deposited into his mailbox. Instead a user is expected to go to the newsgroup himself to read it. Some listservs can also be accessed as a newsgroup. A good analogy to a newsgroup is a bulletin board, *i.e.,* one can go to it, as opposed to having mail delivered to his/ her desk. The mails from newsgroup does not get cluttered and it can be easily regulate how often messages are read.

A drawback of a newsgroup lies in the fact that a user must remember to go out to the newsgroup to look for the information. There are hundreds of newsgroup communities. They centre around topics such as computing, news, recreation, social, and 'alternative' topics. There are newsgroups dealing with virtually every topic under the sun and new newsgroups appear every day.

INTERNET-BASED CONTENT PUBLISHING AND DELIVERY SERVICES

The World Wide Web- know as WWW, W3 or simply, the Web help people to publish, organise and provide access to information on the Internet. The WWW can be defined as a hypertext, multimedia, distributed information system that provides links to hypertext documents, as well as to many other Internet tools and databases.

The Web serves as a platform for several specialised content publishing and delivery services. Some of the important tools for content publishing and delivery services applicable to libraries and information centres are described here.

Blogs

A blog (an abridged form of term web log) is a Web site, usually maintained by an individual, with regular entries of commentary, descriptions of events, or other material such as graphics or video. Entries are commonly displayed in reverse chronological order. Blogs are considered as lightweight publishing tools.

Blogs provide control to an individual or group of individuals for publishing contents or making commentary on it. Technologically, blogs are easier to use, platform-independent, and accessible online over the Internet. Broadly, blogs can be said to be online dairies, however, thousands of blogs are maintained by experts in different subject areas who are willing to share their knowledge, understanding and opinions with other people. Michael Casey, who coined the term 'Library 2.0', for example maintains a blog on Library 2.0 called LibraryCrunch.

The most obvious application of blogs for libraries is to use it as a tool for promotion, publicity and for outreach services. Libraries can disseminate information to their users, make announcements for its new resources and events through its blogs. Blogs can be used to initiate debates and interaction amongst users and staff. Moreover, library staff and user can be encouraged to use Library blogs to get to know each other and interact at personal level.

Wikis

A wiki is a collection of web pages designed to enable anyone who accesses it to contribute or modify content, using a simplified markup language. Wikis are often used to create collaborative Web sites and to power community Web sites. For example, the collaborative encyclopaedia, Wikipedia is one of the best-known wikis, that has broken down one the golden rules of librarianship, *i.e.,* content validation and authenticity of information. Wikis are also used in businesses to provide affordable and effective Intranets and for knowledge management.

Ward Cunningham, developer of the first wiki software, WikiWikiWeb, originally described it as "the simplest online database that could possibly work". Wikis can essentially be equated to open web-pages, where anyone registered with it can publish on to it, add to it, amend it and change it. As in case of blogs, Wikis do not have reliability as traditional resources.

Inspite of this, their value as information resource cannot be undermined. Wikis are not only popular but de-facto source of information for people inspite of the fact that it is not validated or authenticated. The lack of peer review and editorship in case of Wikis is a challenge to librarians. Wikis as items in a collection, and the associated instruction of users in their evaluation, is certainly an important task for libraries. Libraries can use wiki as a communication tool to enable social interaction among librarians and patrons.

Users can share information, ask and answer questions, and librarians can do the same within a wiki. Moreover, a record of these transactions can be archived for perpetuity. Transcripts of such question-answer sessions would serve as a resource for the library to provide as reference. Furthermore, wikis will ultimately evolve into a multi-media environment, where both synchronous and asynchronous audio and video collaborations will take place.

Podcasting

The word 'podcasting' is derived from two words, namely 'broadcasting' and 'iPod' (popular MP3 player from Apple Computer). Podcasting is defined as "process of capturing audio digital-media files that can be distributed over the Internet using RSS feeds for playing-back on portable media players as well as computers.

Users can subscribe to such feeds and automatically download these files directly into an audio management Programme (such as iTunes, Windows Media Player or MusicMatch) on their PCs. When a user synchronises their portable audio device with their personal computer the podcasts are automatically transferred to that device to be listened to at the time and location most convenient for the user. Podcasts can be used with a variety of digital audio formats and play on almost any MP3 player or portable digital audio device - as well as any brand of desktop computer or laptop.

Though podcasters' web sites may also offer direct download or streaming of their content, a podcast is distinguished from other digital media formats by its ability to be syndicated, subscribed to, and downloaded automatically when new content is added, using an aggregator or feed reader capable of reading feed formats such as RSS or Atom. Several libraries use podcasts to support library orientations programmes. Taking advantage of podcasting and other consumer technologies (*e.g.*, PDAs, iPods and other MP3 players) as a deliver media of Library's content and services is a great leap forward for library profession.

Vodcasting

The 'VOD' in Vodcasting stands for 'video-on-demand'. It is identical to podcasting. While podcasting is used for delivering audio files, vodcasting is used for delivering video content. Like podcast content, vodcasts content can be played either on a laptop or on personal media assistant (PMA).

RSS Feeds

RSS stands for Real Simple Syndication or Rich Site Summary. The technology, on one hand allows a web site (or e-publisher) to list the newest published updates (like table of contents of journals, new articles) through a technology called XML, on the other hand, it facilitates a web user to keep track new updates on chosen Web site (s). Like a personal search assistant, RSS feed readers visit pre-defined web sites, look for updated information and fetch it automatically on to the user's desktop.

It provides users a way to syndicate and republish content on the Web. Users republish content from other sites or blogs on their sites or blogs, aggregate content on other sites in a single place, and ostensibly distil the Web for their personal use. Libraries are already creating RSS feeds for users to subscribe to, including updates on new items in a collection, new services, and new content in subscription databases. They can also republishing content from other scholarly web sites on their sites.

INTERNET ACCESS TO LIBRARY NETWORKS

Libraries are at the forefront of providing no-fee Internet access to the public. In 1994, just 8.2 percent of public libraries provided this service; as of 2009, 100 percent of libraries do so. While this is a vital role in every community, the library is the only source of no-fee public Internet access in 71 percent of communities. The core mission of libraries is to connect people with ideas and information. Internet access makes it possible for libraries to fulfill this mission through online resources that can, for example, help people find jobs, improve their skills, access government services, create small businesses, complete school homework, and conduct research. Libraries have reported high demand for Internet access; indeed, in the majority of libraries, the demand for publicaccess computers far outweighs the supply.

As demand for public access to the Internet grows, so, too, does the need for higher bandwidth in the library. In some communities, libraries play the important role of broadband anchor institution; in other words, by obtaining high-bandwidth connections, they drive the deployment of advanced technologies to communities that might be unable to obtain that level of service through residential demand alone.

In short, libraries that are able to meet the demand for no-fee public Internet access play a vital role in serving both their users and their communities. To help libraries achieve this capability, the Bill and Melinda Gates Foundation initiated the Opportunity Online Broadband Grant Programme. This programme provides funding and support to help State Library agencies in seven states—Massachusetts, New York, Virginia, Arkansas, Kansas, California, and Texas—develop leadership and improve library connectivity to the Internet.

The American Library Association's Office for Information Technology Policy (OITP) is participating in this programme, providing research and consulting services to state libraries, as well as developing publications that address key issues salient to the program's goals. The purpose of this publication is to provide a snapshot of five different library networks that provide users with no-fee Internet access.

AGGREGATION OF DEMAND AND SERVICES

Aggregation of demand is an acknowledged successful approach to network management. Among its benefits are:

- Improved planning
- Support for a business case for providers to deploy broadband
- More affordable pricing
- Sharing of costs

Aggregation of demand allowed the establishment of each of the five successful networks profiled here, and its benefits have contributed to the networks' continued success. For example, MSLN aggregates library traffic to two nodes, which results in lower recurring expenses for Internet access. Aggregation offers other, less obvious benefits. An example is streamlining and standardisation of members' E-rate participation. All of the statewide networks profiled here regularly file for E-rate discounts on behalf of their members or offer assistance to members in doing so.

A centralised application relieves the burden on individual libraries. MSLN files an aggregated application for federal E-rate discounts and an application for Maine's state universal service fund. Wisconsin files one aggregated E-rate application that includes every K-12 school district and public library on BadgerNet (about 910 sites), and also completes all the required follow-up.

Considering that the most frequently cited reason for libraries' non-participation in the E-rate programme is the complexity of the process, this is a very real benefit with tangible results. Standardisation is a key requirement for aggregation. OPLIN, MSLN, PLS, and BadgerNet require the same router configuration for every library site; SLN requires that all members have the same network equipment; and every school and library on BadgerNet has the same standard Ethernet interface. Standardisation avoids the logistical challenges associated with customisation. It also allows for aggregation of technical support services.

The benefits of aggregating technical support are readily apparent in West Virginia, where these services are typically beyond the means of individual public libraries with limited budgets and staff expertise. MSLN employs a shared project manager to provide planning guidance to individual libraries, a service that would otherwise be too costly for individual libraries.

LEADERSHIP, COOPERATION, AND THE ABILITY TO LEARN FROM PAST SUCCESSES

Strong leadership was an essential element in the development of each of the five networks. At the same time, leadership was distributed among different players at the state, regional, and local levels and was not the exclusive domain of one person or organisation. Moreover, cooperation among these players was a hallmark of the effort. The case studies also illustrate how the various organisations involved often drew on the experiences of other successful cooperative projects to help in the development of their network.

In the formative stage of the Ohio Public Library and Information Network (OPLIN), public libraries that wanted to emulate successful school and academic networks broached the idea of a public library network with the state library association. This association, later called the Ohio Library Council (OLC), assumed a leadership role, and two OLC staff members organised planning and advocacy efforts that led to OPLIN's development.

The West Virginia Network was the first network to centralise the state's computing and data needs. Statewide Library Network (SLN) leadership acknowledged learning from this first statewide network during the project development. Taking a cooperative approach similar to that applied in the development of OPLIN, Wisconsin's local and regional libraries and State Library officials worked together to define the libraries' role in BadgerNet. A past collaborative project to establish a distance learning video network was a key factor in the creation of a 1993 Governor's Blue Ribbon Telecommunications Infrastructure Task Force, which in turn recommended the creation of BadgerNet.

The Maine School and Library Network (MSLN) was also the result of cooperation between statewide library associations and the State Library agency. Finally, the member libraries of California's Peninsula Library System (PLS) developed the Peninsula Libraries Automated Network (PLAN) based on their past success with a common circulation and catalog system. Perhaps the most important factor contributing to the success of PLAN is the spirit and habit of cooperation among PLS members. Since, 1982, member libraries have been cooperating to operate a joint circulation system.

Such collaborations require that libraries engage in significant give-and-take to modify longstanding local policies and procedures so as to accommodate a centralised system. This habit of collaboration led to the success of other collective endeavors, including PLAN.

USE OF DEMONSTRATIONS

OITP's past research suggests that technology demonstrations are necessary to convince a library's community to support a major new effort such as a regional or statewide network. Such demonstrations, while providing essential training to library staff, also serve a critical outreach and public relations function. For example, during the initial phase of network development, OPLIN staff members visited libraries around the state to demonstrate how access to the Internet would help their users. While demonstrations can be very helpful in growing network membership, their usefulness does not end with the network's establishment.

OPLIN and SLN representatives continue to provide information on network services and their use at annual conferences and meetings. Other library systems offer ongoing training on new resources provided via the network and on how library staff can use these resources to improve library services and ultimately benefit the library's patrons. Demonstrations can also help achieve the network's sustainability when used as an advocacy tool for continued funding and support of network projects.

Bibliography

A.K. Gupta: *Digital Library and Education*, Pearl Books, Delhi, 2012.

Ajay K. Srivastav: *Digital Library Environment and Networking*, Sree Publications, Delhi, 2006.

Beales, G.: *The Evolving Roles of Information Professionals in the Digital Age*, Long Life Publication, New Delhi, 2003.

Bertozzi, S.: *Special Libraries,* Pune Publication, Maharashtra, 2006.

Bloom, B. S.: *Key Concepts in the Architecture of the Digital Library,* Concept Publishing Company, New Delhi, 2003.

C Praveen Singh: *Library Automation in Modern Age*, Alfa Publications, Delhi, 2008.

C.R. Sarma: *Computer Networks*, Jaico Publications, Hyderabad, 2006.

Gibbs, G.: *Library Management and Information Technology*, Cambridge University Press, Cambridge, 2006.

Harris, J. L.: *Training for Change: New Skills for the Electronic Library,* New Technology, New Librarians?, London and New York: Longman, 2005.

Jagadeesha S. and Mahesh V. Mudhol: *Library Automation Using Foxpro 2.0*, Ess Ess Publications, Delhi, 1998

John, V.: *Putting Content onto the Internet: The Library's Role as Creator of Electronic Information,* Mizo History Association, Aisawl, 1995.

K. Nazeer Badhusha: *Digital Library Architecture*, Ane Books Pvt. Ltd., Delhi, 2008.

Kusum Verma: *Digital Library Preservation Strategies*, Akansha Publications, Delhi, 2005.

Kusum Verma: *Metadata and Digital Library Systems*, Akansha Publications, Delhi, 2004.

Manohar Nanda: *Library Automation*, Anmol Publications, Delhi, 2006.

Mukherjee, N.: *Digital Libraries: Principles and Practice in a Global Environment,* Concept Publication, New Delhi, 2005.

N.R. Satyanarayana: *A Manual of Library Automation and Networking*, New Royal Book Co., Lucknow, 2003.

Omesh Aadhavan: *Management of Digital Library*, Oxford Book Company, Jaipur, 2010.

P. Balasubramanian: *Library Automation and Networking*, Deep and Deep publications, Delhi, 2011.

Purushotham Tiwari: *International Encyclopaedia of Library Automation, Vols. I to IV*, A.P.H. Publications, Delhi, 2011.

R.K. Singh and C.K. Sharma: *Library Automation and Total Quality Management*, Shree Publications, Delhi, 2011.

R.K. Singh: *Basic Facts of Digital Library*, Shree Publications, Delhi, 2004.

R.S. Kochar and K.N. Sudarshan: *Library Automation: (Issues and Systems)*, A P H Publishing, Delhi, 2010.

Raghunath Pandey and M.N. Velayudhan Pillai: *Global Library Networking*, Jnanada Prakashan, Delhi, 2011.

S. K. Sangma: *Manual of Library Automation and Networking*, Centrum Press, Delhi, 2013.

S. Yadagiri and R.K. Pavan Kumar: *Library Automation: Perspectives and Challenges*, Swastik Publications, Delhi, 2013.

S.P. Singh: *Library Networking*, Omega Publications, Delhi, 2008.

S.R. Sharma: *Accreditation of Library Education*, Mohit Publications, Delhi, 1997.

Salmon, B.: *The Impact of Electronic Publications on Promotion and Tenure Decisions,* HMSO, London, 2005.

Shiv Ram Verma: *Academic Library System*, Shree Publications, Delhi, 2005.

Swami Chidrupananda: *Making Sense of Library Automation: A Handson Guide*, Meteor Books, 2006.

T. Bala Theresa, C. Ratna Kumari and B.A. Rani: *Information Technology and Library Automation*, Commonwealth Publications, Delhi, 2011.

Thapar, R.: *The Impact of Digital Reference on Librarians and Library Users,* Oxford University Press, New Delhi, 1994.

Vasantha N. and Mahesh V. Mudhol: *Software Packages for Library Automation*, Ess Ess Publications, Delhi, 2000.

Index